Studying the Qur'ān
in the Muslim Academy

AMERICAN ACADEMY
of RELIGION

REFLECTION AND THEORY IN THE STUDY OF RELIGION

SERIES EDITOR
Vincent Lloyd, Villanova University

A Publication Series of
The American Academy of Religion
and
Oxford University Press

LESSING'S PHILOSOPHY OF RELIGION
AND THE GERMAN ENLIGHTENMENT
Toshimasa Yasukata

AMERICAN PRAGMATISM
A Religious Genealogy
M. Gail Hamner

OPTING FOR THE MARGINS
*Postmodernity and Liberation in Christian
Theology*
Edited by Joerg Rieger

MAKING MAGIC
*Religion, Magic, and Science in the
Modern World*
Randall Styers

THE METAPHYSICS OF DANTE'S *COMEDY*
Christian Moevs

PILGRIMAGE OF LOVE
Moltmann on the Trinity and Christian Life
Joy Ann McDougall

MORAL CREATIVITY
Paul Ricoeur and the Poetics of Possibility
John Wall

MELANCHOLIC FREEDOM
Agency and the Spirit of Politics
David Kyuman Kim

FEMINIST THEOLOGY AND THE
CHALLENGE OF DIFFERENCE
Margaret D. Kamitsuka

PLATO'S GHOST
Spiritualism in the American Renaissance
Cathy Gutierrez

TOWARD A GENEROUS ORTHODOXY
Prospects for Hans Frei's Postliberal Theology
Jason A. Springs

CAVELL, COMPANIONSHIP, AND
CHRISTIAN THEOLOGY
Peter Dula

COMPARATIVE THEOLOGY AND THE
PROBLEM OF RELIGIOUS RIVALRY
Hugh Nicholson

SECULARISM AND RELIGION-MAKING
Markus Dressler and Arvind-Pal S. Mandair

FORTUNATE FALLIBILITY
Kierkegaard and the Power of Sin
Jason A. Mahn

METHOD AND METAPHYSICS IN
MAIMONIDES' *GUIDE FOR THE
PERPLEXED*
Daniel Davies

THE LANGUAGE OF DISENCHANTMENT
*Protestant Literalism and Colonial Discourse in
British India*
Robert A. Yelle

WRITING RELIGION
The Making of Turkish Alevi Islam
Markus Dressler

THE AESTHETICS AND ETHICS OF FAITH
*A Dialogue Between Liberationist and Pragmatic
Thought*
Christopher D. Tirres

VISIONS OF RELIGION
Experience, Meaning, and Power
Stephen S. Bush

AMERICAN ACADEMY
of RELIGION

Studying the Qur'ān
in the Muslim Academy

MAJID DANESHGAR

OXFORD

UNIVERSITY PRESS

Oxford University Press is a department of the University of Oxford. It furthers
the University's objective of excellence in research, scholarship, and education
by publishing worldwide. Oxford is a registered trade mark of Oxford University
Press in the UK and certain other countries.

Published in the United States of America by Oxford University Press
198 Madison Avenue, New York, NY 10016, United States of America.

Library of Congress Cataloging-in-Publication Data
Names: Daneshgar, Majid, author.
Title: Studying the Qur'ān in the Muslim Academy / Majid Daneshgar.
Description: New York, NY : Oxford University Press, 2020. |
Includes bibliographical references and index.
Identifiers: LCCN 2019012350| ISBN 9780190067540 (hardback) |
ISBN 9780190067557 (updf) | ISBN 9780190067564 (epub) |
ISBN 9780190067571 (online)
Subjects: LCSH: Islam—Study and teaching. | Islam—Apologetic works.
Classification: LCC BP42 .D36 2019 | DDC 297.071—dc23
LC record available at https://lccn.loc.gov/2019012350

Dedicated to

Seyyed Hossein of Meybod College (Iran), who told 2005 entrants:

This Qurʾanic Sciences faculty is smaller than a high school, so you must always remember to expand your vision beyond its walls!

&

Donald in Dunedin (New Zealand), who told me when I was very much worried about the reaction of readers to one of my works:

Majid, the Earth doesn't rotate around you, me, nor anybody else.

Contents

Figures and Tables

Figures

Tables

Preface

I. *Here Is New York* and My Research Concerns

A few years ago, I read the book *Here Is New York* by E. B. White, which was first published in 1949. It caused me to reconsider the places where I grew up, studied, and worked.

For White, people in New York City are divided into three groups. The first group is made up of "involuntary," native New Yorkers who "take the city for granted and accept its size and its turbulence as natural and inevitable."[1] The second group is the commuters who only come to achieve a certain goal and then get out. The third group is those people, native and not, who view New York as a land ripe for discovery, one in which they can achieve their goals.[2] For them, New York is neither a home nor a place only for specific activity or temporary residence. They love to explore the city and see it as a place whose buildings, shops, and people are full of history. For them, New York is its past and its future: Learning more about it means learning more about both.

Everyone is born and raised somewhere and most everyone both likes and dislikes wherever that place may be; most everyone has a degree of ambivalence toward what he or she calls home.

My own birthplace is Yazd, in Iran, a desert city of the Middle East, where the heritage of Zoroastrianism may still be felt, where the call to prayer (*adhan*) is still heard everywhere.

During Yazd's summer, my brothers and I used to go swimming in the many swimming pools of this hot city. We did not study Yazd history and culture because there were no resources or facilities dedicated for it. Instead, we studied science and biology, for which there *were* resources and facilities. Along with many of our friends and relatives, we were told we had to be equipped with the empirical sciences in high school in order to be *agha-yi khodiman* (our own masters) in the future.

For us, the desert and Yazd the lovely desert-city were a lovely setting and an accommodating birthplace as well as a platform from which we could go on to achieve great things. My brothers and I did not become aware of our hometown's history and culture until we had left it and moved to bigger cities.

Upon returning to Yazd, just after turning twenty, I no longer saw the city as being simply part of the desert. For me, its buildings, people, cafés, food, and soil now all had meaning, reflecting the history that had shaped its identity . . . and mine.

Unlike my brothers, who all studied engineering, I chose to study "Qur'anic sciences" at the Qur'anic Studies colleges belonging to the Ministry of Science, Research and Technology and the Iranian Endowment Organization, which was in close connection with the Ministry of Culture and Islamic Guidance.

I continued to "return" to Yazd and to keep observing its features after deciding to study Qur'anic sciences.

Sometimes I wonder whether it was my own decision to study Islam or a decision that my parents had imposed on me. These good citizens of the desert-city of Yazd believe that not only my existence, but also my name and career, were decreed by God.

During the Iran-Iraq war, my mother, Zari, dreamed that someone gave her a dusty book. In the dream, she cleaned the book's cover and then, with her right hand, picked up a piece of chalk from the floor. Her hand wrote an Arabic-Persian noun phrase: *Qur'ān-e Majid* (The Glorious Qur'ān). The term "Majid," one of the attributes of God in the Qur'ān, became golden. "Majid" was absorbed into the book's cover.[3] Zari then woke.

> She called my father, Rahman.
> She told him: "I am pregnant."
> "Again?" Rahman asked.
> "Yes," she replied. "I am pregnant with a boy whose name is Majid and who will dedicate his life to Islam and the Qur'ān."

For a long time, this story was the motivation for my interest in religious studies. It certainly stopped me from considering studies in urban engineering, textile engineering, and geology, disciplines I was also accepted to study at university.

Unlike my brothers, who began their childhood social interactions in an ordinary kindergarten, at the age of five my parents sent me to a *maktab*, a small school where one learns to recite the Qur'ān and to perform *namaz* (Arabic: *salat*; saying prayers).

In the religious context of post-war Iranian society, a small child with the ability to recite the Qur'ān by heart was the center of every family session and gathering. I was always one of these children. As a result, I received both awards and rewards.

It was a nice feeling for me, at that time, to know that "divine" inspiration was behind my educational choices and future career. I thought that it guaranteed my life, job, and future.

The collectivistic nature of Persian culture, along with our household's top-to-bottom hierarchical rule, always made me say to myself, "Do something, Majid, to meet your parent's dreams! You should grow up to be the man that your parents want you to be!"

So, early in my academic career, I became involved with the media, doing domestic and a few international TV and radio programs and interviews with Iranian newspapers and magazines. This was meant to tell my parents: "This is 'your Majid' who is appearing in the media due to his research activities."

I did all this public activity mainly on the basis of my mother's dream, the reliability of which I constantly wanted to prove to my family. The more media appearances, the better the feeling, for both me and my parents.

The satisfaction I got as a child from good recitation remained with me even after I went to the Qur'anic studies college in Tehran and then to its branch college in the city of Meybod in Yazd province, where I completed my bachelor's degree.

Such colleges, so the dean of the Tehran college of Qur'anic Studies told me in 2003, "aim at producing scholars who are not only obliged to spread the message of God, but also to save people's lives and society from destruction." Saving the world was one thing, certainly, but one of the main educational features of the curricula of both the colleges is an emphasis on *Tajwid*, the phonetic rules of Qur'ān recitation. Indeed, it is a common belief in the Muslim academy that a scholar of Islam and the Qur'ān should be able to beautifully and fluently recite it. I therefore took several courses to improve my recitation ability.

Our lecturer on the subject, Mehdi Seyf, a renowned referee of international Qur'ān recitation competitions, strongly recommended that I work with a tutor and listen to *tahqiq* (lit., "eloquent and gentle recitations") audio tapes of the famous Egyptian reciter Abdul Basit Abdel Samad (d. 1988). I took private recitation classes almost every day for six months, which greatly improved my ability. In order to get my bachelor's degree, I of course also had to pass some courses on Islamic theology, Shari'a, Arabic language and literature, as well as various courses on general psychology, sociology, the philosophy of education, and statistics.

After completing my studies at Meybod-Yazd, and again on the basis of my parents' advice and to honor their opinion on the matter, I went to the city of Qum—renowned as the "Vatican of Iran"—for a masters at the male faculty for Qur'ān and Hadith (prophetic traditions).

I very soon realized that Qum is more complex than might be imagined: Previously part of the megalopolis of Tehran, today Qum is largely independent. Through the thousands of students from around the world who study Islam there, the city now has an extraordinarily significant impact on the wider world, too.

A visitor to Qum will immediately and automatically become a practitioner of Shi'i Islamic teachings and culture, which are largely different from those one learns in Istanbul or Doha, where the Sunni approach to Islam prevails. Shi'i tradition is reflected in Qum's civic life, in restaurants, cafés, and libraries, in the streets around shrines and mosques, even in the few cinemas the city has (which usually do not show the kind of movies that play in Tehran).

As well as reflecting the strong cultural and historical traditions of the lands where the two main strands of Islam were eventually established as dominant, Shi'i and Sunni Islam differ on how the power of Islam's founder, Prophet Muhammad, was passed along. Shi'i theology holds that, divinely inspired, Muhammad named 'Ali ibn Abi Talib as his successor at Ghadir Khumm; Sunni tradition considers that Muhammad named no successor and that the Prophet's intimate circle of "Companions" elected Abu Bakr as successor and leader of the Muslim community by consensus.

In the streets of Qum, one can see students and visitors from every part of the world and hear conversations in the local languages of West Africa (e.g., Bambara), Eastern Europe (e.g., Bosnian), Western Europe (English, French, German), and the Malay-Indonesian world (e.g., Bahasa Indonesia). In Qum, by roadsides, in markets and alleyways, one often passes by the graves of important figures from Islamic history; the small district of Kahak was where the famous and influential Muslim philosopher Sadr al-Din Muhammad Shirazi, known as Mulla Sadra (d. ca. 1640), "spent fifteen years of ascetic devotion and self-purification until he achieved the 'direct' vision of the intelligible world."[4]

In spite of its world renown, Qum as a city remains an untapped source of Islamic knowledge, a place whose archaeology, sociology, and history, especially, deserve better attention.

The Grand Ayatollahs (high-ranking clerics) of Qum have a role and power and influence equivalent to the Mufti of Mecca or Medina.

A Grand Ayatollah of Qum can grant research funds, permanent jobs, and various types of facilities and resources for someone in Islamic—or even plain-old secular academic institutions—in such places as, among many others across the globe, London, Washington, Sydney, Nairobi, Cape Town, Jakarta, and Wellington. A Grand Ayatollah of Qum has the power to issue a *fatwa* condemning to death someone living beyond the borders of Iran and promising a huge financial reward for the eventual killer. Just such *fatwas* (for apostasy) have been, for example, pronounced against the Iranian singer Shahin Najafi, now living in exile in Germany.

Studying the Qur'ān and working with several scientific and research centers attached to *hawzas* (Shi'i seminaries) in Qum brought me up close with Shi'i thinking, traditions, and clerics for some years.

The Qur'ān is not only viewed as a divine revelation but also as the key source for solving every possible national, political and cultural problem. For example, I worked with an institute dedicated to "Qur'ān and science" and "Qur'ān and Orientalism" whose goal is to prove the harmony between the Qur'ān and science and to "decolonize" European Qur'anic studies—to "purify" the Western perspective.

Despite the efforts of my parents to keep me in my Shi'i homeland, after completing my MA in Qum, I went to University of Malaya, at Kuala Lumpur, in Sunni-dominated Malaysia. I decided to experience the Sunni tradition of course but also a social and cultural context that would be, unlike that of Iran, truly pluralistic.

Malaysia consists of communities and ethnicities originally from places as different as Arabia, Yemen, China, India, and Thailand, among other places. Also, Malaysia had a more stable economy, currency, and educational system than those of Iran and some other Islamic societies in the Middle East I might have chosen.

At the time of my stay in the country, the last prime minister, Najib Razak, was still in power. During my time there, however, Malaysia's Islamic context, like that of its institutes dedicated to the study of Islam, remained extremely conservative and orthodox.

Most Islamic institutions tended to be "Arabized." Not only were they financially connected to Arab countries but they also promoted exchange programs such as Malaysian-Arabian/Egyptian (Azhari)/Jordanian intensive or long-term courses that tended to reinforce Arab connections—interest in ties with Iranian Islamic institutions was almost nil. Every month, many, many people from Arab countries came to my institute to speak about (an Arab version of) Islam. I never heard from these guests and visitors any discussion of local—Malaysian—Islamic practice or the effects that the Malay society or culture might have on Islam.

I knew of course that a move from an extremely Shi'i context to an Arabized Sunni institute for the study of Islam in Southeast Asia would be a significant change. Indeed, I found it quite challenging.

My hosts did not welcome Shi'i teachings. The sources I had employed for years—Shi'i-inspired commentaries on the Qur'ān and Hadith—were not considered reliable for the study of Islam. As well, the methodology I had used to study Islamic prophetic traditions (*ahadith*) in Qum was not the same as that used by my new colleagues.

Frankly, I was just astounded by all of it.

What I had heard about the Sunni tradition in my Shi'i homeland was just not the same as what I was now learning in my new Sunni academic context and . . . vice versa: What I was hearing about Shi'i tradition was not what I had learned or experienced.

I very soon realized that there is a dark veil hung between the Sunni and Shi'i traditions. It is a veil of ignorance woven of the culture and political conflicts between the original Sunni and Shi'i lands and peoples. Through this veil—and it hangs not only between Saudi Arabia and Iran but between every Islamic community attached to one of the traditions in respect to the other—one sees a blurred, rather vague, image of "otherness."

For Muslim academia, the veil means that cultural, political and textual ignorance—partly intentional, partly unintentional—permeates Shi'i and Sunni institutions alike. Both students and scholars ignore the other sects, fail to study their theology, literature, culture, and rituals, and are inattentive to any possible literary, ethnic, and cultural connections between the two grand traditions.

The "otherness" of my upbringing and education was a special and difficult challenge for me. When I began studying Islam in general, and the Qur'ān in particular, in Tehran and then in my hometown of Yazd, I had used sources that were not, and still are not, employed in the Sunni academic context.[5]

Indeed, in neither Shi'i nor Sunni academia generally are the methods, syllabi, and styles of the other tradition recognized. For example, although I successfully defended my thesis, during the viva, the chair of the examining committee, after admiring my thesis, reminded me that "here [Malaysia] is a Sunni context," and that I needed to refer to Islamic exegetical works produced by Sunni scholars. Even such classic and modern Shiʿi luminaries as al-Tabrisi (d. ca. 1153) or Tabatabaʾi (d. 1981), respectively, would not do. I should note that the chair had studied at one of the great British universities.

It was not just that Malaysia's Sunni tradition was challenging.

From the very beginning of my time at university, I had been a big fan of European writings on Islam, in particular, those of the late Andrew Rippin (d. 2016), one of the foremost scholars of Islam and the Qurʾān of the last fifty years. In Malaysia, I struggled to find teachers who would take a serious interest in such Western Qurʾān scholars as Rippin and their work—in their eyes, Western analytical readings of the history of the Qurʾān and its commentaries just did not make the grade.

Although Rippin was approved as one of my doctoral supervisors—for which I am still grateful (it was Rippin who persuaded me to carry on when I wanted to drop out of the program)—some of my colleagues and other academic staff did not think highly of him. Recalling the way medieval Christian polemicists and some colonial officials talked about Islam, my colleagues felt that any work by such Westerners as Rippin, who are generalized as "Orientalists," was just not trustworthy scholarship. Once, while passing through a corridor in the department's classroom area, I noticed that a lecturer was presenting Rippin's and other Westerners' pictures on a PowerPoint slide, characterizing them as "Orientalists."

In the most positive scenario, for example, Rippin was viewed as a very severe critic of Islamic history, if not as an actual (so-called) "enemy of Islam." His works are read by Malaysian students of Islam but little-cited and his methodology even less often applied.

As I saw later in my budding career, this dismissive attitude toward Westerners and their work carried well beyond Malaysia. In both Shiʿi and Sunni academia, I found work produced in the West is just not valued. Scholars in the Muslim academy generally were neither familiar with, nor interested in studying, Western work on Islam. They nonetheless frequently produced essays criticizing bits and pieces of such work even when the bits and pieces themselves, let alone a complete work, were generally unavailable or just ignored. I am reminded of Marwa Elshakry's noting how nineteenth-century religious thinkers, Egyptian scholars among them, rejected Darwinism despite never having read any of Darwin's works.[6]

As challenging to my religious point of view and to my Western-oriented academic interests, the Malaysia-government-funded, Sunni-oriented educational institution eventually became my first long-term employer.

As everywhere else, student and colleague motivations at the University of Malaya varied.

Some students *had to* be there and some lecturers *had to* work: These both were a type of what E. B. White called "commuters," "the queerest bird[s] of all . . . [their] entrances and exits more devious than those"[7] of a desert city. Cheek-by-jowl with the commuters were those who had *chosen* to study and work at the university, those who, to paraphrase White, viewed the university as "a land ripe for discovery." For them, education was a means by which they could learn about history, themselves, and their communities.

The next move, premeditated and deliberate, in my early academic career was to one of the most liberal societies in the world. New Zealand's University of Otago, a government-funded, secular university with a highly diverse student body and scholars from many different religious traditions and cultures was almost as opposite as I could find to a government-funded, Arabized, Sunni-oriented Malaysian institution.

After a couple of years living and working in liberal academia, I found that there, as in Malaysia, people fit into E. B. White's typology; I have now concluded that it applies to all communities and cultures.[8] In effect, in each of the three social-academic contexts in which I have lived (Shi'i, Sunni, and Western liberal),[9] studied and worked on Islam's history and traditions, there have been some scholars and students who approach them instrumentally, some who took them for granted, and some who approached them "as a land ripe for discovery."

In New Zealand, it was possible for me to experience and feel concepts such as "individualism" and "liberalism," notions I had heretofore only read about in books and magazines.

I found that New Zealand society *often* proved more open than New Zealand academia.

Indeed, I unexpectedly faced serious opposition from what were, in effect, Muslim fundamentalists there. Some of my Western colleagues, not really familiar with the issues involved, were reluctant to take a hard line against interference from those who wish to impose their particular views on the study of Islam. Although such self-appointed guardians of Islamic "orthodoxy" were often thousands of miles away from their homelands, places such as Afghanistan or Pakistan, they felt fully secure to promote their illiberal values in liberal New Zealand.

As someone who feels himself a native of E. B. White's "third type," I was intrigued as well as troubled when I discovered that, in New Zealand of all places, a group of Muslim students and colleagues objected to my teaching. They said that undergraduates are too young to study such material about Islamic civilization as I was then teaching, especially the work of the scholars Abdelwahab Meddeb and Andrew Rippin. What my critics wanted, instead, they said, was for me to "Islamicize" my teaching by referring almost exclusively to influential traditionalist—Sunni—Muslim scholars.

Two big questions came to me: What was going on *here* (in liberal New Zealand) and *there* (in Islamic academia).

These two big questions resolved into a number of troubling, urgent, and interlocking questions:

- What is the nature of the Muslim academy in general and the study of religion departments in particular, given reigning sectarianism and rampant cultural ignorance (both of which have their root in politics)?
- How do students and researchers study Islam within the Muslim academy?
- Why do Muslim scholars of Islam and the Qur'ān in Iran, Arabia, and Malaysia, among other Muslim lands, not regularly use and reference each others' works?
- Why do Muslim academics so often reject work on Islam done by Western scholars?
- Why do some Muslims want to change the Western approach Islamic studies?
- Why do some Muslims think that reading the works of a European scholar of Islam might hurt their beliefs or ʿaqida?

These questions prompted me to look into the little-explored cultural and educational features of how Islam is studied in the Muslim academy.

In very much the same way as the Bible has done for peoples who historically adopted Christianity, the Qur'ān situates as central to *everything* pertaining to Islam as well as to everything cultural and traditional in a society.

Among people who have adopted Islam, for example, it is a virtually universal belief that the Qur'ān is the key that enables true believers to attain bliss and prosperity. My grandfather, for instance, told me many, many times how he restrained his anger by relying on Qur'anic verses—as he was taught to do by his parents. Grandfather said that he was thereby able to lead a thoroughly "calm and friendly life." What he meant, I believe, was that he felt that reading the Qur'ān had enabled him to attain a form of ethical perfection.

As well, as the central element of Islam, the Qur'ān is of course also a political instrument—it is and has been regularly employed by classical and modern politicians and religious thinkers.

The study of the Qur'ān as an academic subject in universities and colleges (*not* in religiously oriented seminaries and madrasas or in society as whole) is the subject of this work.

It is beyond dispute that, in the Muslim academy, the centrality of the Qur'ān in culture, tradition, and politics, has become an important tool to weed out the European-Christian scholarly approaches in the study of Islam. It is also systemically (and system*atically*) used deny the validity of Western critical historical approaches to the Qur'ān as well as to encourage Muslim students to use the Qur'ān as a way of highlighting and proving political and religious loyalties as well as religious points.

I recently came across an article that illustrates this latter use as a political tool.

Written up as a thesis and presented at the National Conference on New Approaches to the Humanities in the 21st Century in Iran in 2017, a paper titled "The Critical Analysis of the Joint Comprehensive Plan of Action (JCPOA) and Post-JCPOA from the Perspective of the Holy Qur'ān" "defends Islamic values" even as it demonstrates the legal right of the Islamic Republic of Iran to scientifically use nuclear energy in the light of "Qur'ān verses, the lifestyle of Shiʿi Imams and the Iranian Supreme Leader's accounts."[10] The conference was organized by the Female Campus of the Imam Sadiq University of Iran.

Insofar as it sheds light on both my New Zealand critics' demand that I "Islamicize" my teaching and the continuity of politicization in the Muslim academy, the originating institution of the conference is significant.

After the collapse of the Pahlavi dynasty in 1979, the Islamic Republic of Iran focused on "Islamic education" or the "Islamization of colleges" by means of a "cultural revolution" (*inqilab-e farhangi*). In order to unify educational policies, "Islamicize" syllabi, and reassign teaching and administrative staff, colleges and universities were closed from 1980 through to late 1982.[11]

In practice, once reforms were completed, university administrations were charged with eradicating Western social and political doctrines like Marxism while "Islamization" scrubbed out the secularism, "Americanization,"[12] and Western culture that had developed under Reza Shah Pahlavi (r. 1925–1941) and his son Muhammad Reza Shah Pahlavi (r. 1941–1979).

More than any other area or scholarly endeavor, "Islamization" impacted the humanities, "the essence of the university."[13]

Imam Sadiq University, previously the Harvard-affiliated Iran Center for Management Studies,[14] was one of the first post-revolutionary institutions of higher learning to open its doors in 1982. The new establishment sought to train and promote the humanities based on Shiʿi sources, a mission which, as we have seen above, it continues into the present in quite politicized form.[15]

Types of "Islamicizing" educational reforms also occurred in other Muslim societies throughout the period, from around the mid-1970s to the mid-1980s.

For example, the foundation of the International Islamic Universities of Pakistan and Malaysia (IIU and IIUM), in 1980 and 1983, respectively, was the result of a Muslim education reform conference held in Mecca in 1977. The main aim was to help Muslims rediscover and reinforce the dynamics of Islam in their present-day circumstances and, above all, to redefine the Islamic concept of education, thus leading to ways and means of achieving the harmony and unity of the body, mind, and soul for which Islam stands.[16]

Conference participants agreed to produce and unify academic syllabi for Islamic education that would be distributed throughout the Muslim world as well as, in particular, the United Kingdom.[17]

"Islamicization" aimed at enabling university graduates to be experts in their own, specific disciplines, but also in the Islamic faith, making of graduates, ideally, people who could solve human challenges as well as problems related to bring Muslim.

As I have frequently observed, heard, and read over the years, praising and respecting Islamic sanctities is a key aspect of Islamization and is to be practiced in Muslim academic careers as well as applied to published work. For instance, Qurʾanic studies (Arabic: al-dirasat al-Qurʾaniyya; Persian: Qurʾān pazhuhi) graduates from reputed universities in Muslim countries are very frequently called Khadim al-Qurʾān al-Karim ("The Servants of the Holy Qurʾān"), and both academic and nonacademic journals are obliged to print standard blessings (doxologies) after the use of Muhammad's, or his Companions', names.[18]

In light of Islamization, one may legitimately wonder if Muslim universities and other academic institutions are meant as places for students to learn to defend their established beliefs or to learn to think critically about the past, present reality, and future possibilities.

That is the big question.

In the words of Akeel Bilgrami, are academic institutions "sites for students for intellectual inquiry and research, and where one of their chief goals is the pursuit of truth and pedagogical projects for conveying the truth as one discovers it and conceives it in one's research, and to set students on the path of discovering further truths in the future on their own" or . . . not?[19]

***

While previous scholars have examined how Islam is studied, this volume goes one step further to shed light on the role of politics and of religious and cultural conflicts in the study of Islam and to go deeper by studying an underexamined venue: the Muslim academy.

The reception of Islam in Western universities has already been researched by various Muslim and non-Muslim scholars. These works have mostly revolved around the twenty-first-century understanding of Islam in wider secular contexts. For example, *The Teaching and Study of Islam in Western Universities*, edited by four scholars from New Zealand and Australia, was published in 2013. The editors argued that people have become more interested in learning about Islam since the September 11, 2001, attack of the Twin Towers in New York and that, if it is rudderless, a university response has nonetheless been forthcoming:

> Although some of the fear and hostility that followed the events of September 11, 2001 has subsided, there continues to be great deal of public interest in the religion of Islam and the activities of Muslim communities. Universities throughout the West have taken advantage of this interest to establish institutes and programs in the study of Islam. But there has been surprisingly little reflection on the appropriate shape of such programs and the assumptions that ought to underlie such study.[20]

Apart from recent fieldwork dealing with the reception of Qur'anic exegetical and intellectual traditions in Muslim educational institutions, two works have been produced that address the study of religion by Muslims in different countries.

The first, *Schooling Islam: The Culture and Politics of Modern Muslim Education*, edited by Robert W. Hefner and Muhammad Qasim Zaman, which takes a variety of anthropological approaches, gives a general view of "the culture and politics of modern Muslim education." *Schooling Islam*, which is a response to the Western political commentators and media who see Islamic madrasas, mainly those in Pakistan, as the birthplace of radicals, pays particular attention to the situation, confrontation or interaction of a madrasa-based educational system with the policies of both Muslim and non-Muslim countries.[21]

The second work is a recent special issue of Hartford Seminary's journal *The Muslim World*, titled "The Challenges and Opportunities of Teaching Islam in Theological Seminaries" which covers the teaching of Islam in theological seminaries but which also tries to shed more light on the study of Islam in Christian and secular institutions.[22]

Both works definitely fill some gaps for those who wish to assess the difference between radical and ordinary Muslims, the so-called "conspiracy" of the Western media and the real image of Islam, interreligious dialogues, and other current issues.

However, neither *Schooling Islam* nor "Challenges and Opportunities" explores how the Qur'ān is studied in universities, the politics behind the study of Islam in Muslim academic institutions, or the differences in what is produced in the West and in the Muslim world. Neither work concerns itself with the methods and theories produced and practiced in Muslim academia for studying Islam and the Qur'ān. It remains for my book to try to offer some explanation as to why, for example, a William Montgomery Watt (d. 2006) is more popular than a John Wansbrough (d. 2002) in Muslim academia or why Iranian-inspired Persian Shiʿi works are widely read in Indonesian universities and colleges but not in Malaysian ones, or why such new forms of Qur'anic studies in the West as Jane Dammen McAuliffe's *Encyclopaedia of the Qur'ān* have not been warmly received by some Muslim academics.

Acknowledgments

This book is the result of research that began in 2014, when I was exploring various forms of relationship between Western and Muslim academic contexts. A debt of gratitude is owed to many people for helping turn my vision into reality.

I was lucky that I was born in a sort of traditional family in a traditional city, Yazd, in Iran. I thank my parents, Zahra (Zari) and Abdolrahman (Rahman), without whose support I would not have been able to experience different forms of Islamic lifestyles. I also thank my three brothers, Abolfazl, Davoud and Mohammad Mahdi, without whom I could never have realized how much difference there is between myself, as a Qurʾān studies student, and them, as engineers, in the Iranian academy.

I am very much indebted to my supervisors, particularly the late Professor Andrew Rippin, without whose aid and encouragement I would not have continued my academic journey.

I place on record my sincere thanks to Professor Jane Dammen McAuliffe for recommending Oxford University Press (OUP) as a suitable publisher for my book. I particularly thank OUP series editor of the *American Academy of Religion Reflection and Theory in the Study of Religion*, Dr. Vincent Lloyd (Villanova) for reading my monograph and providing me with his feedback as to how the volume could be improved. I appreciate my anonymous reviewers for their constructive comments and suggestions. Working with OUP editor Cynthia Read, her assistant Hannah Campeanue, and Preetham Raj, the project manager from Newgen, one of the partner production companies of Oxford University Press, and their professional team has been a pleasure from the beginning.

I also thank all my colleagues and friends, particularly, Professors Peter G. Riddell (Melbourne), Davut S. Peaci (Düzce), and Gabriel Said Reynolds (Notre Dame), with all of whom I had interesting face-to-face or Skype discussions on many different facets of the Qurʾanic and Islamic studies. I also owe special thanks to my friend Dr. Alex Mallett (Tokyo) for his comments on both language and content of this book.

My thanks go to my teachers, friends and colleagues in Iran, Malaysia, New Zealand, Australia, Canada, France, the United States, and Germany, the remembrance of whom and whose insights prompted me to complete this study. I shall never forget my long conversations with my dear friend Dr. Gholamreza Nui in Freiburg (Germany), Kuala Lumpur (Malaysia), Ankara (Turkey), and Tehran (Iran) about the way Islam is discussed in the Muslim academy and how much freedom there is there. My late night discussions with friends in Dunedin, New Zealand, about public understanding of Islamic history were really helpful. I am also grateful to Dr. Mahmoud Pargoo (Sydney, Australia) for sharing his trenchant comments on my reviews and his disagreement with some of my opinions. I thank Dr. Faisal Ahmad Shah (Kuala Lumpur) for providing me with valuable information about the Malay-Indonesian study of Islam. I am very grateful to my friend, Tim Gerken (New York), for sharing his knowledge and experience with me. My special thanks also go to Dr. Seyyed Hossein Azimidokht (Iran), and Dr. Donald Kerr (New Zealand).

Working with wonderful people and well-established scholars and scientists with global reputations in the Freiburg Institute for Advanced Studies (FRIAS), University of Freiburg, including Professor Bernd Kortmann (linguistics; director of FRIAS), Dr. Britta Küst (FRIAS scientific coordinator), Dr. Carsten Dose (former FRIAS managing director), Professor Günther Schulze (economics; FRIAS social sciences director), Professor Catherine McBride (psychology), Professor Walid A. Saleh (Islamic Studies), Professor Lorena Bachmaier (law), Professor Wolfgang Tschacher (psychology), Professor Ernst Eberlein (mathematics), Professor Nancy D. Campbell (history of science and technology), Professor Kate Burridge (linguistics), Professor Andreas Musolff (intercultural communication), Professor Onur Yıldırım (social and economic history), Professor Henrike Lähnemann (German literature and language), Professor Anne Harrington (history), Professor Paolo Silvestri (legal and political philosophy), Professor Stefan Pfänder (interactional linguistics and multimodal), Professor Stefan Kebekus (mathematics), Professor Nicola Piper (political sociology and migration studies), Professor Dimitris Stamatopoulos (history), Dr. Oliver Bräunling (mathematics), Dr. Michael Staab (ecology and biodiversity), Dr. Anne Holzmüller (musicology), Dr. Jacob Sider Jost (English literature), Dr. Raghid Zeineddine (mathematics), Dr. Lawrence Chua (history of architecture and urban development), Dr. Noa Roei (visual culture), Ms. Petra Fischer (FRIAS fellow assistant), and Mr. Nikolaus Binder (FRIAS fellow assistant), among others, through 2017 to 2018 allowed me to view religion and religious studies from different perspectives. I am thankful to my FRIAS officemate, Dr. Errol Lord (philosophy) whose deep and analytical approach to whatever the phenomena under discussion was always encouraging. This book would not have been possible without the kind support of the FRIAS.

I am also pleased that I have been able to prepare a final draft of the book for publication while joining the department of Oriental Studies at the University of Freiburg, where I have a chance to work as a research associate with amazing people and well-versed scholars of Islamic, Iranian, and Turkish studies, including Professor Johanna Pink, Professor Tim Epkenhans, Junior Professor Dr. Ruth Bartholomä, among others. In addition, Freiburg brought me a good friend, Tracy Danison, who assisted me with further copy editing and comments on my preface and some parts of the introduction and concluding remarks.

Last and by no means least, I am greatly indebted to my true love and wife, Dr. Azar Mirzaei, a tireless listener and sharp commentator and critic of my stories, arguments, and analyses, who also heroically forbore all the absence—mental, spiritual, and physical—generated by writing this book.

Responsibility for all errors, omissions, and follies, big and small, is mine only.

Introduction

I. A Taboo-Breaking Project

This book provides a first-hand look into intra-Muslim critical scholarship and aims to shed light on relatively unexplored issues touching on the political, cultural and intellectual contexts of the study of Islam in the Muslim academy. It breaks taboos on internal self-criticism. It highlights the influence of politics on Muslim approaches to the Qur'ān and Islam. It shows that the study of Islam (and what are called "Qur'anic sciences") is far and away more political than is generally represented. Finally it shows that the challenges of the study of Islam in the Muslim academy are not usually taken up by the best Muslim students, who are most often more interested in the more practical, lucrative, and prestigious fields of medicine, law, and engineering. This is true that most Muslim-born scholars of Islam now in the West work in anthropology, sociology, history, philosophy, and epigraphy and make a good job of it. However, most have been trained in hard sciences such as physics or mathematics or in liberal arts, history, or social science. Very few, if any, have the compulsory background in Qur'anic sciences, let alone degrees in a specialized area of Qur'ān or Hadith studies of their peers in the Muslim academy. Such a difference of training may have spared Muslim scholars working in the West much dry apologetics and confrontation with intellectual inflexibility, but it also ensures that their outlook does not reflect that of scholars of Islam in the Muslim Qur'anic sciences and theology departments.

It is important to understand from go that this book does not investigate the status of Qur'anic studies in the West, a subject that has been amply studied by Western scholars, theologians, Arabists, and historians.[1] Virtually all study done on methods and theory in religious or Islamic studies look exclusively at Western works and contexts.

Rather, from a Muslim academic perspective, I seek to explore the cultural and political aspects of a Muslim academic discipline usually called "Qur'ān and Tradition" (*al-Qur'ān wa l-Hadith*), a form of an independent academic

Studying the Qur'ān in the Muslim Academy. Majid Daneshgar, Oxford University Press (2020).
© Oxford University Press.
DOI: 10.1093/oso/9780190067540.001.0001

program that does not exist in the usual Western university curriculum in which students *mostly* pursue their interest in Islam as a specialty within such disciplines as, for instance, theology, religion, anthropology, history, or sociology.

As a handy summary of how I have come to understand the critical approach to Islam and the Qur'ān within the discipline of "Qur'ān and Tradition," I use the term "Islamic Apologetics." The followings are among the many terms that I had initially thought to emply for "the study of Islam in the Muslim academy": *Islamic Nistudies* (which was the initial term), *Islamic Defensive*, and *Islamic Normativity*. However, I was gradually convinced that *Islamic Apologetics* is rhetorically more powerful than the aforementioned phrases.

Islamic Apologetics refers to "a set of entrenched scholarly approaches and practices within the worldwide Muslim academy that effectively shield Muslims from critical thinking about Islam and the Qur'ān." More specifically, Islamic Apologetics means "an argument or a rhetorical forensic that substitutes a defense of identity or orthodoxy for critical methodology, analysis, or research."

Islamic Apologetics ensures that Muslims are not given access to critical non-Muslim writings about the Qur'ān and Islam while guaranteeing that a customary sectarian divide insulates Sunnis and Shi'i from each other's ideas and works.

A contributing factor to the stranglehold that Islamic Apologetics has gained in the Muslim academy may be a trend in the West to explore contemporary Muslim community experience, using the field techniques and tools of disciplines such as anthropology and sociology.

The trend toward social science-based approaches suggests—if an increasing focus on raising funds and the terms of funding for such projects is an indicator—that Islamic studies in the Western academy are turning away from deep, library-based understandings of source materials—history, language, origins. In short, research knowledge of Arabic, Syriac, Hebrew, Persian, Ottoman Turkish, Malay (Jawi), and other Near Eastern, classical, and South Asian languages is no longer a key factor in helping a good number of scholars to provide readers and the public with the mysteries of Islam and Muslim communities.

The Muslim academy will be increasingly thrown on its own resources in terms of Islamic studies trends toward "Muslim community" approaches that take hold in the Western academy.

We can see this in the development of grant proposal language since the emergence of the so-called "Islamic State of Iraq and the Levant" (ISIL) in areas of Iraq and Syria and the associated innumerable terrorist actions in the world. These developments along with the long-running civil strife in Syria, involving of course Muslims but also ethnic and religious minorities including Kurds, Christians, and Yazidis have created a "refugee and immigration" crisis atmosphere in Europe and North America especially. As a result, many, if not most, scholars now routinely situate or refer to refugee interaction in the West in their research grant proposals.[2]

Indeed, in view of these events and the issues bedeviling public policy that they have given rise to, combined with the way in which grant money is made available, I think it is fair to expect increasingly greater politicization of Islamic studies in the West in coming years.

Understanding the dynamics of Islamic Apologetics and coming to grips with its evil effects in the Muslim academy is especially urgent in view of this trend toward more internal focus and politicization in the West. It is only reasonable to expect that as Western policy-makers, politicians and academies come more and more to feel that understanding Muslim migrants (first, second, and third generations) and war victims is more important than understanding Islam, textual and historical understanding of the Qurʾān will be treated as less important. Indeed, such source-focused study is already being gradually removed in such Western academies as those in Australia and New Zealand.

Serious critical work in the Muslim academy may be facing a perfect storm: not only a decrease in external support for good work but also a decrease in real expertise in the field (a negative complement to the poorer academic quality of personnel in Muslim Islamic studies departments).

As said earlier, many of those in the West currently seen as experts in matters of Islam are anthropologists and sociologists who have not specialized in the history of Islam, the Qurʾān, *Hadith, Fiqh*, or the Arab or Muslim lands and peoples. For example, the views on global religious violence of the insightful scholar Mark Juergensmeyer (b. 1940) are currently prized. However, while attending a talk given by him, I could not help wondering how such a sociologist or anthropologist could help students of Islam without reference to Islam's history or its founding texts and communities.

The big question here is: Specifically, how can contemporary interview-based material help students understand the notions of *jihad* (holy war), *fitna* (sedition/civil war), *Dar al-harb* (the house/land of war) and *Dar al-Islam* (the house/land of Islam) that are put forward as the motivations and justifications for so much religious violence in the Islamic context? The methods employed and the conclusions reached by Juergensmeyer and others working in the field have great informative potential for sociologists and anthropologists whose studies are, to a large extent, based on the results of field observation, and statistical and conventional analysis. But how many students of religion are familiar with such methods? And although combining social science techniques with historical and textual analysis is *supposed* to enhance understanding of Islamic history and its textual base,[3] in reality, learning qualitative and quantitative analysis tends to turn student attention away from historical understanding and toward contemporary-oriented sociological or anthropological approaches.[4] And, frankly, ironically referencing just ISIL's claim to a "caliphate," there is high potential for real tragedy in this seemingly recondite academic trend, for it remains true that one who does not understand the past is condemned to repeat it and repeat it.

Recent developments in the way Western Islamic studies happen and the effect that such developments are likely to have on the Muslim academy's struggle with Islamic Apologetics are troubling. We should also keep in mind that none of this is happening in a vacuum: There is the complicating factor of penetration of Western theology, politics, and religious studies departments by oil- and Sunni/Shi'i-dominated endowments and institutions from the Islamic world, especially since the events of September 11, 2001.[5]

By emphasizing "dialogue between religions" in their funding and grants, many of the actors of this penetration play a significant role in defining historical and textual approaches to Islam. Scholars respond to the emphasis by underlining distinctions between "ordinary" contemporary Muslims and "extremists." This separation usually involves dissociating modern Muslim culture from its pre-Islamic and Islamic formative periods. As a result, such works as produced under the "dialogue between religions" formula generally enable a superficial knowledge of a historical Islam within a framework that treats modern social, anthropological, and ethnographic concerns. Instead of familiarizing readers with Islam as a faith and culture that has steadily and gradually been evolved by specific communities of believers, they present Islam primarily through the acts and behavior of contemporary communities. None of this allows for speculation about how the Islamic teachings, legal rules, and rituals might have changed over the course of history and therefore how they might change today or in the future.

***

Recent methodological studies and theories about Islam and the Qur'ān in European languages largely ignore how the Qur'ān is taught and explored in the Muslim world. If they do consider the role of the Qur'ān in the Muslim world, they often treat emerged trends in readings of it by religious elites such as, among others, Hamid al-Din al-Farahi (d. 1930) and Amin Ahsan Islahi (d. 1997) in Pakistan (South Asia), Muhammad Husayn Tabataba'i (d. 1981), 'Abdolkarim Soroush (b. 1945), and Mohammad Mojtahed Shabestari (b. 1936) in Iran (Middle East), Abdullah Saleh al-Farsy (d. 1982) in Zanzibar and Kenya, and Ali Muhsin al-Barwani (d. 2006) in Zanzibar (Sub-Saharan Africa), or Hamka (d. 1981) and Quraish Shihab (b. 1944) in Indonesia (Southeast Asia).

Western leadership and investment in projects aiming to strengthen the role and reception of female scholars in Islam, in my view, also reveal a certain ignorance about cultural and scientific issues in the Muslim academy. However well-intentioned, such projects may be more a misguided projection of their own local priorities than help where help is really needed. It is somehow true that women scholars of Islam do not have a strong or really visible presence in Muslim higher education. Equally, female voices are routinely disregarded and feminist perspectives are most often drowned out in overwhelmingly male-dominated environments. And getting women the respect and roles that they merit is a hard slog that has a long way to go.

As in the West, women within their own local Islamic environments have progressively been playing increasingly significant roles in the development of the study of Islam, founding scientific associations, leading departments and doing work that is more and more often cited by male scholars. Citing only Aisha Yousef Al-Mannai (author of *Fundamentals of Belief in the Twelver Shi'a and Mu'tazila*, 1992), director of Sheikh Muhammad Bin Hamad al-Thani Center for Muslim Contribution to Civilization at Hamad bin Khalifa University of Qatar, Forough Parsa (author of *Shi'i Commentaries on the Qur'ān during Persia's Safavid Dynasty*, 2013), head of the Qur'anic Studies Department at the Institute for Humanities and Cultural Studies, Tehran, and Raihanah Binti Haji Abdullah (co-editor of *Women and Islamic Law*,

2001), new director of the Islamic Studies Academy, University of Malaya, we can observe that women are steadily more present and active in the study of Islam.

II. Study Organization

My work on the under-development of critical study and the development of what can only be termed defensive literature—Islamic Apologetics—in the Muslim academy has two articulating parts developed in light of both my personal experience and my professional concerns.

Part I considers how the critical methodology and tools of Western Islamic studies are dealt with, and, in interaction with the former, Part II deals with the persistence of sectarian treatment of the Qur'ān and Qur'anic studies.

Part I is made up of two chapters which highlight the notion of Islamic Apologetics in the Muslim academy and Islamic studies in Western ac-ademia as well as the status of Western Islamic-Qur'anic studies among Muslim academics.

The goal of the first chapter is to prepare readers to see how topics discussed in the Western academy are understood differently in the Muslim academy. In it, I try to unpack the motives and intentions behind the development of Islamic Apologetics in the Muslim academy. This, I hope, will enable readers to understand what Islamic Apologetics both is and is not. I also try to out-line the development of an academic approach to the pertinent issues in the Western academy.

The second chapter of Part I considers the ways in which Western Islamic studies in general, and Western Qur'anic studies in particular, are received in the Muslim academy. I compare the promotion of Islamic Apologetics and the approaches taken by Christian theology programs in the West. I consider also if and, if so, how, the Qur'ān is read in light of science, technology, and biblical literature. Finally, I try to describe how the Muslim academy attempts to set apart and keep separate its institutions and publications from those of Westerners.

Part II, like Part I, is made up of two chapters—3 and 4—and explores how the Muslim academy deals with the Shiʿi-Sunni divide, the use of Edward W. Said's groundbreaking work on cultural representation *Orientalism*, and how Muslims viewed Western scientists (not Western scholars of Islam) while defending Islamic teachings.

Chapter 3 shows how Muslim academics are, or are obliged to be, inattentive to the cultural and literary connections both between the Shiʿi and Sunni traditions and the different diverse Muslim academies. These all combine to create a systemic ignorance of, and systematic disregard for, non-Middle Eastern sources and resources.

As noted, not entirely unconnected to the systemic neglect of Western Islamic and biblical studies, I show that Muslim academics too often do not appreciate the views of co-religionists of a different sect, especially in respect to the Sunni or Shiʿi traditions. This neglect of Islamic sources extends to other countries and cultures, even when these are of the same sect. So, for instance, in contrast to European scholars, who were keen to analyze Islamic classical texts and to translate them into European languages, few Muslim scholars pay attention, or have paid attention, to European languages and, perhaps, more importantly, to such Islamic-Asiatic languages as Urdu or Malay. Indeed, in the Muslim academy generally, Middle Eastern sources—Arabic, Persian, and sometimes, (Ottoman) Turkish—are prioritized and other historical and cultural exchanges utterly neglected and treated as unimportant;[6] Qurʾanic literature from parts of the Muslim world other than the Middle East is not taken into account seriously and systematically.

There also exist political academic mechanisms that underpin ignorance about sects other than that which is dominant for a particular Muslim region. Chapter 3 shows why works dealing with sensitive aspects of Qurʾan and post-Qurʾanic literature in Sunni and Shiʿi contexts have been and are largely ignored in one region or another or only very selectively treated when they are not ignored. This chapter also raises important questions about the reception of scholarly works produced by Muslims in the Malay-Indonesian world and in Africa.

Readers should be careful to note that I do not deal with the reception in Iran, for example, of general, neutral, progressive, and apologetic mystical and so-called intellectual works by Malay scholars such as Syed Muhammad Naquib al-Attas (b. 1931), or the warm welcome of the Iranian-American Seyyed Hossein Nasr (b. 1933) in the Malay-Indonesian world and Turkey.

In addition to a discussion of the use and abuse of *Orientalism* and its thesis in chapter 4, in chapter 3, I demonstrate the concerns of Edward W. Said (d. 2003), who wrote, a few years before his death:

To assume that the ends of education are best advanced by focusing principally on our own separateness, or what accords with our own ethnic

identity, culture and traditions, ironically places us where, as inferior or
lesser races, we had been placed by nineteenth-century racial theory: unable to share in the general riches of human culture.[7]

So, where is the Muslim academy in its ability "to share in the general
riches of human culture"?

Indeed, what do we in the study of Islam have to do to move away from
the philosophy of separateness and move toward an embrace of the riches of
human diversity, both within the Islamic faith and outside of it? By sharing
my thoughts and by offering a frank critique of the Muslim academy, I hope
to encourage Muslim academic authorities and faculties to take heed of Said's
strictures.

The Muslim academy needs especially to put on foot strategies for welcoming the diversity of the Muslim world. It must emphasize mutual awareness of Sunni and Shiʻi and other Islamic and non-Islamic traditions as well
as welcome the perspectives of Muslim peoples, countries, and cultures outside the Middle East.

But, as I argue in chapter 4 of Part II, getting the Muslim academy's act together is not just a question of overcoming a non-embrace of Muslim diversity. It also requires recognizing the value of, and welcoming, non-Muslim
critical approaches to Islam and Islamic studies.

Why are a large number of Western Qurʼanic studies so differently—
grudgingly, poorly—received in the Qurʼān and Hadith departments and
Islamic theology faculties of the Muslim world?

To answer this question, chapter 4 focuses its optics particularly on
the influence on Muslim approaches to the West and Westerners and the
study of the Qurʼān in the Muslim academy of Edward W. Said's important
work on cultural representation, *Orientalism*. I look at how Said, whose
works I always impressed with, did *not*, in the nature of things, accurately
depict the West and Westerners and how, in respect to the study of Islam,
Muslims have tended to substitute Western *scientists* and *literary figures*
for Western *scholars* of Islam. Finally, chapter 4 seeks to explain how a
Muslim "inferiority complex" as [tacitly] played out in *Orientalism*, has
over the years been absorbed into the religious teaching of Islam and
given rise to much of the substance to the defensive quality of the Islamic
Apologetics that the Muslim academy has opposed to historical critical
Islamic studies.

I believe that the Muslim confrontation with Western Islamic studies came to a head at the end of the 1970s as the different cultural revolutions that had roiled the world.

At that time, two groups of works on Islam, its texts and its cultures, faced off against each other. The one focused on a critical approach to the history and development of Islamic texts and beliefs. The other focused on how Islam and Islamic culture had hitherto been presented; the former group was largely seen as a "negative" and the latter's as a "positive" view of Islam among Muslim traditionalists, fundamentalists, and revolutionaries.

Foremost of the "negative" group was John Wansbrough's 1977 *Qur'anic Studies*, which denied the divine origin of the Qur'ān. Wansbrough's ideas are explained in chapter 1.

The "positive" group included especially Edward W. Said's 1978 *Orientalism* and Maurice Bucaille's 1976 *La Bible, le Coran et la science* ("The Bible, The Qur'ān and Science"), both of which presented critiques of Western Christian literature.

Muslim scholars countered Wansbrough's and his followers' critical-historical findings with arguments developed, especially in Said's *Orientalism*, an analysis of Western cultural imperialism and orientalism with respect to the Arab world, and Bucaille's *La Bible*, which argued the scientific reliability of the Qur'ān, in contrast to that of the Bible.

Although *Orientalism* was not a Qur'ān-oriented study, in the Muslim world it has served as the primary reference for Muslim "anti-imperialist" works that harshly critique Orientalists, from its publication in 1978 until the present day. In the early years of the Islamic Revolution, for instance, Iranian "religious intellectuals" established journals and magazines and ran special issues dedicated to Islam and the West in which one of the source references was mainly Said's *Orientalism*. In fact, even the briefest review of academic literature and debate since the book's publication shows that, more than that of any other Western philosophical or literary thinker, Said's thesis has pride of place among all Islamic scholarly humors, including traditionalists, nationalists, anti-Westerners and anti-imperialists (anti-Orientalists) in the Muslim academy proper and in the broader Islamic disposition.

The central place of Said's *Orientalism* and its critique of imperializing cultural representation is also present across the different disciplines of the humanities in the Muslim academy, at the expense of other, more contemporary Western thinkers whose concerns focus and develop Said's.

Consider the works of the renowned Nobel-prize-winning African American writer, literary and social critic, and activist Toni Morrison (b. 1931). Hers—like Said's—are popular in the West and cover most of the principal themes covered by *Orientalism*, including otherness, outsider-ship, exploitation and cultural colonialism and imperialism.

Yet Morrison's readership in the Muslim academy is primarily students of English-language literature; one would be hard-pressed to find, for instance, even a free publisher's copy of Morrison's essay *The Origin of Others*, in translation or not, on the bookshelf of one of the Muslim academy's experts on Islam or history, or politics, or sociology.

Morrison, like Said, whose family immigrated to America from another continent and who, despite his significant influence on American society and academia, deeply felt his status as "Other," knows what being on the outside is like. She too is concerned with its destructive effects on the human spirit.

As well, like Said, Morrison is able to take distance from her own pain and see a wider picture. For example, she is able to characterize the Jim Crow laws that enforced racial segregation in the United States as "silly" or absurd insofar as they "prohibited any negro and white, in any public space, from playing together, 'in game with cards, dice, dominoes or checkers,'"[8] even as she recognizes the deeper social and political intentions involved and the terrible consequences for black America in particular and American society in general.

Morrison, in this also like Said, is someone who knows in the gut "the poison of foreignness," "otherness," and "of not being at home in their homeland; of being exiled in the place where they belong."[9]

But Morrison is very different from Said in *this*: Her ancestors were Africans, brought to America as slaves who would be considered *legally* different, if not absolutely inferior, to other Americans until the 1965 Civil Rights Act definitively outlawed all distinctions. Although Arab and immigrants, the Saids were always unquestionable legal equals of their American-born neighbors.

Morrison argues how a black person became the focus of a white scientist's study, in the same way that Said emphasized the way the Orient and Oriental became the focus of study for a colonial officer. Morrison cites Samuel Cartwright (d. 1863) a physician and slaveowner, who said:

Negroes, as a general rule, to which there are but few exceptions, can only have their intellectual faculties awakened in a sufficient degree to receive moral culture, and to profit by religious or other instruction, when under the compulsatory authority of the white man . . . . From their natural indolence, unless under the stimulus of compulsion, they doze away their lives with the capacity of their lungs for atmospheric air only half expanded, from the want of exercise . . . . The black blood distributed to the brain chains the mind to ignorance, superstition and barbarism, and blots the door against civilization, moral culture and religious truth.[10]

I hope chapter 4 stimulates readers to rethink colonial and post-colonial theories through the lens of my investigation of how Said became the author of reference for revolutionary Muslims inside and outside the academy. I hope that readers will begin to reflect, too, on why Said continues ascendant to the exclusion of such powerful contemporary thinkers as Morrison in the Muslim world.

PART I

1

"Islamic Apologetics" and Islamic Studies

I. On "Islamic Apologetics"

I am in agreement with Edward W. Said's comment that "all people share in the making of history, all people make history" and, therefore, making history requires the anti-ethnocentrism of education—viewing other cultures and phenomena from different angles, using different tools.[1] It is also correct that various "oriental" peoples (primarily Muslims, Christians, Arabs and Persians), such as Hunayn b. Ishaq (d. ca. 873 AD) and Avicenna (d. ca. 1037), have had a profound influence on modern European intellectuals and intellectual movements.[2] Furthermore, almost from the very beginning of Islam, Muslims developed scholarly fields related to Islam such as *fiqh, kalam, falsafa, ta'rikh,* and so forth in their religio-theological schools (*madrasas* or *hawzas*), which fall under the broad canopy of *'ulum al-din* ("the religious sciences"), partly for apologetic reasons. By apologetics in general I mean to refer to a set of defensive strategies to preserve and promote religious teachings via scholarly discourse. In this work, I seek to explore the reverse process: how Muslims have, in return, applied (or deliberately not) modern European approaches to the study of Islam in general and the Qur'ān in particular as part of their scientific discipline, and particularly how they have studied and continue to study the Qur'ān and other Islamic sources in both Sunni and Shi'i academic contexts.

As such, this volume sheds light on how the Qur'ān is studied in Muslim academic contexts, from Africa and the Middle East to the Malay-Indonesian world. Of course, this is an extremely broad arena, so much so that it is difficult for a researcher to provide an accurate investigation of every Muslim country and/or context. Thus, the main emphasis will be on the particular academic departments in which the Qur'ān is taught, rather than on the way that Islam is, in general, practiced in different places. As will be seen, these departments are almost always influenced by either Sunni or Shi'i teachings, each of which have essentially shared, common roots across the world. Consequently, the sources and syllabi used in a Sunni context such

Studying the Qur'ān in the Muslim Academy. Majid Daneshgar, Oxford University Press (2020).
© Oxford University Press.
DOI: 10.1093/oso/9780190067540.001.0001

as Malaysia, for example, would be acceptable in other Sunni-oriented departments in Medina, Islamabad, Istanbul, and Abuja. The same is true for Shi'i contexts. However, as shall be seen, those from a Sunni context are *often* not acceptable in Shi'i ones, and vice versa. In so doing, this volume will highlight the various ways in which Islam is discussed and taught in particular departments and by staff and students in Muslim academic contexts.

The phrase "Muslim academy" or "Muslim academic contexts" will refer to academic institutions or publications that are either directly or indirectly dependent on an Islamic government or any type of religious organization or authority. The academic context in the Muslim world, indeed, brings together nationalism, politics, and religion. These academic contexts are not restricted to universities, but also include colleges and academies (Arabic: *al-majami' al-'ilmi al-'aliy*; Persian: *pazhuhashgah-ha*). In such places, students are not only able to pursue their studies but can also make contributions to social and political discussion groups and seminars related to Islamic culture and identity. Muslim academic contexts offer many compulsory Arabic- and some (often optional) English-language courses. The English-language courses are usually based on reading Muslim apologetic texts that are reflective of the country's dominant sect. As such, for example, Seyyed Hossein Nasr's translation of *Shi'ism* by Shi'i theologian and exegetical figure Tabataba'i is read in Iran. In order to improve students' understanding of English texts, some institutes provide them with readings that critique and criticize the writings of the so-called Orientalists' work within the Western academic field of Islamic studies, such as *The Sublime Quran and Orientalism* by Mohammad Khalifa, which is, for example, read in Malaysia.

Some Muslim academic institutes, in countries such as Jordan, Malaysia, and Indonesia, used to provide scholarships for their students to pursue postgraduate Islamic studies in the West; after completing their studies there, they would be employed as a lecturer in their home country. Being familiar with both Islamic and Western contexts, they could defend Islamic civilization and reject the material aspects of the West, such as the "American Dream."

Also, many of them then became a representative or part of an intellectual, educational, or religious movement in their country that wished to reform or establish an educational, social, or political context. One such scholar is Yusuf Rahman, an Indonesian professor for whom I have a great deal of respect. He studied at McGill University and recently spent significant time showing how Indonesian and Western Qur'anic studies scholars can influence each other.

There are also dozens of Iranian lecturers in Tehran and Qum, Iran, who were supported by the Iranian government and who graduated from North American and British universities that are now divided into various ideological groups.[3] Many of them were directly supported by the wealthy religious foundations in Qum that belong to various conservative and fundamental clerics who have close relations with authorities. These scholars are now very influential, and are often called upon to describe and belittle the notions of "the West" or "Westernization" in the media in addition to their academic activities. Some of them also attempted to propagate their religious views across North America through writing theses on various local religious figures. For instance, in a recent article, I highlighted that several Iranians, who were supported by Iranian religious foundations, graduated from highly regarded Canadian and European universities after finishing theses on Tabataba'i (d. 1981) and his exegetical-philosophical approaches (*Tafsir al-Mizan*).[4] Most of them are now affiliated with (*hawza*-based) universities in Iran, where anti-Westernization and anti-imperialist and anti-Orientalist sentiments are widespread.

As may be surmised from above, in this study, the term "Muslim academy" will not be employed to refer to Islamic religio-theological schools such as *madrasas*, *hawzas*, and *pondoks*, where a student is *supposed to be* a *muballigh*, or propagator of Islamic teachings. Yet, in reality, it is very hard to distinguish between the study of Islam in a university/academy and in a religio-theological school within the Muslim world. Both of them offer degrees accredited by the government, and neither is likely to produce controversial or critical statements about the origin and development of Islam.

Scholars in both declare that Islam is the last and most comprehensive divine religion whose principles are and should remain firm. Both are administered by an "*Irshadic* (Guidance/Directing) power"; this is in contrast to the idea of "pastoral power" that was put forward by Michel Foucault (d. 1984) for the Christian European context.[5] *Irshadic* Power, unlike pastoral power, does not need to know "the insides of people's mind,"[6] but does, instead, need to witness their actual and outward obedience to Islamic authorities (Muhammad, the caliphs, the imams, the successors, etc.), who are believed to be the sources of knowledge and bliss, as well as being the link between God and people. Such can be seen in *English for the Students of*

Qur'anic Sciences and Tradition, published by the post-revolution Iranian Organization for Researching and Composing University Textbooks in the Humanities (SAMT), whose authors remind students that "Islam emphasizes practice more than belief."[7] Similarly, the syllabus of the PhD program "Qur'ān and Tradition" at the University of Isfahan, Iran, dated 2014 (08.03.1393, solar calendar/2014) states that: "The discipline of Qur'anic sciences is the blessed offspring of the Islamic Revolution."[8] It then continues by expressing that one of the main objectives of the discipline is "educating well-grounded scholars in order to defend Qur'anic, exegetical and traditional thoughts,"[9] and, after starting their studies, each student is directed toward being a "defender of Islamic teachings."[10]

Irshadic Power has the potential to impact all community members in all parts of their lives, including academia, politics, and religion, particularly through the important Islamic notion of *amr bi'l ma'ruf wa nahy 'an al-munkar* (recommending good and forbidding evil). This principle states that everything that is compatible or incompatible with Islamic teachings must be recommended or forbidden, respectively. As such, lecturers' teaching materials, methodologies, political beliefs, and behavior in class are regularly monitored by departmental committee members and security staff in the Muslim academy. Some lecturers of religion (including myself), regardless of whether they teach in a university or a *madrasa*, have needed to be *irshad* (corrected) after having referred to Western scholars of Islam or having made positive references to another Muslim sect. Unlike (modern) pastoral power, which wants to "ensure people's salvation in this world,"[11] contemporary *Irshadic* Power still prefers to emphasize the salvation of people in the hereafter. This can be clearly seen if one examines both books and media in the Muslim world, which regularly pronounce the prophetic tradition that "the world is the believer's prison and the non-believer's paradise" (*al-dunya sijn al-mu'min wa janna al-kafir*); simply speaking, whoever falls in love with this world, such as someone who follows the American Dream, will automatically be a materialistic disbeliever. *Irshadic* Power dominates, although it is enforced differently, in Sunni and Shi'i contexts (whether academic or non-academic), from North Africa, through the Middle East, and on to South-East Asia.

These two sects give each other almost no academic support, of any kind, although they do follow a common objective: to preserve their own religious teachings. Both also try to distance themselves from the West through processes of de-Westernization. For both, the modern West is the result of degeneracy, not evolution. As part of such processes, for example, Muslims have their own academic journals and their own peer-review standards, merits, and criteria by which they evaluate and promote their own religious, cultural, and political teaching.[12] Muslims even have their own international publishing houses, which include an army of translators and editors, through which they can, if they want to, produce anti-Western Islamic studies or apologetic material for their own religious beliefs. For instance, Mohsen Alviri, an Iranian cleric, published with SAMT a Persian-language book titled "Islamic Studies in the West," which gives readers a taste of anti-Orientalist ideas and which has been translated into Russian and widely distributed across that country.[13]

The main difference between a Muslim university/academy and theological school is in the way its students approach Islamic texts. In some universities/academies, and due to the presence of scientists, literary figures, and artists, students often have more options to read critical translations of foreign, non-Islamic texts alongside more traditional Islamic sources. In addition, university students may attend classes and gatherings in departments other than religious studies, such as mathematics, physics, chemistry, sociology, and demography, which allow them to move outside the Islamic religious sphere for a time and learn about some non-religious topics. However, the stance toward Islam in both educational contexts is, and has to be, the same. It is very rare to see a university scholar of Islam challenge the divine origin of the Qur'ān. If anyone does, they will be warned and reprimanded.

For example, some years ago, a Qur'ān lecturer was almost expelled from a university in a Shi'i context as a result of some controversial comments he made frequently on the originality of the revelation and the foreign vocabulary in the Qur'ān. During a meeting on the Qur'ān and its language that was held at a university in Qum, which was supposed to be groundbreaking and innovative, he decided to engage the audience with innovative discussions on the presence of Hebrew and Syriac terms in Qur'anic and post-Qur'anic literature. Very soon, he was warned and then stopped by fundamentalists and traditionalists in the audience who explicitly and publicly objected to his approach and called him an infidel. In response to them, this lecturer, who became rather nervous, said: "Here, the policy of university is, unfortunately, the policy of stick and carrot!" He was then silent for the remainder of that meeting and did not share anything with the audience. The lecturer had hoped that he could open up new avenues for young scholars, but even in class his critical approach was not warmly welcomed by students, who had among them some traditionalists and clerics. I observed many times that students believed that he was going astray and needed to be guided. Yet despite intense pressure, he did not give up. To circulate his critical approaches methodology, he ran a blog in (about) 2006 in which he published his thoughts. Despite receiving encouraging comments from the general public outside the university and anonymous readers, the lecturer frequently received summons from the security and the administrative departments commanding him not to propagate his controversial ideas in classes, meetings, or cyberspace; thus, he was essentially banned from talking about his views anywhere. This monitoring, through *Irshadic* Power, aimed to ensure that he would not be critical or controversial. As such, the "Muslim academy" restricted his ideas, not only within academia but also online. However, he did talk about his ideas with me in private, for example in his car, where he was not monitored by anyone. Indeed, it reminded me of how the inside of the Muslim academic context is very different from the outside. Also, I can clearly recall how students were cautious when choosing him to be their supervisor when writing their theses. They were worried that they could be influenced by him or warned by traditionalists or the security department. I have not had contact with him for a long time, but I have heard that he has given up his discussions regarding intertextual connections in religious studies and the historical context of the Qur'ān. As such, it seems his thoughts were successfully suppressed by his opponents.

This volume will not discuss the personalities and research of Muslim scholars such as Nasr Hamid Abu Zayd (d. 2010), 'Abdolkarim Soroush, Mohammad Mujtahid Shabestari, or Mohammad Arkoun (d. 2010), whose works are influential but are not usually used in departments and faculties of religion across the Muslim world. This is because an overview of the syllabi of universities in Medina, Beirut, al-Azhar, Tehran, Isfahan, Aligrah, Kuala Lumpur, and Jakarta—some of the places on which this study will focus—shows that almost in none of these are the works of these scholars placed into either the "readings" or the "further readings" sections. Likewise, works by Muslim scholars that have been published in Western peer-reviewed journals and publications in European languages, which are supposed to be assessed academically, are not addressed in this book. On the other hand, it does examine why some important publications by Muslims in Islamic languages, written outside the context of academia in the Muslim world, are usually not part of syllabi in Muslim academic contexts.[14] The Muslim academy does not address Muslim individuals and thinkers "in the real world outside the academy," [15] where they are not closely monitored by the government and act as individuals. Instead, Muslim academic contexts deal with the specific scholarly framework in which Muslims' *academic* understandings of religion are shaped. Indeed, scholarly concerns in a seminary, *madrasa* or *hawza*, where students are supposed to be propagators of Islam, are intertwined with those of Muslim academic contexts, particularly their universities and colleges.

This volume also unpacks different layers of the Muslim academy in which selected sources are read and examined, and explores various courses and programs in which Islam is studied—but which are not *Islamic studies*, per se—at both undergraduate and postgraduate level in Muslim academic contexts. The "religion of Islam" that is presented in these contexts is different from that seen in the *Islamic studies* discipline that has emerged in the West and from that seen in the academic context of the "other" sect (Sunni or Shiʻi). It will be seen that modern Islamic studies in the West, based on historical and textual analysis, not those that try to peddle a liberal form of Islam, do not seek to convince readers about a certain fact or to provide them with certainty (*yaqin*) but to offer alternative methods for exploring the dark layers of history. In contrast, the study of Islam and the Qurʾān in the Muslim academy falls into three categories: apologetic, neutral, and critical. Some works are produced in order to preserve Islamic identities and promote Islamic values throughout society, which are apologetic. Some studies are neutral, as they do not deal with controversial matters; instead, they resemble an academic report or encyclopedia entry about a specific character or idea within the history of Islam or about a European scholar of Islam (see chapter 2). Some studies are critical, and these are divided into either (1) intra-Islamic polemics or (2) criticism of Western studies of the Qurʾān. The former is produced in considerable numbers, usually for political and sectarian reasons, while the latter views Westerners as Orientalists who are generally seen as distorters of Islamic teachings (see chapters 2 and 3). For instance, in Arabia, Iran, and Malaysia, among other Muslim countries, there are bilingual journals (Arabic-English/Malay-English/Persian-English) devoted to criticizing Western Islamic studies.[16] As such, people within the Muslim academy monitor both external and internal rivals.

Islamic Apologetics, Not Islamic Studies

The study of Islam and the Qur'ān in Muslim academic contexts not only seeks to negate (*nafy*), reject (*naqaḍ*), and interdict (*nahy*) the Western *Islamic studies* model that has emerged since the post-Enlightenment period, but to do the same to the other Muslim sect's approach, too. As such, Muslims' study of Islam and the Qur'ān "is not" Islamic studies nor is it comprehensive nor anti-sectarian. Thus, it is "Islamic apologetics." This term shows how modern (Western) Qur'ān scholarship is rejected or modified in Muslim academic contexts and how Sunni sources are rejected in Shi'i academic contexts, and vice versa. It does not lead to the presentation of new global theories and/or methodologies. "Islamic apologetics" encompasses *Islamic religious studies*, a phrase recently laid out by Aaron W. Hughes about North Americans' approach to the study of Islam, one which is "theological in orientation, manipulative in its use of sources, and distortive in conclusions," and which has the aim of showing a merciful and less controversial picture of Islam, its emergence and development.[17] As will be seen in the next chapter, Islamic apologetics allows an author to censor a text, misrepresent it, and be selective in choosing various types of sources. Islamic apologetics is a specific method of studying Islam that is not and, from an insiders' perspective, *should not* be compatible with modern (Western) scholarship. In Islamic apologetics, a "relentlessly erudite researcher" is not to be an archaeologist of knowledge, aiming to "dig up [different] documents, raiding archives, rereading and demystifying texts";[18] instead, he is forced to trust, follow, study, and live with his past and tradition. Islamic apologetics both is and is not an indigenous approach toward teaching and studying the Qur'ān in Muslim academic contexts, one which is tied in with reformism, nationalism, and sectarianism.

As such, its flexibility is limited, although it does vary region by region, government by government, and period by period. For instance, the study of Islam before and after King Faisal in Arabia (r. 1964–1975), before and after the Iranian revolutions (of 1909 and 1979), before and after Atatürk in Turkey (r. 1923–1938), before and after Mahmoud Ahmadinejad in Iran, and before and after any other religious or political movement, are all very different.

Islamic apologetics is mainly based on the central tenets of Islam,[19] which should, it is decreed, be preserved from generation to generation. Everything else, that which falls outside of these main tenets, is negotiable by local intellectuals or reformists. For instance, while Muhammad Khatami (b. 1943), the former President of Iran, could shake hands with a woman in Europe—for which he was criticized—he and his followers in universities were not able to freely challenge the Qur'anic verse related to the wearing of the *hijab* in Iran. Although, in Indonesia, a public event can start with the recitation of the Qur'ān by a woman, which really surprised me, it is very unlikely that someone could freely and frequently challenge the divine origin of Islam, the revelation, and Muslims' dogmatism in an *akademi pengagian Islam* (academy of Islamic studies).

Islamic apologetics, as will be seen, is selective, and through it the authorities decide which works should be translated and studied in the Muslim academy and which should not. For instance, works by influential Iranian figures are very rarely translated into Malay by Malaysian publishers. For example, despite post-Khatami and post-Rouhani cultural attempts to translate Persian and Shi'i works in Malaysia, not many of them take into account in the Malaysian academic context in general and their *jabatan* (Department of) *Sejarah dan Tamaddun* (History and Civilization), *Aqidah dan Agama* (Theological Doctrine and Religion), and *al-Qur'ān dan al-Hadith* in particular. Recently, the cultural center of the Embassy of Iran in Kuala Lumpur supported the Malay translation of the Persian poet Sa'di's (d. ca. 1291) masterpiece, the *Gulistan* (The Rose Garden) in Malaysia. Whether he was a Sunni or a Shi'i believer, Sa'di is currently one of the main representatives of Persian literature, something that has no place in Malay-Indonesian academies that more widely study Islam and the Sunna.[20] Very soon after its publication (in which the name of its translator is deliberately left blank on the cover), the Malaysian editor and novelist Nazmi Yaakub argued that Sa'di's book should not be considered as a uniquely Persian piece of heritage,[21] as it was written in the pre-Safavid period of the Islamic world, when Shi'ism was not yet the state religion of Persia, and thus it is the property of all Muslims, including Malays. The *Gulistan* or *Taman [Bunga] Mawar* was cited by various scholars of the Qur'ān and Islamic literature over the course of history, though it is not seen on the syllabi of courses on Islam and civilization in Malaysian academic contexts, which are heavily politicized and Arabized. Likewise, the Persian translation of the Malay classical figure Hamzah Fansuri's (d. ca. 1590) works (discussed in chapter 3), which are replete with Persian elements, are missing from Iranian academic contexts. Recently, three of his mystical treatises were translated into Persian under the supervision of the cultural center of the Embassy of Iran in Kuala Lumpur, but if this is the case, it will not be done as a result of Fansuri's significance in the Malay-Indonesian world but because of references to Persian elements, and it is not clear whether such will be used in the Iranian academic context. On the other hand, many Persian works by Ali Shari'ati and Khomeini, among others, are frequently translated and reproduced by Indonesian institutes and publications such as *Mizan*, and more recently the Shi'i-dominated *RausyanFikr* institute. These works are widely read by students in Indonesian universities and colleges.

As such, this is governmental and religious politics directing people as to what to read and not to read within the Muslim academy. As will be seen, the Iranian government is currently extremely influential across Indonesia, and it is exporting Iranian revolutionary, religious, and political ideas to that country. On the other hand, Malaysian Islamic scholarship is deeply dependent on Saudi Arabia and so, unsurprisingly, Persian works are marginalized there; this is very likely to be true for other Muslim communities around the world, too. Being religiously or politically Sunni or Shi'i, Arabized or Persianized, affects the way Islam is taught in Muslim academic contexts in Africa (e.g., Kenya, Nigeria), in Eastern Europe (e.g., Bosnia and Herzegovina), and in South Asia (Sri Lanka, Bangladesh). It is Islamic governments' sectarian and racist attitudes and their strong religious basis that dictate the features of Islamic Apologetics.

It must be admitted that the case becomes more complicated if we assess the study of Islam in some Lebanese, Egyptian, Qatari, and Emirati colleges and institutes that are connected and affiliated with Judeo-Christian, British, Australian, New Zealand, and American institutes, universities, and people. Whether the study of Islam in their departments and faculties are closely linked to the main poles for the study of Islam, philosophy and the Shari'a in Arabia (in Mecca and Medina), Egypt (in al-Azhar), and Iran (Qum, Mashhad, Rayy) is unclear.[22] Many of these faculties and their academic staff are operating between modernity and tradition. They want to or must become modern while at the same time preserving their traditional identity. Yet a review of the publications of American and European scholars (without wishing to mention any of them by name) based in Arab academic contexts demonstrates that, up to now, none of them has produced any study of the origin and early period of Islam, nor of related topics that are likely to prove controversial, to say the least, in their place or country of work. Many of them instead produce "neutral" works, dealing with safe, or even "approved" topics, that address contemporary debates on Islamic law and the Shari'a,

Islamic finance and education, Muslims in Europe, etc. Many of these are also influenced by Muslim and mystical scholars in the West such as Seyyed Hossein Nasr, Hamza Yusuf (b. 1960), and Tariq Ramadan (b. 1962), who usually present only a mystical, ethical, or holistic spiritual image of Islam.

II. Western Islamic Studies

Naturally, the Qurʾān and other scriptures have played an important role in Western Islamic studies. Within this context, scholars used to study the Qurʾān and biblical literature together, as part of their studies of Islam, which surely was not always an innocent endeavor.

In the second half of the eighteenth century, historians, Arabists, and literary figures accompanied Christian priests and missionaries in order to study Islam. Instead of choosing an apologetic or a polemic approach to Islam, *many of them*, regardless of whether or not they were helping to promote Western colonialism and imperialism, based their work primarily or exclusively on a personal scholarly passion, thus choosing an *academic* approach to the religion. In modern Islamic scholarship, "the emphasis has not been upon whence the Qurʾanic worldview derives, but rather what the Qurʾanic text can tell us about the man who presented it to the world, the community that grew up in response to its message, and the history of the earliest period of this community's life."[23]

A new generation of Western scholars came after Leopold von Ranke (d. 1886), who, having been impressed by Kantian philosophy, declared the primacy of official documents over any historical information that was based on "tradition." For such scholars, original sources, including Islamic manuscripts, became more valuable for post-eighteenth-century European scholars of the Orient; this was not in order to rule over or civilize *Orientals* but to acquire knowledge.[24] Many of them were also impressed by Karl Lachmann (d. 1851), who "raised the science of textual criticism to a higher level by developing a set of instruments to analyse the reciprocal relationship between the surviving manuscripts of one particular text."[25]

This new approach, which spread throughout Europe and North America, was mostly the result of human rational progress and the post-Enlightenment era—*not* religious missionary concerns. In contrast to Christian polemicists and apologists, they tried to put aside the holiness of religions and their scriptures. Finding "possibilities for further source analyses [rather than to establish] historical facts"[26] became the priority of Western scholars of religion in general, and Islam in particular. Offering new insights into puzzling historical events became more important than describing the (im)purity of particular people or the quality of rewards and punishments in Paradise and Hell respectively. This was, in fact, inherited from Ranke, who, while studying the Psalms, tried to "connect one and another with specific events in the history of the Kings."[27] The objective of academic works by Western scholars of Islam was to help scholars complete the puzzle of the history of religion. Therefore, they had to be equipped with knowledge of other scriptures, texts, and historical documents and manuscripts.

Abraham Geiger (d. 1874) was the first scholar to perform textual and historical analyses comparing Islam and Judaism. As such, scholars abandoned medieval Christian views of Islam and gradually became interested in adding one or more alternatives into the field in order to specify the textual and conceptual connections of early Muslims with Jewish literature. Geiger's work *Was hat Mohammed aus dem Judenthume aufgenommen?* was a fresh approach at that time that "helped to foster a more objective and less overtly polemical approach to the life of Muḥammad."[28] Later, Theodor Nöldeke (d. 1930),[29] whose *Geschichte des Qorāns* achieved a "default position" for Qur'anic study in the late nineteenth and early twentieth century, also followed this approach.[30] He emphasized the chronological order of Qur'anic chapters and connected Qur'anic and post-Qur'anic literature. As such, "Nöldeke's work has set the agenda for subsequent generations of Qur'ānic scholarship by emphasizing concerns with chronology in the text and the text's biblical background."[31]

Unlike colonial officers' political application of language, which was "generally used as the medium of official communication over the vast extent of Your Majesty's Asiatic dominions,"[32] modern scholars of Islamic studies, for sure not all of them, have shed light on the application of philology and textual sources in academic contexts. According to William A. Graham (b. 1943) at Harvard University, the factors that are basic to modern Qur'anic scholarship are:

(1) The semantic background of the Qur'anic text, (2) the particular nexus of previously existing vocabulary and ideas that provided a medium for the Qur'anic revelation, and (3) the strong continuity—something firmly asserted in the Qur'ān itself—of Islam with its monotheistic predecessors, especially the Jewish and Christian traditions.[33]

As such, textual sources have shaped modern scholarship within Islamic studies; this is what Graham calls the "textual orientation"[34] of the academic study of the Qur'ān.

III. Modern Trends in Qur'anic Studies

It was the famous and influential Hungarian scholar Ignác Goldziher (d. 1921) who presented perhaps the most strikingly different modern study of the Qur'ān compared to his contemporaries. He highlighted how an understanding of Islam and modern Muslims could be connected to early Islamic exegetical-*hadithi* literature. He wrote "we are also greatly indebted to al-Tabari (d. ca. 923 AD) for variants in the text of the Koran. The example which I used [above] to demonstrate this problem originates almost exclusively from his *tafsir*."[35] As such, Goldziher's *Die Richtungen der islamischen Koranauslegung* is regarded as the backbone of modern studies of Islamic exegetical works. That book examines how Egyptian reformers of the nineteenth century received and applied classical interpretations of Islam.[36] To describe the emergence of modern movements in India, Goldziher analyzed both Islamic traditions and Syed Ameer Ali's (d. 1928) interpretation of Islam.[37] His work clearly shows the interdependence of Islamic scripture and the Muslim community throughout history. Subsequently, other studies on the Qur'ān were produced by Friedrich Zacharias Schwally (d. 1919), Gotthelf Bergsträsser (d. 1933), and Otto Pretzl (d. 1941), all of whom prepared volumes regarding the collection and variant readings of the Qur'ān.[38] What Ranke, Geiger, Nöldeke, and Goldziher, among others, presented was convincing enough to stimulate future generations of scholars to continue along the path (not the result) they had forged and to analyze "the formal, stylistic and linguistic aspects of the text, as well as . . . the terminology of the Qur'ān and . . . its semantic and conceptual" aspects.[39]

From the late nineteenth to the early twentieth century, both the Qur'ān and Muhammad's life were subjected to detailed scrutiny by scholars of Islam, such as in the three-volume set by A. Sprenger. From the first decades of the twentieth century, significant numbers of meetings and conferences were held annually in various places in the West, which, along with encyclopedic movements (such as the *Encylopaedia of Islam* first published by Brill in the Netherlands in 1913), prompted scholars to consider specific terms, names, events, concepts, and works related to the Qur'ān, *hadith* compendia,

sira (Muhammad's biography), commentaries, and Judeo-Christian literature in light of the early Islamic Arabian context. Yet there were few studies
written before 1950 on various individual Muslims; one article that was
written before then examined the life of Fakhr al-Din al-Razi (d. ca. 1209),
the famous theologian and Qur'ān exegete.[40]

The second half of the twentieth century saw further textual orientation
projects based on: (a) the semantic analysis of Qur'anic notions, such as those
by Toshihiko Izutsu (d. 1993), who opined that a term makes sense in the
context of its use; (b) the emergence of literary analysis, seeing the Qur'ān as
the product of literary activity [fictional literature],[41] started by Wansbrough
and developed by Rippin; (c) the profound study of the historical and cultural
context of Late Antiquity developed by Patricia Crone (d. 2015) and Michael
Cook (b. 1940);[42] (d) the examination of the "liturgical and heavily sym-
bolic nature of the language of the Qur'ān"[43] by Angelika Neuwirth (b. 1943);
and (e) the analysis of Qur'anic hermeneutics through classical exegetical
works (*tafasir*) by Gerhard Böwering (b. 1939) and Jane Dammen McAuliffe
(b. 1944).

Subsequently, scholars have generally become either supporters or
opponents of one or more of the aforementioned trends. A further helpful development has been the use of various new techniques alongside one or more
of the above-mentioned approaches from Qur'anic studies. It is too difficult,
at present, to find a work that fully covers all modern trends in the academic
study of the Qur'ān, but Powers' books, particularly *Zayd* (also related to his
previous book: *Muḥammad Is Not the Father of Any of Your Men*), provide
readers with an overview of the evolution of theories on the originality of the
Qur'ān and the development of Muslim communities as they were discussed
by Wansbrough, among others. It is true that many of Wansbrough's ideas
regarding the collection of the Qur'ān are controversial. As Schöller says, "to
clarify this issue will be a major challenge for the modern study of the Qur'ān
in the years to come,"[44] while Robert Irwin has stated that Wansbrough's
publications in the 1970s were "devastatingly original and controversial."[45]
Powers not only analyzed the historical context, literature, and original texts
but also highlighted the significance of the imagination in shaping human
identity and history. While employing various methods to interpret the
history of the Qur'ān, Powers' work also renders Wansbrough's "ideas into
straight-forward, [concise,] and readable English."[46] Readers might know
how difficult it is to understand Wansbrough's analysis in his controversial

book *Qur'anic Studies*. Many Muslims who did not have access to (a translation of) *Qur'anic Studies* and could not read English well simply rejected
Wansbrough's ideas. This is despite the fact that anyone who wants to analyze his approach should, according to Charles J. Adams (d. 2011), be fully
familiar with several different languages and cultures.[47] Despite this, in the
Muslim academy students never study non-Islamic languages and cultures
such as Greek, Hebrew, Syriac, and Aramic. Yet any critic of Wansbrough
(and Powers)

> must also have a thorough grounding in biblical and rabbinic studies as well
> as Islamic studies. Needless to say, perhaps, not many of those of us whose
> primary interest is the Islamic religious tradition have those qualifications,
> particularly the acquaintance with Jewish studies that is evident on every
> page of Wansbrough's work.[48]

Wansbrough was called by Adams the mentor of Britain's "revisionist
school of Islamic scholars,"[49] the main emphasis of which is on the canon-
ization of the Qur'ān in the second and third centuries of the Islamic calendar. Wansbrough showed how Muslims competed with Jews in the second
century (AH), as a result of which they tried to develop their own unique
identity and "invent an Arabian background for the rise and early history
of Islam. Such a background would distinguish Muslims quite sharply from
Jews and guarantee a true factor of uniqueness to Islam."[50] Nonetheless, in
contrast to Wansbrough, who did not suggest "who was responsible for deciding what did, or did not belong to the Qur'ānic canon,"[51] Powers studies
both well-known and neglected Muslims from the early period of Islam,
whose names and roles are frequently mentioned in early Islamic literature. Moreover, Powers used many innovative methodologies and added
historical texts that were not employed by Wansbrough and others. It
seems that Powers, like Rippin, echoes Fred M. Donner's (b. 1945) research
concern that

> we must be able "to say who was responsible for deciding what did, or did
> not, belong to the Quranic canon . . . ." To put the responsibility for such a
> process simply on "the continuity" or "the scholars" is too vague; we need to
> have some idea of what individuals, or at least what groups, were involved
> in making decisions, and what interests they represented.[52]

Donner has raised various objections to Wansbrough's thesis, and asked a number of questions:

- Does the Qur'ān really have the characteristics of a text that crystallized over two (or more) centuries, and largely outside Arabia, as Wansbrough's hypothesis implies?
- If the Qur'anic text is really a product of the same milieu that produced the *hadiths* and the origins narratives, so that the *hadith* and various passages in early narrative sources contain (to use Wansbrough's own phrase) "sub-canonical" versions of Qur'anic material, why is the content of the Qur'ān so different from that of the other materials?[53]

Powers tried indirectly to provide an answer to these questions. He not only built his studies upon on available textual sources, but also on rare manuscripts. For instance, to find out more about the term *kalala* (lit., "the one that has no parent or child") in the Qur'ān (4:12), in *Muḥammad Is Not the Father of Any of Your Men*, after first referring to François Déroche's (b. 1952) Qur'anic manuscript analysis, Powers expressed:

The word *kalāla* is packed tightly between the word that precedes it and the word that follows it: only 2 mm separate the initial *kāf* of *kalāla* from the final *thā'* of *y-w-r-th*; and only 1 mm separate the final *hā'* of *kalāla* from the base of the initial *alif* of *aw*.[54]

After a comprehensive study of a number of manuscripts, Powers concluded "I have argued that the original meaning of *4:12b was forgotten and that a *better* version of this was produced: 4:12b. I also have argued that a new and improved version of 4:12b was *formulated* and inserted at the end of *Sūrat al-Nisā*."[55] To write his book on Zayd, the temporarily adopted son of the Prophet, Powers also combined different approaches. The result is most thought-provoking.[56] Q 33:37, which mentions by name the Prophet's adopted son Zayd, together with the pericope in which it is embedded, vv. 36–40 of *Surat al-Ahzab*, are the focal points of Powers' book *Zayd*. In the conclusion, Powers postulates that Q 33:36–40, which link a domestic crisis within the Prophet's family to the doctrine of the finality of his prophecy, were added to the Qur'ān during the caliphate of 'Abd al-Malik b. Marwan, fifty years or so after the Prophet's death, by the caliph's agent al-Hajjaj b. Yusuf al-Thaqafi. The interpolation, Powers speculates, served the political interests of the Umayyads by "eliminating the argument for leadership based on sonship." It also served "to silence 'false' prophets," "to promote Islam and its prophet as the culmination of sacred history," and to illustrate God's power and ability to protect a prophet from committing sin. This conclusion agrees with that of Alphonse Mingana, which was published about a century ago, and which highlights "the dating of the final official version of the Qur'ān . . . to the time of the caliph ʿAbd al-Malik."[57] Mingana refers to a report dealing with collection of the Qur'ān by ʿAbd al-Malik himself in the month of Ramadan.[58]

Powers' innovation is to ask the reader to consider the possibility that the figure of Zayd as depicted in the Islamic sources is not identical with the historical Zayd. He examines a wide range of Islamic sources that contain narrative reports about Zayd, his son Usama, and Zaynab bt. Jahsh al-Asadiyya, who was the wife first of Zayd and, subsequently, of Muhammad.

Zayd is the only Muslim apart from Muhammad who is mentioned by name in the Qur'ān. The reference occurs in the chapter al-Ahzab, which currently has 73 verses, although, according to various Companions, it originally had either 129, 200, or 286 verses. If fifty or more verses could be removed from this sura, Powers asks, echoing the "interpolation hypothesis," could not also a number of verses have been added? The possibility that verses were added to or removed from the Qur'ān is a subject that has long been discussed by both Muslim and non-Muslim scholars. According to Amir-Moezzi in The Silent Qur'ān and the Speaking Qur'ān, some Shiʿis, for example, claim that references to ʿAli, his descendants, and their enemies were removed from the Qur'ān.[59] According to Powers, Zayd was marginalized in the earliest biographical sources on Muhammad, such as the Sira of Ibn Hisham, because he posed serious threats—both political and theological—to the leaders of the early Muslim community and to Shiʿis, Umayyads, and ʿAbbasids, whose supporters were among the compilers and editors of the Qur'ān, Sira, and other texts. As the son of Muhammad, his credentials for leadership were arguably as strong as, or stronger than, those of any other Companion, including the first four caliphs. This claim closely resembles that of some Shiʿa, who opined that ʿAli, the fourth caliph, and his family were marginalized in society and their names removed from the Qur'ān by their opponents after the death of the Prophet.

Although Powers does not present any physical evidence to support the interpolation hypothesis, he does argue that "timing of the revelation of verse 40 [on the finality of Muhammad's prophethood] is odd" and that the claim of "finality" makes better sense in the historical context of Umayyad Damascus around 700 than it does in the context of Medina between 622 and 632, when Muhammad was struggling to establish his status as a true prophet in the face of opposition from Jews and others. To highlight the significance of the finality notion as well as the possibility of a significant revision of the Qur'ān, it might have been worthwhile to pursue the findings of Amikam Elad and Yehuda Nevo, which mention that "the first true glorifications of Muhammad as the prophet of a religion independent of both Judaism and Christianity also date from the period of 'Abd al-Malik."[60]

By uncovering and exploring layers of early Islamic and non-Islamic texts, Powers shed new light on the creation and development of a new religion in Late Antiquity, a new religious culture in Arabia, and a new religious figure among the Arabs, although the question of interpolation and omission, particularly during the Umayyad period, could have been discussed in more detail. Regardless of the accuracy of the scriptures, Powers raised serious questions, and, in so doing, attempted, using various methods, to shake up the history of Late Antiquity. It is worth mentioning that, despite being supported by learned scholars based in the West, such as Mohammad Ali Amir-Moezzei (b. 1956), who said that "Il est indéniable que c'est de l'examen critique et comparatif de toutes sortes de sources, sans en négliger aucune, que pourront jaillir quelques lueurs sur l'histoire encore énigmatique des débuts de l'islam et de ses sources scripturaires."[61]

David Powers' *Zayd* has not been well received in Muslim academic contexts. The reasons for this will be examined in the next chapter.

IV. Studying Islam outside Its Core Lands

In addition, some Western scholars have focused their attention outside the core lands of Islam, toward places such as South Asia and the Malay-Indonesian world. In contrast to colonial anthropological studies of Muslims' lives and behavior, some modern Western scholars, such as Anthony Johns (b. 1928) and Peter G. Riddell (b. 1951) from Australia have used original *Jawi* (Arabic-Persian alphabet) manuscripts and printed volumes to analyze the emergence and development of Qur'ān translations and commentaries in the Malay Peninsula.[62] Johns and Riddell also explored the Arabian and Middle Eastern roots of classical and modern Malay Qur'ān commentaries, translations, and literature, which had only rarely been examined, by a small

number of colonial officers, such as Sir Richard Olaf Winstedt (d. 1966).[63]
For instance, Riddell's 1984 PhD thesis and some of his publications have
concluded that *Tarjuman al-mustafid*, the oldest known Malay Qur'ān interpretation, which covers the whole of the Qur'ān and was compiled in
the seventeenth century by Shaykh 'Abd al-Ra'uf, is a translation of well-
known classical Arabic exegetical works, mainly *al-Jalalayn* and, second-
arily, *al-Baydawi* and *al-Khazin*. Through his discovery, it became clear that
Malay-Indonesian Qur'anic educational systems were closely connected to
medieval Arabo-centric sources; such classical works were and still are frequently taught in Middle Eastern *madrasa*s and seminaries.[64] Furthermore,
other scholars (from Germany), such as Roman Loimeier (b. 1957), have
paid attention to translations of the Qur'ān produced in Africa,[65] an approach which has been only rarely pursued by Muslim scholars, such as
Hassan Ma'ayergi.[66]

   Recently, a number of learned societies in the North American context have been established, such as the new International Qur'anic Studies
Association (IQSA) and the Qur'ān panel of the American Academy of
Religion (AAR), and these, despite the lack of unity, put particular emphasis
on Islam in Late Antiquity and Qur'ān commentary, among others. Through
these, and particularly their annual conferences and discussion forums, ever
more Western scholars are working on neglected issues within Qur'anic
studies.

   Also, some emerging scholars have been keen to work on the Late Antique
Persian Sassanid Empire, the "opponent" of the Byzantine Empire, making
use of the work of Iranologists such as Touraj Daryaee (b. 1967), among
others. This is because, as Daryaee notes, knowledge of Iran at that time is
"important for understanding the development of world civilization."[67]
Therefore, Islam, Persia, and all other so-called ancient civilizations and communities are not regarded as separate, and analyzing the origin and evolution
of Islam outside the Arabian Peninsula will not only connect the Qur'ān to
its socio-cultural context and audience but also suggests that the "Islams" in
Persia, Africa, South- and Southeast Asia, and Europe are all interlinked and
should, from the very outset, be deconstructed and examined through the
lens of relevant texts and history.

2

The Qur'ān in the Muslim Academy

What Should Be Censored?

I. Muslims' Views of Western Islamic Studies

While growing up in the Middle East, I used to wonder about how religion is taught in the Western academy. What was available to many of us with a traditional background (and without access to satellite television) was either news about or translations of Western academic achievements, particularly in the fields of technology and engineering. There was, however, a dearth of information regarding the study of religion in the West. Perhaps the easiest way to guess how religion was being taught there was to generalize everything coming from *there* under the canopy of the Enlightenment and the academic context. As such, I considered myself to be a member of a backwards community (*us*) who saw the West (*them*) as more advanced in every academic field, including religious studies. At that time it was not known, neither by me nor by many others, that Western Islamic studies, despite its groundbreaking productions, was largely Eurocentric and only rarely does it include allusions to [non-elite] Muslim scholars of Islam who have actively participated in different scientific events in the Muslim academy. The works produced in the West are extremely interesting, yet they mostly suffer from viewing Islam through the lens of a specific community of Islamic and non-Islamic elites.[1]

Although some readers may consider this an exaggeration, we imagined the West as a land of classy people with colorful eyes. One became proud of oneself for visiting a Western country. Indeed, *there* was everything many of my friends wanted, too. They left their country to become civilized and classy! For many Middle Easterners, the *West* was and is known as *onvar-e ab* or *al-kharij* (literally "overseas"). Overseas for them was never regarded as being in an easterly direction! Recently, some of them have moved to countries that are Oriental allies of Western societies (India, Singapore, South Korea, Japan, China, Malaysia, etc.), where they plan to live for a time.

Studying the Qur'ān in the Muslim Academy. Majid Daneshgar, Oxford University Press (2020).
© Oxford University Press.
DOI: 10.1093/oso/9780190067540.001.0001

Studying, working, or living in South, Southeast, or East Asia—which are areas perceived as better than the chaotic Middle East—is viewed as being a platform from where they can reach the West.

From the mid-twentieth century, and particularly in the last decades of the twentieth and the early twenty-first century, many Middle Easterners have paid significant attention to learning English. They have established foreign language courses and provided government-sponsored masters and PhD scholarships for talented students who are supposed to come back and serve in the Middle East upon graduation from universities in the West. Following the early-nineteenth-century acts of Muhammad ʿAli (d. 1849), who sent the first group of Egyptians to Paris to study,[2] modern Islamic governments have done so too, yet this time not only to Paris but to places throughout the West. Unlike Muhammad ʿAli, who sent students to study law,[3] Muslim countries, especially Iran and those of Arabia, have paid little attention to the humanities.[4] Most students sent to the West are graduates of engineering, science, and medicine, while very few have been from law and economics. Authorities did not and still do not send Islamic studies students to the West.[5] Unsurprisingly, for the Muslim authorities, the study of Islam and its Scriptures in an academic context should be done in *umm al-qura* ("The Mother of the Cities") of the Islamic lands, such as Mecca, Medina, Qum, Rayy, and Mashhad.

Western Scholars of the Qur'ān: Popular or Unpopular?

As mentioned already, Muslim scholars who reside in the Islamic world who want to learn about Western knowledge of religion in general, and of Islam in particular, have to refer to translations of Western works. However, translations of all such "alien" works are not available; indeed, much of Middle Easterners' understanding of Islam is based upon selective translations of Western outputs. To be eligible for translation into local languages and be well received by academics, the general public, and the government, a work should be one of the following: (a) supportive and compatible with Islamic—and sometimes governmental—teachings; (b) neutral essays or reports that do not address controversial issues regarding the origin of Islam; or (c) critical and anti-Orientalist works presenting Westerners' unfamiliarity with the "greatness" of Islamic civilization or their attempts to ruin Muslims' identity.

It is, therefore, possible to find translations of some Western scholars' works, including those of Andrew Rippin, a famous historian of Islam, within the Muslim world. I will discuss the status of his works in the Muslim academy shortly. However, publishing a translated work is not easy and the conditions vary from country to country. Western works that echo Shi'i teachings are not usually translated in Sunni-majority countries, and vice-versa. Instead, they may be critiqued. For instance, some Persian Shi'i scholars have argued that both Orientalists and Sunnis have attempted to downplay the role of the first Shi'i imam, 'Ali b. Abi Talib, in the collection of the Qur'ān:

> In Orientalists' studies, the intention [of distortion] is to some extent seen. They, following Sunni people, push aside Imam 'Ali from the virtue of the Qur'ān collection . . . the Qur'ān as collected by Abū Bakr has no annotations or commentary and he had a political motive for his work.[6]

In this regard, the famous contemporary Shi'i clergyman Makarim Shirazi (b. 1926), whose works are taught in different institutes throughout the world (e.g., in Jakarta, Washington), contends that there is a group of Orientalists whose "one-sided" approach toward Islam is entirely based on Sunni sources; "they know nothing of Shi'i sources and so they might work in favor of Sunnism, which ends with loss for us [the Shi'a]."[7] Thus, to be known as fair Orientalists, according to Makarim Shirazi, Western scholars not only need to be uncontroversial but should not attack the Shi'i school. Sunni scholars such as Himmich (b. 1948), who wrote on Edward Said, among others, also believes that some Orientalists, including Henry Corbin (d. 1978), echoed Persian and Shi'i Islam and mysticism, which led to the expansion of Persian Shi'i authorities over Sunnis and the Arabic language.[8] Nonetheless, there are so-called Orientalists who have been admired, to some extent, by different Muslim communities.

John Burton's *The Collection of the Qur'ān* (1977), which has been translated into some Asian languages, was fairly well received by Muslims compared to works by other Western scholars of Islam, such as Wansbrough. Because Burton's opinion regarding the collection of the Qur'ān during the life of Muhammad was compatible with that of Islamic teachings,

> Burton's analytical methods regarding the collection of the Qur'ān's traditions proves that he considers the Qur'ān as the earliest and most

common source used for Muslims' legal and jurisprudential instructions. Thus, his method, . . . unlike that of [other] Western scholars, is not to prove that the Qur'ān is an immortal literary book.[9]

Although Burton is accused of having been influenced by Joseph F. Schacht (d. 1969), who "claimed and popularized the theory that all _hadeeth_ literature are forgeries of the scholars of the second and third century of the hijrah,"[10] the contrast of his conclusion with that of other Western scholars of the Qur'ān such as Arthur Jeffery (d. 1959) is praised:

> For Burton's honesty, at least, he must be given greater credit than Jeffery. He states, ". . . one must either accept all _hadeeth_ impartially with uncritical trust, or one must regard each and every _hadeeth_ as at least potentially guilty of a greater or lesser degree of inherent bias . . . We cannot in our arrogance continue to presume that guided by mere literary intuition we can safely pick our way, selecting or rejecting hadeeths . . . ."[11]

It is the work of Richard Bell (d. 1952), as well as that of William Montgomery Watt (d. 2006), who edited and revised Bell's writings, that are admired more than other Western works within Muslim academic contexts. Bell's _Introduction to the Qur'ān_ and _The Qur'ān Translated_ were both rendered into various languages, including Persian and Indonesian.[12] The thing that distinguishes Bell's, and particularly Watt's, works from those of other Western scholars is their acceptance of the divine origin of the Qur'ān and the prophecy of Muhammad. This is why Watt's _Muhammad in Mecca_—with a slightly changed title; _Muhammad, Peace Be Upon Him and His Household, in Mecca_—was translated into Arabic in Cairo in 1994.[13] Also, Baha'iddin Khurramshahi, one of the most famous Iranian translators and scholars of the Qur'ān, contends that Watt was the one who first moved from polemical approaches to the Qur'ān to academic ones.[14] However, when translating Bell-Montgomery's book, Khurramshahi still omitted some of it, and stated:

> In general, due to their contradiction with the holy religion of Islam, some paragraphs and sentences were removed from the whole body of the book; those were neglected even from the detailed eye of book's editor, Montgomery Watt. The omissions, that are a few in total, have no scientific significance and do not include any important content . . . .[15]

Some works have been completely ignored by both publishers and Muslim academics. For instance, Wansbrough's *Qur'anic Studies*, later revised and annotated by Andrew Rippin, and his *Sectarian Milieu* were not translated into any Islamic language. This is despite the fact that many of Rippin's Qur'anic exegetical studies or encyclopedia entries have been translated into different Islamic languages due to their perceived neutrality. Some of Rippin's neutral exegetical works do not, in fact, reflect his concerns about the contribution of early Muslims and non-Muslims in shaping of Islamic scriptures. Powers' *Muḥammad Is Not the Father of Any of Your Men* and *Zayd*, as well as Shoemaker's *The Death of a Prophet*, have not been translated either. All these three works, while not admired by some Western scholars due to their methodology, invited scholars to observe the other side of the coin, showing other possibilities about the origin of Islam. Shoemaker, through assessing various non-Islamic sources, tried to examine the traditions regarding the death date of Muhammad. He believes that

> [i]n light of the rather negative assessment that this report of Muhammad's vitality during the Palestinian invasion has received in recent publications, it seems necessary to revisit the question of Muhammad's death, not so much with the goal of determining when he really died, but with an eye toward whether these non-Islamic sources may in fact preserve an early tradition that was subsequently revised as Islam's self-image and self-understanding were transformed.[16]

My short note describing the story of Muhammad's death in Shoemaker's book was not allowed to be published by an online Islamic journal. The editor assumed that Shoemaker's books are problematic:

> Most probably, we cannot publish the article online due to the particular conditions [i.e., restrictions] of Iran.[17]

It was obvious that the editor did not have any problem with the publication of such works; rather, his concern was related to others' potentially negative (including for him personally) feedback or reactions. On the other hand, the review of Powers' *Muḥammad Is Not the Father* by a professor at the University of Toronto, Walid A. Saleh (b. 1966), along with the short preface to the book, were translated into Persian.[18] Perhaps unsurprisingly, the reviewer's criticism was a good excuse for an Islamic journal to introduce Powers to the Iranian academic community. Saleh wrote:

The monograph reviewed here consists of a series of hypothetical or, rather, fanciful presuppositions that are hardly sustainable, let alone cogent; confusing and confused, they claim both one thing and its opposite at the same time... The fact of the matter is that every assertion made by Powers is shaky.[19]

Regarding the translation of neutral works, many of Rippin's works were translated in the Middle East (e.g., Iran and Turkey) and the Malay-Indonesian world (particularly Indonesia). The translated works are chiefly focused on the history of Islamic exegetical works or are encyclopedia entries on religious notions and individual exegetes (*mufassirun*).

Apart from translations of Rippin's work, some Muslims, either in the West or the Muslim world, believe that Western scholars of the Qur'ān in general, and contributors to the *Encyclopaedia of the Qur'ān* (*EQ*) in particular, are fighting a "Cold War" against Islam, one by which non-Muslims seek to seize authority over the Qur'ān.[20] Rippin was one of the key editors of *EQ* and as such he was sometimes accused of attacking Islam (as will be seen soon). The opponents of *EQ* may be termed one-sided critics, something apparent in a controversial article by Muzaffar Iqbal (b. 1954). Iqbal's essay was initially published in English in the Arabic *Journal of Qur'anic Research and Studies* in Saudi Arabia in 2008 and later republished as a book by the Malaysian Islamic Book Trust (Kuala Lumpur) in 2009.[21] It caused both Arab and Malay scholars to adopt a polemical stance toward Rippin and many contributors to the *EQ*.

While delivering a lecture during the celebration of a Festschrift in honor of Andrew Rippin, which I co-edited with Walid A. Saleh, we both agreed that Rippin has been one of the most popular scholars of Islam among Muslims, and that his works need greater attention in the Muslim world. In this regard, drawing the attention to the reception of Rippin's works in different Islamic contexts might be helpful.

II. Western Works in the Muslim Academy: Rippin's Qur'anic Studies

Arabian Contexts

Although it is difficult to find reliable translations of Rippin's works in Arab academic contexts, the names of Rippin and other non-Muslim Islamic scholars are frequently seen in Arabic articles and blogs. Yet they are not called researchers (*bahithun*) but, rather, Orientalists (*mustashriqun*). Rippin was not only fully familiar with Islamic sources, but he was very much interested in communicating with Muslims. He delivered many lectures and conducted several projects in various Islamic countries including the UAE, Turkey, Egypt, Kuwait, and so on (though not in Saudi Arabia, Iran, Jordan, Syria, Malaysia, or Indonesia).[22] However, his name carries a negative sense in some Muslim academic institutes, where he is viewed as a critic of Islam.

In this spirit, the Islamic Center for Strategic Studies, funded by the government and based in Iraq, created a panel called *al-Istishraq* (Orientalism), which introduces the names and publications of Western scholars. Rippin is one of them, and his academic career is described and some of his publications translated into Arabic.[23] A 2006 article on Orientalists' Qur'anic studies written during the first quarter of the fifteenth century AH (AD 1979–2004), published in Saudi Arabia, highlights five different aspects of the Orientalists: (a) new movements/trends of Orientalists' Qur'anic studies at the beginning in the fifteenth century; (b) Orientalists' Qur'anic studies subsequently; (c) Orientalists' activities related to Qur'anic studies; (d) the decreasing number of studies on Orientalism with regard to the Qur'ān in this period; and (e) the most famous Orientalists engaged in Qur'anic studies. According to this article, Orientalism has, in recent decades, taken one of three forms. The first is a classical or traditional movement; the second is "New Orientalism"; the last is "Journalistic Orientalism." It also divided Qur'ān-related publications by Western scholars into: (i) translations of the Qur'ān; (ii) encyclopedic works; (iii) academic writings; and (iv) investigations, indexing, and cataloguing.

Renowned Orientalists (*ashhar al-mustashriqin*) are divided into two groups. The first group comprises those interested in Qur'ānic codices and manuscripts and who are fully familiar with Muslim textual sources, such as Solange Ory, Frédéric Imbert, and François Déroche.[24] The second group of scholars are those who participate in Qur'anic studies (*al-dirasat al-Qur'aniyya*) using an analytical-historical approach; this includes Angelika Neuwirth, Claude Gilliot, Andrew Rippin, and Sergio Noseda. For an Arab scholar, Rippin, rather than being known as a fair scholar or the writer of neutral works, is an Orientalist, one who, according to Iqbal's article, contributed to the production of a dangerous encyclopedia:

Those who have doubts about the dangers inherent in this work may wish to investigate what the editors and most of the contributors of the work [*EQ*] have written elsewhere; here is a specimen from Andrew Rippin, one of the four associate editors of *EQ*....[25]

Iranian Contexts

As well as the importance of the translation movement to the Persian Constitutional Revolution from the late nineteenth century onwards, connections with Euro-American academic institutions and scholarship programs available for outstanding students and elites led Iranian thinkers to familiarize their compatriots with the modern (scientific) achievements of the West.[26] The attempts of twentieth-century thinkers such as Ahmad Aram (d. 1998), 'Abbas Zaryab Khu'i (d. 1994), Najaf Daryabandari (b. 1929), and 'Izzatullah Fuladvand (b. 1935), among others, to offer Iranian communities translations of the philosophical, mystical, and historical works and treatises of Western scholars were developed by subsequent generations and divided into various branches. A "young" branch, with a particular focus on modern Western Qur'anic studies, was officially established after the Iranian Revolution and peaked in the late 1990s.

Young Iranian scholars have spent considerable time translating modern Qur'anic-studies pieces into Persian. In addition to the importance of Rippin's works for them, they also referred to Rippin's *informative*, rather than, *critical* essays. Among early Persian translations of Rippin's works is 2000's "Literary analysis of the Qur'ān, *tafsīr*, and *sīra*: The methodologies of John Wansbrough," by Morteza Karimi-nia. One may wonder how it is possible to introduce Wansbrough to an Islamic academic or public sphere through another work which analyzed Wansbrough's approach, yet Rippin could be the bridge between Iranians and Wansbrough. Rippin's less controversial work on his mentor allowed not only Iranians but also other Muslims, who did not or were not able to translate Wansbrough's work, to learn about the latter's ideas. Later, other young scholars including Mehrdad 'Abbasi, 'Ali Aqa'i, and Muhammad Kazim Rahmati translated more of Rippin's works.

It was on the basis of these translations that the Iranian public became familiar with the modern Qur'anic studies works of Rippin and his colleagues before other Muslim communities.[27] Moreover, the publication of *EQ* edited by Jane D. McCauliff and the growing number of translations and discussions of Western works on the Qur'ān by the aforementioned Iranian scholars drew attention to various encyclopedia entries they had written. In this field, two types of translation were performed. The first was pure translation, with no analysis, while the second entailed appraisals or critical translations or reports in which the author adds notes to critically analyze such European-language works on the Qur'ān. In fact, and unsurprisingly, the more translations and "domestications" of Western works that are carried out, the greater the number of critical analyses of Western works in the Muslim world.

Regarding the first of these types, prior to translating, a scholar does not usually address Westerners' views on the "divinity," "accuracy," and "history" of the Qur'ān and revelation. 'Abbasi, professor of the Qur'ān and Hadith at Islamic Azad University (Science and Research Branch, Tehran), was the first to officially establish a school of translation dedicated to encyclopedia entries and Western Qur'anic publications. Today, along with his colleagues, he leads the editorial team at Hikmat Publications Inc., Tehran, with the academic translation of *EQ* into Persian. However, this large translation project is subject to the supervision of an overseer, who has strongly criticized Rippin, and it is funded by the Islamic Development Organization of Iran (*Sazman-e tablighat-e Islami*). However, it is reported (according to the overseer) that upon the completion of the project, Hikmat Publications Inc. will publish an additional volume that will be a critical review of *EQ*.[28]

Therefore, 'Abbasi, Karimi-Nia, Aqa'i, and others have been trying to change public perceptions of Western scholars from being regarded as Orientalists to being seen as Western Qur'anic studies scholars—a notion promoted by Schöller—by emphasizing their literature, methodology, and innovations, rather than their nationality, religion, or affiliation.

The second type of translation involves a critical reading of Westerners' works. In this, a group of scholars holds the view that most works in Islamic-Qur'anic studies written by Westerners should be analyzed through the lens of Islamic teachings. Although it is unusual to find a critical analysis in Persian of a Western Qur'anic work without a translation, it is occasionally evident that some critical essays (*maqalat-e intiqadi*) published in peer-reviewed journals (*'ilmi pazhuhashi*) analyze the methodologies of Western Qur'ān scholars. In an essay titled "An Analysis and Criticism of Orientalists' Qur'anic Studies," the authors (one of whom is the supervisor of the *EQ* translation project) argue that analyzing Rippin's works makes clear that he did not use reliable sources. They opine that Rippin was inattentive to Shi'i exegetical works when attempting to elaborate on *ta'wil* in his *tafsir* entry and criticize him for not referring to modern Iranian Qur'ān commentaries either. According to this essay, Rippin's main sources are *Isra'iliyyat* (Jewish Lore), which are not accepted by many Muslims, acquired from early exegetical works such as the commentary of al-Tabari on the Qur'ān and the *qisas al-anbiya'* (stories of the prophets) of al-Kisa'i. For instance, they argue that Rippin's reference to Noah's intoxication and the cursing of Ham for laughing loudly at his father Noah's nakedness is based on the works of al-Tabari and al-Kisa'i,[29] which are, according to the Iranian authors, very weak compared to other Islamic sources. The authors ask why Rippin did not mention that al-Tabari is the only Islamic thinker who noted such trifling points. This part of the article ends acerbically, with: "these cases were merely some apparent works of a 'scholar' who has been writing on Qur'anic studies since 1978 and is considered a prominent scholar in the West."[30]

Indeed, the reception of Rippin's works in Iran is controversial. An article published by the Islamic journal of the Iranian ministry of science, research, and technology, Rippin is still accused of promoting the thought of the so-called "opponents" of Islam, including Ibn Warraq, Christoph Luxenberg, Mohammad Arkoun, Shabbir Akhtar, and Michael Lecker.[31] It suggests that, despite the effort of the younger generation to highlight the fairness of Westerners such as Rippin, anti-Orientalist or pro-Neo-Orientalist movements, which want to say that mocking Islam by Europeans still occurs, are still strong movements that are attempting to prevent the circulation of foreign voices in Iran.

Other works written in the Iranian academic context attempt to analyze Rippin's view on the historiography of exegetical texts, in line with John Wansbrough. It is argued that, according to Rippin, scrutinizing the *sanad* is not a *very* reliable criterion for dating a text. However, such scholars believe that Rippin was deeply influenced by Wansbrough in terms of literal analysis which, according to them, is not sufficient for dating a text.[32]

South and Southeast Asian Contexts

Looking further east, a number of translated Western essays have been published by South Asians. Although far fewer than those produced by Iranians, a number of critical essays targeting the methodology or perspective of "Orientalists" have been produced. Some of these refer to the *mis*guidance, *mis*understandings, and *mis*readings of Westerners.[33] However, a few informative essays have familiarized Pakistani and Indian scholars with the efforts of Rippin. For instance, Tauseef Ahmad Parry, assistant professor of Islamic Studies in Kashmir, unlike Muzaffar Iqbal, emphasized Rippin's and McAuliffe's important contributions to the history of Islamic interpretations.[34]

Not surprisingly, and regardless of their familiarity with the English language, it is very hard to find informative essays about, or translations of, works by Western Qur'anic studies scholars in the Malay-Indonesian world, where local scholars and students mostly see the former as Orientalists who attempt to *deny* the divine origin of the Qur'ān. This could be related to the significant influence of Arabo-centric sources/institutes on Malay Islamic works, as well as to the historical Malay connection with Azhari and Meccan scholars, both groups that have developed an inflexible perspective on Islam with an emphasis on tradition (*naql*). An example of this one-sided viewpoint is the translation of the Arabic *Mawsu'a al-mustashriqin* (*Encyclopedia of Orientalists*) into Indonesian by 'Abd al-Rahman Badawi in January 2003. Although the original Arabic work is mostly a bio-bibliographical sketch of Western scholars of Islam,[35] the cover of the translation has the popular Malay-Indonesian [anti-]Orientalist concept. It shows a man wearing a coat and tie with a bilateral face, one side being human while the other is a monster's (or pig's) head (Figure 2.1).[36] Thus, after seeing such images, the first thing that comes to a reader's mind about a Western scholar of Islam is not, of course, the time and effort he or she spent to demystify a part of history, but a hypocritical face, invented by a Muslim artist. For the reader, the mind and behavior, as well as both the inside and outside of a Western scholar (an Orientalist), come to be viewed as poisonous. As such, a Muslim reader will not examine Westerners' works critically, but instead critique Westerners in light of their beliefs and teachings in order to downplay their ideas and achievements.

In addition, the main source at some Malaysian universities for a course on "The Qur'ān and Orientalists," which I had to teach, too, is a bilingual version of *The Sublime Quran and Orientalism* by Mohammad Khalifa, which is critical of Western scholars of Islam.[37] The Malay translation was published by the state publisher, the Dewan Bahasa dan Pustaka (DBP). The cover of the original book also reflects how the author and the publisher visualize the study of the Qur'ān by non-Muslims. It shows the Qur'ān, surrounded by a

Figure 2.1 The translation of the Arabic *Mawsu'a al-mustashriqin* (*Encyclopedia of Orientalists*)

halo, under attack by many arrows fired from all around (Figure 2.2). Upon reading the book, the reader will fully comprehend that these are shot by the Orientalists, who are attempting to annihilate the Muslims' Holy Book.

Furthermore, due to socio-political supervision by the religious authorities, whether in organizations or departmental committees, the translation process of Western Qur'anic works is slow in the Malay-Indonesian world in general and Malaysia in particular. It is significant that, despite Darwin's work being available in the original language in Malaysia's bookstores, the

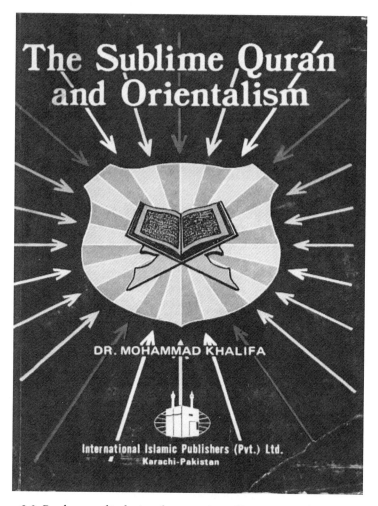

Figure 2.2 Book cover displaying the reception of Western Qur'anic studies among traditionalists

distribution of translated copies to the public, and particularly to the younger generation, is banned.[38] This is true for other controversial works, too.[39] Although there are Malays who are proficient in reading English works, the younger generation, with insufficient knowledge of European languages, suffer from this lack of translated works.

However, having a slightly more flexible context, influenced by pluralism, has allowed Indonesians to translate the Islamic-Qur'anic works of non-Muslims. As in Iran, a very early Indonesian translation of Rippin's work was

Table 2.1 A Malay-Indonesian classification of "Orientalist" attacks on *hadith*

Hadith *and Its* Text	Hadith *and Its* Isnad	Hadith, History, and Sira	Hadith, Islamic Law, and Fiqh	Tafsir (tafsir hadithi)
Sprenger	Horovitz	Kister	Schacht	Wansbrough
Muir	Schacht	Scholler	Powers	Rippin
Goldziher	Juynboll	Motzki	Calder	Gilliot

his chapter pertaining to John Wansbrough's methodology, which is included in Richard C. Martin's *Approaches to Islam in Religious Studies*, translated by Zakiyuddin Bhaidhawy in 2001.[40]

Rippin is known as a *murid* (disciple) of his master Wansbrough, which is why his views are often found under the rubric of studies on Wansbrough. In a Malay classification of Orientalist "attacks" on *hadith* (*serangan orientalis terhadap hadits*), Rippin's name is mentioned after Wansbrough's (see Table 2.1).[41]

Turkish Context

Although there are a few scholars who are trying to popularize the concept of "Western scholars' Qur'anic studies," the terms *Orientalism* and *Orientalists* are more common in the Muslim academy, where they are also regarded as polemicists. Turkish sources suggest that Wansbrough's book has distorted the image of Islam and "the Muslim world has still not found the time or opportunity to write a sufficient and scientific response to the work of John Wansbrough . . . which is one of the most offensive works conveying its own vision of the Qur'ān."[42] In this respect, Rippin is also positioned in the same line. Muslims opine that although they have the strong academic basis required for this confrontation, they had not had any opportunity or enough time to provide an answer for Western scholars of the Qur'ān. Scholars in Turkey have also tried to critique and/or reject "Orientalist" analyses of the Qur'ān, hoping, it seems, to thereby expand "Islamic consciousness" (*İslâmî bilinç*). For instance, Selahattin Sönmezsoy published a book titled *Kur'an ve Oryantalistler* (*Qur'ān and Orientalists*) in 1998, in which, after providing readers with his critical approaches to the notion of Orientalism

and (Jewish and Christian) "Orientalists" (*Oryantalizm Nedir?*), critiqued
Orientalist propositions in respect to the divine origin of the Qur'ān, its
revelations (*vahy*), content (*muhteva*) and translation (*tercümesi*).[43] Turk
scholars were impressed by Mohammad A. Chaudhary's "Orientalism on
Variant Readings of the Qur'an: The Case of Arthur Jeffery" in which the
author asserts that

> Jeffry has failed to camouflage his prejudice against Islam and the Qur'an
> when dealing with its compilation . . . Finally, it seems appropriate to sug-
> gest that such orientalists [. . .], who continues to pursue Jeffery's mission to
> invalidate the character of the Qur'an as an unadulterated revealed book,
> should apply the principles of higher criticism in an affirmative way.[44]

In addition to garnering attention in Turkey,[45] this article was translated into
Turkish by Mahmut Ay and published in the *Journal of Faculty of Theology
Istanbul University* (*İstanbul Üniversitesi İlahiyat Fakültesi Dergisi*) in 2011.[46]

Two of Rippin's neutral works were translated in Turkish in 2002 and
2003.[47]

****

Interestingly (and in the most positive scenario), some Muslims (like
Khurramshahi) have agreed that the concept of Orientalism has changed
the academic study of Islam not through Goldziher, Nöldeke, Crone,
Wansbrough, and Rippin, but via Montgomery and his followers, whose
thoughts are partially compatible with Islamic teachings. For Khurramshahi,
other works are not scholarly but polemical, ones which not only fail to promote Islamic values but also lead scholars astray.

What has reached Muslim students and scholars of Islam is a selective, partial, and censored amount of the wide-ranging results of Western
Qur'anic studies. Within the Middle Eastern and Southeast Asian academic
contexts, the image of Westerners' academic study of religion is opaque, and
it is one that is combined with traditional interpretations that do not allow
a reader to map correctly the evolution of scholarly understandings of religion in the West. Indeed, the connection between rational progress and the
research concerns of scholars is lost; the links between Goldziher, Nöldeke,
Bell, Burton, Wansbrough, Rippin, and Powers, and also Watt, among others,
are ignored, and with it an optimistic view toward these scholars is replaced
with a skeptical and pessimistic one. That the works by these scholars are
all positioned within modern scholarship studying the Qur'ān can help to

suggest that they are not the enemies of Islam; they are, instead, critics of each other, helping to pave the way for future generations of scholars.

III. Studying the Qur'ān in Muslim Universities and Seminaries

A Shirazi friend who studied comparative philosophy told me ten years ago that scholars believe that it is unlikely that the tree of modernism will bear fruit in the Middle East, the region from which the monotheistic religions with their vast numbers of believers worldwide emerged. Traditionally speaking, in the Near East, the land of many prophets and their schools of thought, narratives and traditions play a more important role in people's lives than modernism may ever do.

Nonetheless, Western technology and science have entered the Muslim world much more readily than Western culture and ideology. To prove this, it is only necessary to observe how Muslim countries compete with each other to produce industrial science.[48] Apolitically speaking, approaches to religious sciences ('ulum al-din) are in a different category from other sciences, engineering, and the social sciences. While the competition to attain modern technology and industrial science is intense, the study of religion has remained in its classical (i.e., unmodernized) form.

The *madrasa* (in the Arab-Sunni world), *hawza* (in the Shi'i context), and *pondok* (in the Malay-Indonesian world) are traditional Islamic versions of the seminary, temple, and monastery, places where people learn about and defend their religion. They can also be places to educate students to become theologians, known as *mutakallimun* in Arabic. Speculative theology, or '*ilm al-kalam*, is one branch of the religious sciences ('ulum al-din) and "is the science which concerns firmly establishing religious beliefs by adducing proofs and banishing doubts (from the *Mawāḳif of al-Īdjī*, 8th/14th century)."[49]

The study of Islam in Muslim academic contexts largely follows the agenda of Islamic traditional schools (*madrasa, hawza,* and *pondok*). To prove this, *large* similarities between the subjects that students are enrolled in, in both Islamic traditional schools and the Muslim academy, are displayed in Table 2.2.

The above comparison between major subjects taken by students indicates that these subjects are largely similar, as are the end results. It is expected that students who graduate from these schools/universities should further incline

Table 2.2 Common subjects in both Islamic traditional schools and the Muslim academy

Traditional Islamic School in the Malay-Indonesian World	Muslim Academic Context in the Malay-Indonesian World (BA Course)	Muslim Academic Context in the Middle East (BA Course)
Fiqh (Jurisprudence)	An Introduction to *Usul al-fiqh* (Principles of Jurisprudence)	*Fiqh*
Comparative *fiqh*	An Introduction to Islamic Philosophy	Islamic Theology (*Kalam*)
Tafsir ayat al-ahkam (Commentary on Verses of the Rules)	Ethics and *Tasawwuf* (Sufism)	Islamic Ethics and Training
'*ilm al-tafsir* (Exegetical Science)	Islamic Thought	History of Islam
Hadith (Tradition)	Science of the Qur'ān	History of the Qur'ān
al-Balagha (Eloquence)	Science of *Hadith*	Qur'anic Sciences
'*Ulum al-Qur'ān* (Qur'anic Sciences)	Principles of *Da'wa* (Islamic Missionary Activity)	Science of *Hadith*
al-Mantiq (Logic)	Religions	Logic
Tawhid (God's Unity)	*Shari'a*	*Tafsir*
Da'wa Methodology	Prophetic *Sira* and Rightly-Guided Caliphs' Thought	Arabic Literature
Qira'at (Qur'anic Readings)	'*Ilm al-qira'at* (Science of Qur'anic Readings)	*Tajwid*
al-Sarf wa'l-nahw (Arabic Grammar and Morphology)	*al-Jarh wa l-ta'dil* (Critique and Fair Evaluation)	Principles of Sociology
Islamic Culture	Research Methodologies	Research Methodologies
Scientific Research	Scientific Project	Research Project
=====	*Isra'iliyyat* (elective)	Application of Computer (elective)
=====	Orientalists and the Study of Qur'ān	Orientalism (elective)

toward *propagating* and *defending* Islamic teachings rather than studying and analyzing those of modern Qur'anic studies.

Such approaches to the study of religion in the Muslim academy resemble the study of Christianity in theology departments in *some* Western universities and seminaries, such as those of New Zealand, where I have taught, and where it is known as "academic theology" (see Table 2.3).

Table 2.3 Academic theology subjects in New Zealand

Bachelor of Theology in a New Zealand University	Description of Subjects
The History of Christianity	"if you believe God works through the Church today, you must also believe God has worked through the Church in the past"
Doing Theology	"What is Theology? . . . Why do Christians confess that all of human history turns upon Jesus' life, death, and resurrection?"
God and Ethics in Modern World	"This paper . . . challenges you to think afresh above how life is changed through the life, death and resurrection of Jesus."
Interpreting the Old Testament	"When Jesus made his identity known to the disciples, he used the language and thought of Scripture. When the earliest Christians tried to understand who Jesus was, they looked to Scripture for the answer . . . this paper will immerse you in these books and how they have been interpreted throughout the ages and in the modern world, focusing on Genesis to Kings."
Interpreting the New Testament	"How do we understand Jesus? Who was the apostle Paul? . . . It covers the Jewish background to the New Testament, methods for reading the text, the vital dimensions of Jesus' ministry . . ."

Note: Based on the brochure produced by the theology department.

One may wonder whether the bachelor of theology degree in a New Zealand university is idiosyncratic and can represent academic theology in western universities and seminaries. I think, however, that the objective of Christian theology is more or less similar worldwide. In such contexts, students are encouraged, according to the Boston University School of Theology, "to pursue knowledge of God, to cultivate leaders for communities of faith, to enrich the academy, and to seek peace with justice in a diverse and interconnected world" on the basis of Christianity.

IV. Reading the Qur'ān with Other Materials

Rippin viewed knowledge of Islam as both simple and complicated. It is simple because it could be learned easily everywhere in the Middle East, New Zealand, Brazil, and North America, but it is complicated as it has been treated differently at different periods in time. The digital age has made it easier for scholars and students to read Islamic texts, yet how Islam is read in cyberspace is still quite a new topic. Rippin was undoubtedly one of the pioneering scholars who linked the study of Islam and the Qur'ān with modern technology and the digital age.[50]

Rippin showed how cyberspace is Islamicized not only in the Muslim academy but also in Muslims' daily lives. As the Internet is sometimes sectarianized, so is modern scholarship in Qur'anic studies divided into Sunnism and Shi'ism.[51] Indeed, this is one of the main features of the Islamic context. It is not just technology but modern philosophical and linguistics theories that also have the potential to be applied for the sake of Islam within Muslim academic contexts. Today, some Muslim Qur'anic works apply knowledge of phonetics, syntax, pragmatism, etymology, and semantics to their studies[52] in order to "present a logical response for the immortality and comprehensiveness of the Qur'ān."[53] These groups of scholars, some of whom have contacted me, are particularly interested in reforming Islamic theology—they have so far received significant support from their governments. Nonetheless, the growing interest in *The Qur'ān and Science* and *The Qur'ān and the Bible* is both more obvious and more controversial within the Muslim academy.

The Qur'ān and Science

As mentioned earlier, the French [Christian] physician Maurice Bucaille (d. 1998) published a revolutionary work titled *La Bible, le Coran et la science: Les écritures saintes examinées à la lumière des connaissances modernes* in 1976, which was quickly translated into various languages. Its English translation was printed in 1977 and could confront the publication of controversial books including that of John Wansbrough, *Qur'anic Studies*, which had been published the same year. By relying on Bucaille's work, Muslim scholars have tried to prove the compatibility of the Qur'ān with modern science and to challenge the accuracy of biblical literature, through which they sought to reject the claims of the so-called deniers of the divine origin of the Qur'ān. Indeed, Bucaille's book became an instrument by which Muslims not only tried to prove the inimitability of the Qur'ān (*i'jaz*) but also to promote "the Qur'ān's immunity from distortion."[54] Very soon, his book was translated into Islamic languages, including Arabic, Persian, Urdu, and Turkish.

Although Bucaille presented a "comparative work" about *Science, the Bible, and the Qur'ān*, his study did not enjoy the popularity among Christians that he had expected. Bucaille claimed that the Bible contains some ridiculous statements and that the Qur'ān is the most infallible scripture.[55] In the preface, he declared that the Bible is full of mistakes that fall into one of three categories: "historical inaccuracies or anachronisms; (ii) implausible statements; (iii) blatant contradictions."[56] Bucaille referred to historical data, scientific knowledge, and other scriptural statements with the aim of highlighting the obvious mistakes in the Bible.

From Bucaille's perspective, many points found in the Bible are inaccurate, and there is no reason to compare biblical scripture with scientific facts.[57] Bucaille also believed that contradictions in the Gospels indicate a confusion as to the genealogical background of Jesus. In his opinion, the disjointed literature in the Gospels is part of this paradox. After claiming this about biblical ideas, Bucaille then moved on to look for any compatibility between the Qur'anic text and modern science. This scientist was convinced that the Qur'ān did not contain a single questionable statement from a modern perspective.[58]

Muslims in Arabia, such as the Yemeni scholar (Abdul-Majeed A. Azzindani), India (Maulana Wahiduddin Khan), the Philippines (Suleiman Qush), and Jordan ('Abd al-Rahman Salih 'Abd Allah, Nasir Ahmad Khuwalidih, and Muhammad 'Abdallah al-Samadi), among others, were greatly influenced by Bucaille's thesis when they wrote their works on the Qur'ān and nature.[59] Beyond the academic arena, Bucaille's works were very much admired by politicians and religious thinkers, particularly in the late 1970s and 1980s. It is said that "the former king of Saudi Arabia, Faisal, appreciated Bucaille's books,"[60] although he was killed one year before the publication of Bucaille's *chef-d'œuvre*.

His works are also widely available in mosques and Islamic centers and used "in *da'wa* efforts in the West."[61] His discussions on the relationship between Islam and science are still popular, particularly across the Muslim world. For example, the famous Arab director Farouq Abdul-Aziz ran an Internet web page titled "bucaillelegacy," which seemingly is "supported by the Nasser al-Sa'eed Charitable Foundation of Kuwait." Abdul-Aziz directed the two documentaries *Maurice and the Pharaoh* and *From Microcosm to Macrocosm*, for which he won the most creative Islamic work award of 2010 from the Sheikh Fahad Al-Ahmad International Award for Charity. Both of them were screened by the al-Jazeera documentary film festival in 2010, too. It seems Bucaille's explicit interest in Islam and the Qur'ān was the main reason Arabs and the al-Jazira Documentary Film Festival nominated it as the best documentary work. The film addresses the primary reasons why Bucaille began investigating the relationship between religion and science.

Later on, the Western embryologist Keith L. Moore, who spent part of his life in Saudi Arabia, studied the embryological notes found in Islamic texts and particularly in the Qur'ān. He published his embryological interpretation of Q 22:5; 23:13–14; 32:9; and 39 in the *Journal of the Islamic Medical Association of North America* in 1986.[62] With the help of Azzindani, former professor of Islam at King 'Abdul Aziz University in Jedda and the founder of al-Iman University in Yemen, Moore later expanded his embryological thoughts. He referred to Q 39:6 in order to develop his scientific account and attempt to prove a connection between embryological statements and the accuracy of the verse: "He makes you in the wombs of your mothers, in stages, one after another, in three veils of darkness." Moore not only presumed that the scientific boundaries in the Qur'ān will not be restricted in the future, but various other Qur'anic verses related to human beings, with new interpretations, will soon to come to light.[63]

Moore's publications regarding the embryo and the Qur'ān led to the production of an impressive body of work by Muslims subsequently. He had formulated his ideas after joining the Embryology Committee of King 'Abdulaziz University, where he assisted researchers with commenting on Qur'anic and Sunna phrases pertaining to "human reproduction and prenatal development." He himself expressed his surprise at the accuracy of these phrases as they were recorded in the seventh century AD and Muslims' important contributions to various fields of knowledge (e.g., medicine) in the tenth century.[64]

After Moore, the number of Western scholars who devoted their time to learning about the scientific elements of Qur'anic verses increased. William W. Hay, a geologist/oceanographer, stated at an official gathering that the scientific information in the Qur'ān is really interesting and noteworthy.[65] Later on, Azzindani, also as the main member of the Commission on Scientific Signs in the Qur'ān and Sunnah in Saudi Arabia, brought together a number of questions dealing with scientific discoveries. These were being asked by scientists including Keith Moore, William Hay, Yushidi Kusan, Alfred Kroner, Gerald C. Goeringer, T. V. N. Persaud, and E. Marshall Johnson.[66] It is important to note, however, that one of these figures confirmed via email that they had never said what is attributed to them on various websites.[67]

Thanks to the work of Azzindani, Bucaille, Moore, and other scientists familiarized people with the novel doctrine of *i'jaz 'ilmi,* or the scientific inimitability of the Qur'ān, and explored other qualities that they found in the Qur'ān that they believed enabled them to predict scientific findings. Scientific inimitability of the Qur'ān was able to emerge on the basis of specific debates about science and Islam that took place during the second half of the twentieth century. Indeed, due to the particular socio-political conditions of the post-colonial and post-war periods in both East and West, the period from the 1970s onwards saw the emergence of different groups surrounding various rulers (e.g., King Faisal, Muhammad Reza Shah Pahlavi) and thinkers who debated the relationship between Islam, science, culture, and Western technology.

Academic Courses on the Qur'ān and Science

Since then, and due largely to the efforts of Azzindani, courses titled either "The Qur'ān and Science" or "The Scientific Inimitability of the Qur'ān" have been added to the syllabi of Qur'anic studies program at some universities in Islamic countries. The earliest institute was the Commission on Scientific Signs in the Qur'ān and Sunnah, part of the Muslim World League established in Mecca in 1983, which aims to link Qur'anic verses, faith, and modern science. Very soon, other similar institutes were founded throughout the Muslim world, particularly in Arabia, Iran, Turkey, and Malaysia. One of the main purposes of these institutes is to show the uniqueness of the Qur'ān. Due to the increasing number of scientific disciplines, new types of scientific inimitability of the Qur'ān are introduced yearly. As well as the embryological miracle presented by Moore, numerical,[68] biological, zoological, oceanographical, physical, and other aspects have all been investigated by Muslim scholars.[69]

The emergence of such approaches within Qur'anic studies has encouraged scholars to include the similar topic "The Qur'ān and Interdisciplinary Studies" within Islamic studies programs. It may be wondered if this topic resembles the new approach of Western scholars who deal with the anthropology of Islam; however, in this case, disciplines such as psychology, sociology, medicine, computer science, and others are used not only to show the level of faith or the health of people but to prove the inimitability of the Qur'ān or its unique role in society.[70] This is what the Muslim *'ulama'* (religious figures) refer to as the application (*istikhdam*) of modern science in *'ulum al-din wa l-ijtima'* (the religious and social sciences), and vice versa.

In this respect, the most pioneering center dedicated to the study of Islam and interdisciplinary topics is the Islamic Economics Institute of King Abdul Aziz University, Saudi Arabia. It was established in the 1970s following the first international conference on Islamic Economics (al-Iqtisad al-Islami) in 1976. This institute has collaborated with some European universities and offers Islamic finance degrees that are compatible with Islamic-Qur'anic teachings.[71] For about a decade, Arabia was the educational starting point for Islamic economics and finance in the Muslim academic context. Subsequently, Turkey, Iran, Pakistan, Malaysia, Qatar, and some European colleges (e.g., Durham, United Kingdom) have established centers and research teams to employ Islamic teachings within modern scientific disciplines.

The Qur'ān and the Bible

Biblical literature played an important role in shaping Islamic history. As well as references to Jewish and Christian sources in the Qur'ān, Muhammad's biography (sira) and early exegetical and traditional (hadithi) works also refer to biblical and post-biblical sources. Yet, as Walid A. Saleh says, "Muslims hardly, if ever, used the Bible to argue for a religious truth or to deduce from it a divine message or a legal ruling."[72] As is widely known, classical exegetes of the Qur'ān, such as Ibn Barrajan of Seville (d. ca. 1141) and Hasan al-Biqa'i (d. ca. 1480),[73] unlike the critics of both biblical and Shi'i doctrines such as Ibn Taymiyya (d. ca. 1328) and Ibn Kathir (d. ca. 1373), frequently referred to the Arabic version of the Bible in order to present a fully developed interpretation of the Qur'ān.[74] This allows us to infer that Hebrew was not systematically taught in Islamic schools at that time. The dominant view regarding the Bible, as a scripture, and biblical literature as source for Islam, was often polemic as it was mixed with the medieval understanding of [anti-]Isra'iliyyat to identify material with a Jewish background, which were consequently "alien to Islam."[75] Partly as a result of medieval Europeans' anti-Islamic works, Muslims continued to develop their anti-Judeo-Christian stance.

Among modern Muslim scholars, Muhammad Tawfiq Sidqi (d. 1920), a famous and pioneering Qur'ān scholar, published, with his close friend Rashid Rida (d. 1935), a work titled 'Aqida al-salb wa l-fida (The Doctrine of Crucifixion and Redemption). He paid close attention to modern exegetical sources and modern science, as well as to biblical literature, in an attempt to eliminate the many doubts about the Qur'ān, Muhammad, and Islam that were chiefly emanating from medieval and modern European studies of Islam. His main works were a response to Christians who, according to him, claimed that the Qur'ān is a distorted scripture. Likewise, Sidqi opined that reading biblical sources leads European and Muslim scholars, as well as the general public, to fail to see the truth, particularly that displayed in the Qur'ān. This is clearly obvious in his article "The Rocky Tract in the Holy Qur'ān: Correcting the Errors of the Orientalist Margoliouth," published in 1942, which is about Q 15:80–82.[76] Apparently, unlike in the Classical period, "from the first quest in the nineteenth century, Muslims have increasingly utilised historical criticisms of the New Testament for apologetic purposes."[77]

Subsequently, in the early twentieth century, exegetical works that make mildly supportive rather than harshly critical references to the Gospels were written. When the English version of the Gospel of Barnabas by Lonsdale and Laura Ragg was published in 1907, Egyptian (e.g., Rashid Rida) and Indian scholars, who were the forerunners of the reformist movements in the Muslim world, provided religious thinkers ('ulama') with Arabic (1908) and Urdu (1916) versions of it.[78]

Tantawi Jawhari (d. 1940) paid attention to Europeans' thoughts regarding biblical literature and the *Gospel of Barnabas* for his interpretation of *sura Al-'Imran* (Q 3). He declared that his commentary benefited from the recent discovery of the Gospel of Barnabas (*afa-laysa min al-'ajab 'an yakun hadha al-tafsir akthar hazza wa-awfar sa'ada bi-zuhur injil Barnaba fi hadhih al-yawm*),[79] as it agrees with the Qur'ān (*wa-injil Barnaba yuwafiq al-Qur'ān*). In order to stop controversies associated with the death of Jesus, Jawhari, along with Abu Zahra (d. 1974), mentions that the Gospel of Barnabas replaces Jesus with Judas (Yahuda) on the cross, as is stated in the Qur'ān.[80] It is clear that modern exegetes, on the basis of the Qur'ān, have given credit to this Gospel. This recalls al-Biqa'i who "was giving the Torah the same status as that of the Qur'ān."[81]

Indeed, various modern Muslims, including Jawhari, publicly announced the importance of Occidentalism (*istighrab*), the interdependent knowledge of the culture, religion, and literature of Europe. However, other thinkers quickly rejected Jawhari's references to European sources and failed to appreciate his commentary on the Qur'ān, thus marginalizing him. The majority of Qur'ān exegetes and scholars again, gradually, and during the final years of the colonial period, took up an anti-biblical and anti-Christian stance, which,

along with the work of Bucaille, discouraged students from examining biblical literature.[82] For those in the Muslim academy, biblical knowledge could
do nothing except lead them from the right path (*sirat al-mustaqim*).

Some Muslims, among them Muhammad Yahya al-Hashimi, published
an article "in the influential organ of the World Islamic League of Mecca"
(*Rabitat al-ʿAlam al-Islami*) in Muharram 1397/1977,[83] which declared
Muslim references to Barnabas to be a conspiracy to scatter the *umma*:

> [He] refers to the famous Christian-Muslim dialogue in Tripoli (Libya) in
> 1976, in which some Muslims tried to put the Gospel of Barnabas at the
> center of their arguments. He dismisses the gospel as a document of du-
> bious value, comparable to the innovations of the Ahmadiyya movement
> who claim that Christ did not die on the cross but survived it, went to Asia
> and died in Kashmir. He even contends that it might have been composed
> by a Jew in order to instigate hatred between Christians and Muslims.
> A refutation of the gospel's authenticity is also found in a newspaper ar-
> ticle from 1959 by the Egyptian biographer of Christ ʿAbbas Mahmud al-
> ʿAqqad, who comes close to standard historical-critical positions taken by
> Western scholars.[84]

Additionally, post-colonial movements, the de-secularization and
Islamization of knowledge program in 1970s, and the 1979 Iranian
Revolution increasingly led to the prohibition of the teaching of Biblical literature in Muslim academic contexts. However, it should also be noted that in
the last years of the twentieth century, apologetic comparative works related
to Mary and Jesus in the Qur'ān and the Bible were gradually produced in
some Muslim academic contexts.[85]

V. Self-Sufficiency in Academic Production

From ISI to ISC: Immortal Dream of Islamization

Due to the significant growth in Islamic-Qur'anic programs, special attention will now be paid to academic journals in the Muslim academy. Not only
is publishing in such journals a requirement for MA and PhD students but
it is also used to judge whether a university lecturer should be promoted.
Unlike the paucity of English-, German-, and French-language academic

journals in Muslim academic contexts, there are hundreds of active Arabic monthly, quarterly, semi-annual, and annual journals on Islam and the Qur'ān published, from North Africa, the West Bank, and Lebanon[86] to Pakistan and the Malay-Indonesian world. In addition, there are many journals in other Asian languages including Persian,[87] Malay,[88] Indonesian, Turkish, and Urdu.

Upon reviewing these journals, it is apparent that the methodology used in Muslim academic contexts is different from that of the West, as it sees the religion only through the lens of theology, makes reference to only a limited number of scholars, and only employs descriptive and apologetic methodologies. The main thing that they shed light on is the *greatness* of Islam rather than any crucial research concerns. Any innovations are limited to internal-sectarian Islamic teachings, including Qur'ān, *hadith*, or *fiqh*. The Islamic exegetical works are examined, in the best scenario, comparatively, neutrally, and outside of their socio-political contexts. For instance, the environment from which the new genre of the theological exegesis of the Qur'ān appeared are less important than the way a theological exegesis describes a verse or term.

Furthermore, the level of innovation produced by scholars is tightly controlled so that nothing too controversial is produced. Nasr Hamid Abu Zayd, among others, is one example of someone who fell afoul of such rules, as his claims and opinions regarding the Qur'ān and Islamic thought and politics led an Egyptian court to call him an apostate in 1995. He

> strongly condemns the belief in one single, precise and valid interpretation of the Qur'ān handed down by the Prophet for all times . . . in Abu Zayd's view, an individual's interpretation is never absolute (*fahm mutlaq*). It is always relative (*fahm nisbi*), since the "information" in the divine "message" varies according to whoever "receives" it.[89]

Abu Zayd's intention was to "focus on the following problems: how to achieve a scientific understanding of the Qur'ān, how to brush aside layers of the ideological interpretation, in order to unearth the historical reality of the text."[90] But we should bear in mind that the *scientific* understanding of the Qur'ān in Muslim academic contexts is defined within the traditional framework of Islam. If it goes beyond that, it will be removed from the academic corpus. One example, mentioned earlier, was that some parts of Watt's work were removed by the translator as he believed they contained points that were not significant from a scientific perspective.

Thus, questions such as the following, dealing with research methodology, are rarely addressed in studies published in Muslim academic journals:

> Do our methods and methodologies teach us something, or reveal some new and interesting facet about *religion* as an aspect of human life and experience in the world? And what, in turn, does the study of religion teach us about the nature and character of humankind?[91]

Likewise, describing Islam from an insider's perspective can also be considered one of the main reasons for the very high levels of rejection of Muslim scholars' work by Western academic journals, particularly those that are indexed and abstracted by Web of Science (ISI) and Scopus. Publishing in the journals included in these two databases elevates the global level of universities. Consequently, Islamic countries have been trying to become independent from the Western educational system, and have established an Islamic version of ISI/Scopus called ISC or *Islamic World Science Citation Center*. ISC, also connected with the *Islamic Educational, Scientific and Cultural Organization* (ISESCO), officially started its work in Iran in 2004 as a result of the "Recommendation of the Supreme Leader regarding the establishment of a citation system for Iran and the Islamic World."[92] Although there are still some Islamic centers and institutes (often Sunnis) that do not recognize ISC, this database covers academic journals in all scientific disciplines from various Muslim countries with the purpose of

> [p]roviding incentives that would increase the Islamic countries researchers' zeal for initiating innovative research in the humanities, while considering local needs and Islamic values, such that would encourage all Islamic countries to adopt such incentives.[93]

The establishment of ISC underlines that the objectives and methodologies used in the West and the East are different.

Following this, Muslim countries have tried to become more global, cultural, and educational, and less oil-based. For instance, the Iranian educational authorities wish to establish a comprehensive university system in Iran with civilization-building (civilizing) ability (*tamaddun-sazi*) by 1404/2025—five years earlier than the Vision of Qatar and Arabia for

2030. This educational system will reflect that "Iran should be able to in-spire the Muslim world and achieve the first rank in science and economy in the region [viz., the Middle East]"[94] by then.[95] As mentioned previously, Muslims took steps to Islamicize university and knowledge and obtain sci-entific and educational independence in the 1970s and, even more so, in the 1980s. Pioneering Muslim scholars, including, among others, Ismail al-Faruqi (killed in 1986), established the International Institute for Islamic Thought (IIIT) in the United States. According to Faruqi and his fellows, Western human knowledge and education, affected as it is by Darwinism, Freudianism, and Marxism, contradict Islamic values.[96] In this regard, Brohi says:

> Much of the dissatisfaction expressed against Islam by modern educated Muslims is a result of the kind of textbooks they have read and so-called sci-entific thoughts, presented to them in the name of modern knowledge. We, therefore, would like to sponsor a world-wide movement for securing rec-ognition of the paramount need and so reorganize the elements of modern knowledge and to purge it of the deleterious elements, which are currently at war with the sanctity of our religious beliefs and practices and tend to give to the believers a sort of schizophrenic personality, so that when they are in a religious mood they do not unconditionally accept principal contributions of modern knowledge and when they are thinking about modern knowledge, their religious beliefs do not undergo a sort of heretical transmutation.[97]

As should be apparent, Brohi suggests that Muslims should create a ver-sion of knowledge that is compatible with human nature.[98] This is also what Christopher Furlow argues, that through such approaches Muslims should want to reform their educational systems to produce "individuals who have a unified knowledge of both rational and Islamic science which is relevant to the Islamic civilization."[99] According to Faruqi, European colonialists tried to destroy "everything Islam," including

> [t]he integrity of the Qur'ānic text, the genius of the Prophet (ṢAAS), the veracity of his Sunna, the perfection of the Sharī'a, the glories of Muslim achievements in culture and civilization—none of these were spread. The purpose was to destroy the Muslim's confidence in himself, in his 'Ummah . . .[100]

Preserving the Islamic identity through education and knowledge has become the duty of Muslim communities, and something that goes one step beyond the medieval de-Hellenization movement. Thus, it is no surprise to see that the works of Nöldeke, Goldziher, Wansbrough, and Crone, among others, are not taught or studied in Muslim academic contexts.

Islamization of Encyclopedias

On the other hand, Muslims have also attempted to Islamicize Western Qur'anic studies and to do so through the use of modern technology. For instance, in order to reject Brill's *Encyclopaedia of Islam* (*EI*) and *Encyclopaedia of the Qur'ān* (*EQ*), both published in Leiden, the Netherlands, Muslims have produced their own versions of Islamic and Qur'anic encyclopedias with particular reference to either Sunni or Shiʿi sources.

Historical records show that Persians, Turks, and Indo-Pakistanis were at the forefront of producing encyclopedias from the late nineteenth century until the middle of the twentieth. However, the majority of their works were informative rather than critical, and dealt with *rijal*: religious, political, and otherwise influential figures. For example, *Nama-yi danishvaran-e Nasiri* (*The Book of Scholars from the Time of Nasir al-Din Shah*) was published in Persian from 1879 until 1906,[101] and the Turkish-language "Grand Viziers of the Late Ottoman Period" project was started by Muhammad Kemal Inal in 1913, and was republished in Ankara and Istanbul in 1969 and 1982 respectively.[102]

However, the first comprehensive Islamic encyclopedia was published in Urdu in Lahore between 1964 and 1993. According to Rizwanur Rahman:

> Initially, the encyclopedia was conceived as a mere translation of the Encyclopedia of Islam, published under the aegis of the Dutch Royal Academy, Leiden between 1913 and 1936, but in the course of the preparation it developed into an independent, more comprehensive and original work.[103]

However, since the late 1970s, Muslims have been producing various Islamic encyclopedias and glossaries that speak of their specific religious identity (e.g., encyclopedias of Sufism and of Shiʿism), their national-cultural identity (e.g., *Iranica*), or political attitudes (reformist movements).[104]

In fact, self-sufficiency and anti-Western Islamic studies are the main reasons that Islamic institutes and centers have produced their own encyclopedias. During the launch of the *Encyclopaedia of Qur'anic Sciences*, replete with Shi'i accounts, the general editor stated:

> At the outset we decided to produce this work when it came to our attention that Leiden University [*sic*] in the Netherlands has published an Encyclopaedia of the Qur'ān (*EQ*). When we checked the list of contributors, we found that all of them were written by non-Muslims . . . I wrote a letter to the *EQ*'s editor and mentioned that we have some critiques on the entries, and we are able to write some essays and point out Shi'i teachings. I sent the letter to the University of Leiden in the Netherlands, but I received an answer from the United States . . . Zionists have a particular and profound influence on the Netherlands.[105]

It seems that some institutions and individuals assume that the *EQ* and its contributors are not permitted to write on the Qur'ān because they are not Muslims and are presumed to be connected to anti-Palestinian parties; this recalls that such ideas were frequently mentioned by Edward W. Said in his books and interviews. Thus, in Muslim academic contexts, a Western scholar of the Qur'ān is often viewed through the lens of politics (rather than science) and might be a reminder of Zionism, occupation, and exploitation. Unsurprisingly, not only Rippin but also other Western scholars run the very real risk of being labeled as an enemy of Muslim identity if they want to write on their scriptures critically.

This was also seen, earlier, in Iqbal's criticism of *EQ*. After its publication, Iqbal directed the project *The Integrated Encyclopedia of the Qur'ān* (*IEQ*), which was a response to the *EQ*'s approach to Islam. The first volume of the *IEQ* was launched in various Islamic societies and centers in North America and some copies were sent to various Islamic centers, such as those in Kuala Lumpur, among others.

Andrew Rippin reviewed the first volume of the *IEQ* and criticized its approach of not including modern Qur'anic scholarship produced in the Western academic context (by both Muslims and non-Muslims). According to Rippin, the *IEQ* was a sectarian encyclopedia, too:

> As a result, the encyclopedia is solidly Sunni: Ash'arī-Māturīdī theology and the four legal schools monopolize the sources employed. Only very occasionally are Shī'ī sources, for example, mentioned.[106]

Subsequently, Rippin's idea regarding the dearth of modern scholarship was rejected by Gibril Fouad Haddad (b. 1960), one of the *IEQ*'s associate editors and a lecturer at the University Brunei Darussalam, in the Malay-Indonesian world. In response, he stated that "serious scholarship on Islam is defined by Orientalism *sine qua non*,"[107] and he viewed all Western scholarly approaches to the Qur'ān as a neo-Orientalism project. Haddad ended his statement very harshly:

> Biased as it is, Rippin's review is nevertheless helpful. He critiques from the very perspective that *IEQ* is warning against and which he insists is the only valid one. The pulpit of Orientalism, born out of medieval heresiography, morphing into missionarism, then colonial *littérature de surveillance*, and finally area studies, still has its preachers to the converted; but from the perspective *IEQ* has defined as its own, such fault-finding is a confirmation that *IEQ* is in fact on the right track. There is an Orientalist *EI*, an Orientalist *EQ*, now even a syncretistic '*Study Quran*"; let there be an "'Ulematic" *IEQ*, a work that keeps faith with the field's oldest standards, a work that refuses to put everything on a par and in which there is qualitative and epistemological differentiation between *Ṣaḥīḥ al-Bukhārī* and *1,001 Nights*! It is not all literature and intertextuality. This is just one of many unsound doctrines against which it is hoped that *IEQ* will serve as the antidote of choice in our time.

To my utter lack of surprise, Haddad published this review in the journal of *Islamic Sciences* (previously known as *Islam & Science*), edited by Muzaffar Iqbal, who is the director of the center with same name, the Center for Islamic Sciences (certainly not Islamic Studies!). His review aptly reflects the perspective of the study of Islam under anti-Western Qur'anic studies, which rejects Brill's *EI* and *EQ*. Such views have the potential to deal with sectarianism.

As such, according to this, the "'*ulematic*" version of *Islamic studies* (as a subset of Islamic Apologetics) should be accomplished without any reference to modern (Western) academic approaches to the Qur'ān. Therefore, it is to be expected that a rejection of the research methodologies used by the majority of Western scholars of the Qur'ān—using biblical literature or intertextual analysis—will be seen in Muslim academic contexts.[108]

VI. Muslims' Reading of Muhammad's Adopted Son, Zayd

An Example of Islamic Apologetics

I have noticed several times that the relationship between Zayd, the *temporarily* adopted son of Muhammad, his wife Zaynab and Muhammad have been the central point of discussions in the Muslim world. Outside the academic context and in the private sphere, over which the authorities have less control, people argue that Muhammad loved the wife of his son. They know that this is a controversial topic which needs to be expressed cautiously. Many of them declare their opinion on the basis of classical sources, including *The History of al-Tabari*, a work which is not particularly admired by Muslim fundamentalists. Such ideas are scarcely heard among academics in universities. Regarding an earlier piece titled "Censored Manuscripts, Censored Intellects: Can We Trust the Past?," in which I depicted how modern Muslim exegetical figures have been trying to marginalize the historical significance of Zayd, I received feedback from colleagues and friends who were worried about the publications of such pieces. On one occasion, a non-Muslim colleague of mine said: "I'm very curious and slightly concerned about any reactions."

Muslims academics need to meet the expectations of the authorities in order to save their lives and jobs. I fully understand their concerns, yet I am always asking myself why I, or anyone else, should do what others force us to do.

Even my Muslim and non-Muslim colleagues in the West, with one of whom I recently had an Indian lunch in the heart of Europe, are worried about the reaction of Muslim fundamentalists and authorities if they write something critical about Islam or Muslims. He said that he is a white European and might become a dartboard for Muslims. Thus, they prefer to write neutral pieces on safe topics and publish them with reputed publishers. This also occurred to some other colleagues. A few days ago, I met a Muslim scholar and a member of the American Academy of Religion who had come from the United States. During the lunch, he was full of questions and asked me many things about my collaboration with Andrew Rippin and others with whom I had edited a volume. Among the big questions for him was whether Rippin respected the religion of Islam and Muslims, and whether he was influenced by so-called Orientalists who wished to downgrade Islam. Apparently, he was rather pessimistic about Western scholars of Islam. I think that the younger generation of scholars, who have graduated from Western/European contexts are cautious. They do not want to be marginalized or be known as Orientalists by Muslims. Such things always remind me of a classical and very popular Yazdi (from my hometown) expression which simply instructs people to be conservative: *assa bero, assa biya: ke gorba shakhet nazana*, which means: "go slow and gentle, come slow and gentle: so you are not attacked by a cat."

It is true that authorities, politicians and some fundamentalists and radicals are everywhere trying to prevent us from being critical, and ground- and taboo-breaking. As such, Muslim scholars are automatically ordered to be conservative and to ignore controversial issues and serious historical questions. Therefore, most publications on important Islamic topics such as Zayd are superficial and inattentive to earlier sources. To show Islamic Apologetics in Muslim academic contexts, this section examines three essays on *Zayd* and allows readers to compare the approaches used by Muslim scholars with that of Powers seen in the previous chapter:

- "Research on Adoption and Zayd b. Haritha" ("*tahqiqi darbara-yi Tabanni va Zayd b. Haritha*") is a Persian essay published in 1995 that is divided into two parts. Part one addresses "adoption" in the pre-Islamic and Islamic periods. Along with a terminological investigation, the author says that those men who did not have any male children practiced "adoption" and, relying on Jurji Zaydan, opines that the Hamurai of Babylon was the oldest nation practicing this custom. He also dedicated a section to the "disadvantages of adoption." It is said that those who adopted a son did not pay attention to his family background or to the "purity" of child (i.e., whether the child was born within or out of wedlock).

   As well as this, after the battle of *Ahzab* ("the parties") and his defeat of his enemies in the sixth year after his *hegira* (emigration) to Medina and the commencement of his power and authority, the Prophet derogated the custom of adoption, along with various others. Using classical Qur'ān commentaries, such as that of al-Zamakhshari, the author says that Muhammad is not the father of any of your men from a biological perspective. However, he is the spiritual father of the whole nation (*umma*). In addition, the emphasis of Islamic narratives, including

Shi'i ones, on the rejection of adoption, which forbids Muslims from adopting a son for their family, is addressed. After that, the importance of Zayd in Islam and for Muhammad, merely through describing the Islamic narratives, is related.[109]

- "Zayd b. Haritha al-Kalbi: The Martyred Leader" ("*Zayd b. Haritha al-Kalbi: al-Qaʿid al-Shahid*") is an Arabic article published in 1406AH/1985AD. This work, which uses only Sunni narratives, is particularly focused on Zayd's life as well as his role in battles and his military campaigns. It shows how Muhammad trusted him and appointed him to be the leader of the army. It recounts the intervention of God and Muhammad in satisfying Zaynab to marry Zayd.[110]

- "The Pride of the Young Muslims: Zayd b. Haritha" ("*Fakhr al-Shabab al-Muslim: Zayd b. Haritha*") is another Arabic essay, published in 1404AH/1983AD. This article, also using Islamic sources, describes the importance of Zayd in the Muslim army and how Muhammad relied on him in a number of battles.[111]

The main point of commonality between these three articles is their reference to Islamic traditions. However, these references are incomplete. None of them discuss Muhammad's marriage to Zaynab after Zayd divorced her. This is the story that is, with slight differences, discussed in the books of history, Muhammad's biography, and early Qur'anic exegetical works. The authors also fail to mention that, from the beginning of the fourteenth century AH, commentators began to reject the claim of earlier exegetes that Muhammad had expressed love for Zaynab by exclaiming, "Glory be to God, the Creator of light, blessed is God the best of Creators" (*subhann allah khaliq al-nur tabarak Allah ahsan al-khaliqin*).[112] Some Shi'i scholars, for example, argued that al-Zamakhshari and other exegetes falsely claimed that Muhammad had a (sexual) interest in Zaynab, that he loved her, and that he kept his feelings for her a secret. According to these scholars, Muhammad did not say, after encountering Zaynab, "Glory be to God who can overturn [men's] heart" (*subhan Allah muqallib al-qulub*).[113] They could also have referred to al-Tabrisi's work *Jawamiʿ al-Jamiʿ*, in which we read that, after Zayd returned home, Zaynab told him about Muhammad's visit and his infatuation with her beauty. Zayd then offered to divorce Zaynab so that she might marry Muhammad.[114] One wonders: Did Zayd not know that "sexual relations between a man and his daughter-in-law are prohibited"? If he did, why did he suggest that Zaynab marry her father-in-law?

Indeed, it would have been more appropriate for each of the authors to have discussed the diversity of stories regarding Zayd in the Islamic sources in the following five source-types:

1   -Qur'ān: mentions Zayd by name and his divorce from *an unidentified* woman.
2   -*Sira*: presents information about Zayd, his military career, his wife, and his son, albeit *without mentioning Muhammad's sexual interest in Zaynab or his repudiation of Zayd*.
3   -Early narratives: the fullest account of the lives of Zayd and his son Usama; of *the relationship between Muhammad and Zaynab; of Zayd's repudiation; and of the marginalization of Zayd and Usama.*
4   -Early exegesis: explains that *Zayd was aware of Muhammad's interest in Zaynab*; otherwise very similar to (3).
5   -Islamic theology and later exegesis: *highlights the infallibility of the Prophet* and *downplays the importance of Zayd.*

The early exegesis (4) was influenced by the *Sira* (2) and the early narratives (3). Subsequently, theologians and exegetes of the Qur'ān (5) either removed or refuted narratives about Zayd, Zaynab, and Muhammad found in source-types (2), (3), and (4) in order to preserve the doctrine of Muhammad's sin-lessness and the integrity of his status as a true prophet. What is clear is that although Zayd's name is mentioned in Q 33:37, making him the only Muslim apart from the Prophet mentioned within it, he is *not* the focal point of the exegetical or historical interest of Muslim scholars. If we examine the same body of narratives but shift our attention from Zayd to Muhammad, the following special qualities of the Prophet emerge in sharp relief: (1) magnanimity (Muhammad frees his slave Zayd and adopts him as his son); (2) trust (he appoints Zayd as the commander of numerous military expeditions); (3) closeness to God (who intervenes in history to reinforce the Prophet's decisions); (4) virtue (by exercising control over his sexual urges and instructing Zayd not to divorce Zaynab); and (5) obedience to God in the face of sharp criticism from the Hypocrites.

PART II

3

The Sectarian Study of Islam

A Culture of Isolation and the Isolation of Cultures

When they are asked about Islamic sectarianism by non-Muslims, I have often heard some of my Muslim friends and students (often Sunnis) in the West say that Islam is one religion and is not divided into different branches. They claim that Islamic sectarianism is a "Western" or an "imperialist" conspiracy concocted by Europeans in general, and the British Empire in particular, with the aim of breaking Muslim unity. How, though, does this relate to earlier periods of Islam? It is rather improbable that the Byzantines, for example, caused Muslim warriors such as al-Mukhtar (d. ca. 687) to create various sub-branches of Islamic belief. It has become clear to me that many classical works show that Muslims, depending on geography and politics, have established their own sects, mystical paths, and school of thoughts. The evidence outlined in this chapter shows not only that Islam does include different branches in the modern world—which predate the colonial era and cannot be said to have been the result of foreign actors—but also that Islam is taught and studied differently in Muslim academic contexts depending on which branch of Islam—here focusing on the main split between Sunni and Shi'i—is politically dominant.

I. From the Islamization of Biblical Literature to the Sectarianizing of the Muslim Academy

An emeritus professor of Lutheranism shared with me his confusion as to why a student of Christian theology prefers to read the Bible in English. "Did Jesus talk in English?" he asked. He was dissatisfied with the limited number of Hebrew, Greek, and Latin language courses in the history, classics, and theology departments of his institution. Such growing unfamiliarity with the languages, cultures, and literature of other, earlier communities, suggests that religion, culture, and history will be studied differently in the future.

Studying the Qur'ān in the Muslim Academy. Majid Daneshgar, Oxford University Press (2020).
© Oxford University Press.
DOI: 10.1093/oso/9780190067540.001.0001

What a student will prefer to work with is the *modern* English, or any other *modern* translated version of the Bible, doing practically nothing with the classical Hebrew language that was used by ancient Jews and other citizens of the Near East. The student will be disconnected from philology, which is supposed "to make sense of the term."[1] A modern English translation of the Bible cannot really allow students to imagine the past and to understand the transformations of ancient rituals and biblical theology over the course of history. What about the Arabic language? Modern Christian theology seems to have limited place for an Arabic translation of the Bible. Yet historical reports suggest that the Bible was translated into Arabic, and priests, following Muslims, used to translate and study the Arabic Pentateuch in churches from the earliest period of Islam.[2] For example, Reed MS 11 kept in the Heritage Collection, Dunedin Public Library shows part of the Arabic translation of the Pentateuch by the priest Sulayman, the son of the priest Fanus, the son of Archbishop Salib (?), the servant of Dayr al-'Adhra' (Samalut), produced in 1429 of the Coptic calendar (1713 AD).[3]

One may wonder how many of these documents are studied by Christian theology students. It seems that almost everything *biblical* is nowadays seen through the lens of the modern world and modern language, instead of history.

Related to this issue is the question of what the status of Islamic languages and Arabic translations of the Bible is in Muslim academic contexts. It can be said that, as well as the de-Biblicization of syllabi in Islamic academies, Muslims used to Islamicize biblical teachings. In the academies (*kulliyyat*) of Islam, students used to read the Qur'ān, a text that is called a miracle, in Arabic. However, it was not until the time of the famous grammarian and theologian (*mutakallim*) al-Rummani (d. 996) that it was officially announced that both the Qur'ān and its language are a miracle, and this was only in order to reject the Christian al-Kindi's claim regarding the non-divine origin of the Qur'ān; as such, al-Rummani established the doctrine of the inimitability of the Qur'ān.[4] This doctrine later became the backbone of the study of Islam in the Muslim world. Accordingly, the Qur'ān, the word of God (*kalima Allah*), came to be seen as unique and incomparable with other scriptures. This reason is enough to see why neither the Hebrew Bible nor its Arabic version were or are taught in the Muslim world. It recalls the rejection of al-Biqa'i's commentary on the Qur'ān, entitled *Nazm al-durar fi tanasub al-ayat wa-l-suwar*, because it employed the Hebrew Bible and the New Testament.[5] Following the official promulgation of Rummani's doctrine, Muslim theologians and scholars began the de-Biblicizing process of Islamic literature in general, and of exegetical works in particular, very quickly. As mentioned in the previous chapters, allusions to the story of Zayd and to David in early works were replaced with those of upcoming religious thinkers and commentators who ignored the similarities between Islamic and biblical material. Prior to al-Rummani's doctrine of inimitability, early Muslims attempted to apply biblical narratives for the sake of Islam; for example, Wahb b. Munabbih (d. ca. 732) had alluded to the Torah, the Psalms, and the Gospels in order to support Muhammad's prophecy, which, according to them, was predicted in the Bible.[6] Later, in the tenth century, Muslims substituted the "Biblicizing of the Islamic prophetic claims" with the "Islamization of whole biblical narratives."[7] The point has been made by scholars such as Griffith that "the availability of the Bible in Arabic in oral or written form played an important role in the formation of early Islamic religious thought and in Muslim responses to challenges from Jews and Christians."[8]

While investigating an Arabic translation of the Bible from the late eighteenth century in the Otago University Special Collections, it came to my attention that the translator Islamicized Genesis and Exodus. For example, the common Arabic translation of Genesis 20:1, compatible with the Hebrew version, says: *intaqal[a] Ibrahim[u] min hunak ila ard al-janub wa sakan[a] bayn[a] Qadish wa Shur wa tagharrab[a] fi Jarar*: "Now Abraham moved on from there into the region of the Negev (*e.ngb*) and lived between Kadesh and Shur. For a while he stayed in Gerar." However, the Otago manuscript says: *thumm[a] rahal[a] min thamm[a] Ibrahim ila balad <u>al-qibla</u> wa aqam[a] bayna <u>Raqim</u> wa <u>l-Ghifar</u> wa sakan[a] fi l-<u>Khulus</u>.* The underlined terms, added by the translator, are clearly Islamic-Qur'anic names, and do not make sense when compared to the Hebrew and the normative Arabic versions.

John Gill (d. 1771), an English Baptist pastor, in his *Exposition of the Bible Commentary*, interpreted Genesis 20:1 as follows:

> And Abraham journeyed from thence towards the south . . . . He returned from the plains or oaks of Mamre, where he had lived fifteen or twenty years, into the more southern parts of the land of Canaan: the reason of this remove is not certain; some think, because he could not bear the stench of the sulphurous lake, the cities of Sodom and Gomorrah were become; and others, because of the scandal of Lot's incest with his daughters, which prejudiced the idolatrous people in those parts more against the true religion; neither

of which are likely, by reason of the distance; but the better reason seems to be, that it was so ordered in Providence that he should remove from place to place, that it might appear that he was but a sojourner in the land:

and dwelt between Kadesh and Shur; two wildernesses, as Jerom says (y), one of which joined to Egypt, to which the people of Israel went when they passed over the Red sea, and the other, Kadesh, reached to the desert of the Saracens.[9]

The term *balad al-qibla* is the place toward which Abraham is moving, and it only makes sense if we consider that the Otago manuscript's translator has referred to the original *qibla* (direction of prayer for Muslims), in Jerusalem. Using the term *raqim* (Q 18:9), "the name of a leaden plate on which the names of the Seven Sleepers were inscribed,"[10] again shows that this translator Islamicized the Bible. Replacing *Kadesh* with *Raqim* makes no sense here, unless we refer to early Qur'ān commentaries such as *Tanwir al-Miqbas min Tafsir Ibn 'Abbas*.[11] In this commentary, the interpreter writes that "the inscription refers to the valley where this cave was; and it is also said that it refers to a city (are a wonder among Our portents) such as the sun, the moon, the sky, the earth, the stars, the oceans and even that which is more wondrous than this?"[12]

On another occasion, unlike אֲדֹנָי (*adonai*: my Lord) of Genesis 19:18 ("And Lot said to them, oh no, my lords"), which is commonly rendered as *Sayyidi*, the translator has replaced it with "Rasul Allah," the *Messenger of God*. Yet Gill's commentary does not suggest in any way that *my Lord* could be interpreted as *Rasul Allah*:

And Lot said unto them, . . . Supposing three present, not observing that the two angels had left him that had brought him thither; though it is but to one of them he addresses himself, even to him who had bid him make the best of his way to the mountain, as appears by what follows: oh, not so, my Lord; that is, let me not be obliged to go so far as to the mountain; though R. Samuel takes it to be an assent, and interprets the phrase of his being willing: but this does not agree with what follows, and is rejected by Aben Ezra, who relates it; and who also observes that the word "Lord" is a common name, that is, that belongs to a creature; but Jarchi says their Rabbis take it to be an holy name, that is, a name that belongs to God, and gives a good reason why it is so to be understood here; since the person spoken to had it in his power to kill or make alive, to save or destroy, as the following words show; so Ben Melech and the Targum of Oukelos render it by Jehovah.[13]

It thus seems clear that there were some Arabic translators who deliberately changed the meaning of certain terms. It is not surprising that many translators were influenced by Muslims and supporters of al-Rummanis including Jalal al-Din al-Suyuti (d. ca. 1505), whose works, including *al-Itqan fi 'ulum al-Qur'ān* (*The Perfect Guide to the Sciences of the Qur'ān*), are still used by MA and PhD Qur'ān students throughout the Muslim world.

Nonetheless, nothing like the Arabic translation of the Bible exists to show Muslim students how the scriptures that are read by Jews, Christians, and Muslims are interdependent. A Muslim reader will be able to find various points, notions, stories, and figures in the Bible that are also mentioned in Qur'anic and post-Qur'anic literature. Having access to either the Hebrew or the Arabic translation of the Bible would allow them the opportunity to observe the evolution of the Qur'ān and of its exegetical (*tafsiri*) literature over the course of history.

Such Islamicization of biblical literature or de-Biblicization of Islamic sources is similar to another type of censorship, which can be termed the "sectarian study of Islam." It must be stated here that both Sunnis and Shi'is, regardless of their supposed emphasis on integration and brotherly bonds, essentially prevent their own students from reading the sources (esp. recent publications) of the other sect.

We know that there are hundreds of extant classical treatises and manuscripts that display the earliest conflicts between Sunnis and Shi'is. For instance, the book by Sulaym ibn Qays (d. ca. 696), *Saqifa*, which was read by Shi'i devotees for centuries, includes the following topics:

> The power struggles and the violence marking the succession to Muhammad, the turbulent history and the problematical elaboration of the Qur'anic text and the body of hadith, the connivance between the circles of power and the religious scholars, the articulation of the civil conflicts, and the constitution of the scriptural sources.[14]

Sulaym had also a special status among Shi'i imams, as Amir Moezzi states:

> Certain early sources record a tradition going back to the forth imam, 'Alī b. al-Ḥusayn Zayn al-'Ābidīn, who supposedly said, after hearing a disciple

recite the *Book of Sulaym* to him, "Everything that Sulaym says is truthful, may God have mercy on him. All of this forms a part of our teaching (i.e., we imams) and we recognize it."[15]

As such, Sulaym's book clearly threatens the status of the first successors of Muhammad, particularly Abu Bakr (d. ca. 634) and 'Umar (d. ca. 644), who, according to Sulaym, usurped the place of the Prophet. I am not going to write more on this issue but it is worth noting that although Sunnis and Shi'i had and have a peaceful relationship—although this does, of course, depend on the time and place—it does not mean that they approve of each other's approach to the fundamental tenets of Islam.

The syllabi of traditionalist sources (*naqli-hadithi*) used in Sunni and Shi'i seminaries and universities are very different from each other. Currently, the de-Sunnization or the de-Shi'itization of Islamic literature has become a project that now prevails in most Muslim institutes, carrying on an approach that has been tied in with nationalism and racism. One example of this is that way that Safavid Persians (Shi'is) and Ottoman Turks (Sunnis) confronted each other and trained their people to reject one other by various forms of censorship.

Logically speaking, the scholars studying in or influenced by these contexts had lost or eventually would lose their connection to other civilizations, and subsequently other cultures.

II. The Forgotten East

Shahab Ahmed (d. 2015), in *What is Islam?*, used the term "the Balkans-to-Bengal complex," covering a wide area from Saray Bosna and Anatolia to Bengal and, according to a map designed by Ahmed, on to Mindanao and Mataram, where a metaphorical and *love-based* language and culture was dominant from the fourteenth to the late nineteenth century.[16] This geographical-cultural notion is correct in terms of removing the excessive focus that was, for a long time, given to "Persianate or Turco-Persianate civilization."[17] However, his notion is not applied to this chapter, as I think it still displays a unilateral power of particular languages, one community (Muslims), or region (the Muslim world). It does not reflect on a cultural *exchange* and a political *competition* that led to the contribution not only of Bengali but, even further east, also of Malay-Indonesian literature to the dominant culture of the Balkans and the Middle East. This is because Ahmed employs a term that Islamicizes Muslim civilization and separates it from the global culture. Rather, Ahmed's work seems to be attempting to conceal the real "sectarian" problems across the Islamicate world. Thus, this chapter tries to highlight the intra-sectarian disagreements in Muslim academic contexts.

Sectarianism in Qur'anic Exegetical Works: Connections

For centuries, a commonly held view among classical Muslim and Arab scholars was that Dhu l-Qarnayn, the famous Qur'anic figure from chapter 18 (*surat al-Kahf*) who supposedly suppressed Gog and Magog, refers to Alexander the Great (*Iskandar*). However, Indian Muslims, including Maulana Muhammad ʿAli (d. 1951) and Abu'l-Kalam Azad (d. 1958), declared that Dhu l-Qarnayn does not refer to Iskandar, but a Persian king. Azad argued that classical Qur'ān commentators wrongly interpreted Dhu l-Qarnayn because Alexander was not a God-fearing, just warrior or a kind ruler to the people of his time. By referring to biblical literature, scientific-historical discoveries from 1838, and Karl F. Geldner's (d. 1929) findings, it was suggested that Dhu l-Qarnayn was an honorary title used to praise Cyrus. Iranians, who highlighted Alexander's affiliation with a list of betrayers who had invaded and destroyed the ancient capital of Persepolis, warmly welcomed this new interpretation. Along with Azad and other South Asian scholars, including Mawdudi (d. 1979), Iranian Shiʿi commentators, reporters, and authors included Cyrus the Great, rather than Alexander, in their works. Muhammad Husayn Tabataba'i and Makarim Shirazi, among others, were at the forefront of writing such works, which met the expectation of Iranians (and particularly nationalists). In these, they replaced the view of Alexander the Great as Dhu l-Qarnayn, something which is still generally accepted by Sunni scholars, while Makarim Shirazi suggested that the title of Dhu l-Qarnayn obviously refers to Cyrus' personal features, something which has been widely accepted by Shiʿa the world over. This was an important step in the "Persian-Shiʿitizating or Pershiʿitizating" of the Qur'ān and its exegesis within the Muslim world. Thus, today, the answer to the question *Who was Dhu l-Qarnayn?* is inextricably linked with Muslims' national and racial identity.

Nonetheless, fewer Iranians or Arabs are aware that there is a Malay folk tale (*hikayat*) dating back to the fifteenth century that is profoundly influenced by Qur'anic stories, prophetic statements, and other (non-Islamic) Asian legends called *Hikayat Iskandar Zulkarnain* (*The Tale of Alexander Dhu l-Qarnayn*). This story displays the profound influence of Middle Eastern and Asian traditions on Malay literature. Here, Alexander is presented as a "propagator of Islam" who is thought to have been the true ancestor of the kings of Malacca. As Othman contends, "the story of Iskandar Zulkarnain is to realize the sacredness of royal families, their protectors and guardians."[18] In contrast to such traditionalists, there are some Malay scholars who instead claim that the real father of their kings of Malacca was Cyrus, as he showed ethical virtues such as kindness and integrity. As such, Afareez Abd Razak al-Hafiz sought to refute the view that Dhu l-Qarnayn was Alexander the Great (*Iskandar Maqduni* or *Iskandar-i Kabir*, often referred to as "Iskandar Zulkarnain" in the Malay tradition). To explore the identity of Dhu l-Qarnayn, Afareez analyzes classical literature on four great kings, two of whom are presented as believers in the Abrahamic tradition, and two of whom are presented as unbelievers. Afareez allocates one chapter to each of the four: Nimrud, Sulayman (Solomon), Nebuchadnezzar (Bukhtanasar), and Dhu l-Qarnayn. Through a historical discussion, he concludes that Alexander the Great cannot be linked historically with Dhu l-Qarnayn based on the description of the latter in the Qur'ān. In line with other contemporary Muslim thinkers (such as Azad and Mawdudi, as well as some Shi'i commentators), Afareez argues that the ethics, morality, and history of Alexander the Great make it impossible for him to be the Dhu l-Qarnayn mentioned in the Qur'ān. Afareez considers that Cyrus' birthplace, empire, territory, authority, and morality make it likely that he is Dhu l-Qarnayn. In addition to his textual study, Afareez also made a documentary, titled *Iskandar/Alexander Bukan Zulkarnain*, for the Malaysian Communication and Multimedia Commission (MCMC). This documentary may have resulted in his study, and indicates Afareez's concern with the Malay context of this discussion. In it, Afareez also argues against the notion that the Malay kings were genealogically related to Alexander the Great, a man guilty of corruption and widespread destruction.[19]

By contrast, a few Arabic works have highlighted that there are Malay-Indonesian scholars who have agreed with the recent notion presented by a Saudi scholar, Hamdi Ibn Hamza Abu Zayd, that Dhu l-Qarnayn could be Akhenaton (Amnihobit IV), an Egyptian pharaoh. Subsequently, other Malay scholars, including a famous pro-Shi'i scholar and novelist, have inferred that this is part of an anti-Persian-Shiʿi act to derogate the dependency of Dhu l-Qarnayn to Persia:

> This "strategic assumption" is to divert people [from the fact that] that *Iskandar Zulkarnain* is Persian. To them, being an Egyptian is far much safer. It is said that Akhenaton replaced his father, Pharaoh as the king, and he ruled Egypt justly and extend his empire. This idea originated from a Saudi scholar name Hamdi bin Hamzah Abu Zaid. Therefore, as we can expect, *Yajuj Makjuj* [Gog and Magog] will be Persian (and thus, of course, a Shiʿa).[20]

In fact, there are very few Middle Easterners who pay any attention to the controversies surrounding the Persian background of Dhu l-Qarnayn in the Malay-Indonesian world, even though they are rooted in Middle Eastern sources. Malays' ideas on this subject are directly linked to whether they use Sunni or Shiʿi sources as the basis of their ideas.

The "sectarian study" of Islam is not restricted to the Middle East, where Iranian or Iraqi Shiʿis and Sunni Arabs rarely study the sources of the other sect. Of course, it is not to be expected that every religious teaching of the Shiʿa and the Sunnis be read in the other context. However, this chapter wants to show that this *ignorance of the other* has become widespread across the Muslim world. Annually, the Middle East hosts hundreds of Sunni and Shiʿi Malay-Indonesian students who are in various ways influenced by pieces of propaganda produced against the identity and politics of the other sect. Neither the Sunnis nor the Shiʿa study each other's legal treatises (*risalat-e fiqhi*) and writings. It is thus not surprising that a Sunni Malay university professor who graduated from a famous Middle Eastern university told me, without reference to a source, that "temporary marriage, *mutʿa*, allows Shiʿis to have intercourse with an immature girl!"[21] Such unfamiliarity is often related to a sectarian evaluation of Islamic sources. For instance, very few Malaysian students study the famous Shiʿi commentaries by al-Tabrisi (d. ca. 1154) and Tabatabaʾi.[22] Likewise, and despite recent enthusiasm for comparative interpretations (*tafsir tatbiqi*) of the Qurʾān in some colleges in the Middle East, only a few Shiʿi scholars argue for the importance and contribution of Sunni exegetical works to the study of Islam. In some comparative studies, Sunni works are critically rejected in the light of Shiʿi theology. For instance, to analyze the possibility of visiting graves (*ziyara*) by referring to Q 9:84, a Shiʻi author expresses the objective of his research as being "to study the reliability and authenticity of narratives regarding the occasions of revelation of this verse because of the statement of ʻUmar b. al-Khattab."[23] Here, "to study the reliability" implies that there are weak points in narratives by ʻUmar. Then, after displaying some minor similarities between Sunni and Shiʻi sources, the author ends his examination with several questions, including: "as said, the revelation of this verse from ʻUmar's note is problematic. Sunni people attempted to provide answers for these problems. Thus, analyze [and describe] the answers and critique Sunni responses and justifications regarding this point."[24] Foreign students coming from other countries, including the Malay-Indonesian world, will study such books, which are generally published by Shiʻi institutes.

What is clear is that the geographical movement of the sectarian-based study of Islam from the Middle East to the Malay-Indonesian world disconnects students from other cultural and literary contexts.

Foreignness of Other Languages

There is dearth of studies that redress such cultural omissions. For instance, there have been only a few studies written by Iranians, Malays, and Turks that have highlighted the fact that there are hundreds of Arabic, Persian, and Turkish terms in Bahasa Melayu, whose classical written form was constituted by *Arabic-Persian* alphabets, called *Jawi*.[25]

Authority of Arabo-Sunni and Persian-Shiʻi Sources in the Malay Peninsula

The Islamic studies programs in the Muslim academy do not offer courses on these comparatively new Islamic languages. The main language taught in the Muslim world is still Arabic, rather than Persian, [Ottoman] Turkish, Malay, or Indonesian. Even today, there are few native Islamicists of the abovementioned languages who can read and make use of classical works. For instance, I have a Persian friend (a PhD holder) who is not able to read early-eleventh-century Persian manuscripts or a Qajari source.

While in New Zealand, I went through several Islamic and Middle Eastern manuscripts preserved in the Otago University Special Collections and the New Zealand National Library.[26] The majority of works produced in the sixteenth, seventeenth, eighteenth, and early nineteenth centuries had been written or annotated in Persian using *nastaʿliq* or *shikasti nastaʿliq* calligraphy. These texts were also translated into other languages, in Persia, Hindustan, or elsewhere, and they thus shaped the cultural and historical identity of Muslims both *inside* and *outside* those lands.[27] European travelers, colonial-era book collectors, and politicians all collected and studied many of these manuscripts. Therefore, Occidentals likely would have viewed Islam not as a purely Arabic faith, but as a multicultural and multi-linguistic religion stretching from Morocco, Cairo, the Hijaz, and Syria to Hyderabad, Pattani, and Northern Sumatra.

This recalls the emphasis of linguists on the fact that language and culture are strongly connected: "Culture is the product of socially and historically situated discourse communities, that are to a large extent imagined communities, created and shaped by language."[28] The host community of a foreign language and literature naturally and gradually changes its global and cultural perspective. Thus, the long-term reception of Arabic Sunni or Persian-Arabic Shiʿi sources is likely to form a Sunni or Shiʿi perception of culture(s), one that will not be able "to discover and travel among other selves, other identities, other varieties of the human adventure."[29]

Arabic and Arabizing Beyond Borders

As a further example, the teaching of Arabic in a Malay-Indonesian department of Islam (*pengajian Islam*) is almost always not sufficiently deep to understand the cultural and literary background of the Arab world. The Arabic language courses in Malay-Indonesian departments help students to converse, to specify the tense of sentences, and to translate a text from or into Arabic. Yet the connection between Arabic tales, particularly those with a global reputation (e.g., *1001 Nights*), and the development of Arabic [Islamic] culture is not discussed. This is despite the fact that studying Arabic stories can connect Malay students with alien cultures, including Persian, one that is not taken seriously into account by authorities. The Persian language was originally a cosmopolitan language that was "not forced upon cultures" but borrowed, one that began "to dominate as a language for elites" in the Malay-Indonesian world.[30] Historical sources suggest that Malays started to become oriented toward Arabia and India from the late sixteenth century. Subsequently, Malay students (*morid atau pelajar*) then started to read different versions of Islamic commentaries translated from Arabic.

Nonetheless, Hamza Fansuri (fl. c. late sixteenth century), a noted Malay Sufi poet, whose works are now mostly circulated across the

Malay-Indonesian world, regularly referred to Persian characters in his works. In *al-Muntahi* ("The Adept"), after first praising God and blessing the Prophet Muhammad and his companions, Fansuri gave a narration by 'Ali b. Abi Talib: "'Ali (may God be well pleased with him) said: 'I see nothing except that I see God within it.'" He went on to develop his prose work with several verses from the Persian 'Abd al-Rahman Jami, such as: "And Mawlana 'Abd al-Rāḥmān Jāmī (God's mercy be upon him) said, in verse: 'In neighbor, friend, and travelling companion—all is He / In the veils of beggars and in the robes of kings—all is He.'" Some of 'Attar's couplets from his *Mantiq al-tayr* (the Conference of Birds) were also cited by Fansuri, for instance: "Furthermore, Shaykh 'Attar (may God be well pleased with him) said: 'Some from among them returned, after beholding, leaping for joy; their souls have been given release from seeking.'"[31] Fansuri did not restrict himself to Jami and 'Attar alone, but also referred to other Persians, such as Fakhr al-Din Iraqi (d. ca. 1289) and Shaykh Mahmud Shabistari (d. ca. 1320). It is no wonder that Persian concepts of the philosophy of the unity of existence (*wahdat al-wujud*)—inspired by Ibn 'Arabi (d. ca.1240)—are visible in Fansuri's oeuvre. Shams al-Din al-Sumatrani (d. ca. 1630), a disciple and possibly student of Fansuri, elucidated some of the latter's notions through Arabic and Persian, and some modern Southeast Asian scholars and Islamologists recognize Fansuri as a "Shi'a" who knew both Arabic and Persian.[32]

Standing in opposition to this was the influential scholar Nuruddin al-Raniri (d. ca. 1658), originally from Gujarat in the northwest of India, who moved to the Malay Peninsula. He was particularly influenced by Arabo-centric sources, and opposed the mystical and poetic works produced by Fansuri, burning them near the Banda Aceh mosque.[33]

> By using the rhetoric of plurality, pitting the *ulama*'s more legalistic Islam against "indigenous mysticism," Raniri and his fellow *ulama* defined Arabic as the supra-language of the Malay world . . . . Arabic silently assumed supremacy as the supra-language when enough Arabs occupied the Malay world."[34]

During the colonial period (the nineteenth century), Malays, although not Indonesians, also received many of their religious and non-religious texts from Bombay (modern Mumbai) and Calcutta (modern Madras, both in

British India); the main sources of these, whether translated into Urdu or English, came from southern Arabia.[35]

From the beginning of the twentieth century, as a result of many socio-economic and political factors such as the opening of the Suez Canal, Egyptian and Arabian universities such as al-Azhar became more important and began to host many Malay students. Thus, "it is not a surprise that after 1900 the number of translations from Arabic sources into Malay [and vice versa] also grew, among them various texts of a political nature."[36] Via the translation of socio-political works produced by Egyptian reformists and nationalists in the late nineteenth century, Malay publishers, mainly those based in Singapore, informed Malays about the ideas surrounding reformism and pan-Islamism. Famous Arabic journals and magazines of the twentieth century, including *al-Manar*, contain communications that detail how Malays (and Singaporeans) sought a legal response (*fatwa*) from muftis and thinkers in Egypt in order to experience a "real" Islamic life. Indeed, the reception of large volumes of Arabic sources forced Malays to define and imagine the world as Arabs were defining and imagining it. Not surprisingly, modern Malay interpreters of the Qur'ān were significantly influenced by Sunni Arabic sources. Muhammad Saʿid bin ʿUmar, who studied in Mecca, wrote many parts of his Qur'ān commentary *Nur al-ihsan* ("The Light of Kindness") on the basis of Sunni Arabic exegeses.[37] This commentary is still taught, examined and studied in Malay *pondok*s and universities.

Modern Controversies on Arabo-Sunnism and Persian-Shiʿism

The modern controversy surrounding Shiʿi sources in the Malay Peninsula began much earlier than the 1979 Islamic Revolution in Iran. As well as being a result of Saudi financial support, which was used to propagate "conservative and puritan brands of Islamic teaching"[38] in Indonesia in the 1960s, it primarily happened when Middle Eastern rulers visited Malaysia, particularly Muhammad Reza Shah Pahlavi of Iran in 1968 and King Faisal of Arabia in 1970.

In the 1960s and 1970s, Iranian academics paid particular attention to Islamic civilization and culture. As part of this, they tried to highlight the contribution of the Persian language and Persian thinkers to world civilization, and extended the Persian dominion to the Malay-Indonesian world. For instance, Alessandro Bausani (d. 1988), a famous Italian scholar, gave a lecture at the University of Tehran in 1966 dealing with the influence of Persian culture and language on the literature of Malay-Indonesian people, which was later published in Persian in the University of Tehran's journal of humanities.[39]

King Faisal, known as the modernizer of Arabia, donated $240,000 to the Muslim College in Petaling Jaya, suggested the Malay authorities to set up "a permanent secretariat for the Conference of Islamic Nations,"[40] and paved the way for the Sunnization of knowledge in Muslim academic contexts. Therefore, the former rivalry between the "Persianizing and Arabizing" of Malay Islamic civilization and history was changed to "Persian-Shi'itization vs. Arabo-Sunnization" of the Malay-Indonesian world in the early 1970s.

A review of the literature shows that the majority of studies pertaining to Persian-Shi'ism in the Malay-Indonesian world before 1969 examined the contribution of Persian to Malay literature.[41] It seems that Muhammad Asad Shihab (Syihab), who had previously been editor of Indonesian newspapers, was the first to write a book on *al-Shi'ah fi Indonisia* ("The Shi'a Indonesia"), published in Najaf, Iraq. Its review was later published in the journal *Manabi' al-thaqafa al-Islamiyya* in Karbala. This review was soon translated into Persian and published by the new Shi'i revolutionary magazine *Darsha'i az Maktab-e Islam* (*Lessons from the Islamic School of Thought*), edited by the young clerics Ja'far Subhani (b. 1929) and Makarim Shirazi, in Qum in 1962.[42]

However, publications discussing the significance of Persian-Shi'i elements increased in the 1970s and peaked after the Islamic Revolution in Iran in 1979. Prior to the revolution, Iranian intellectuals and clerics both announced the result of their activities as being a "new Shi'ism . . . not solely occupied with doctrine and metaphysics, but also with acquiring political intelligibility."[43] Furthermore, many works by Iranians thinkers, such as *Dastan-e Rastan* ("The Story of the Righteous," 1960) by Murtaza Mutahhari (who was assassinated in 1979), which used Islamic-Shi'i elements in order to describe an imaginary just, ethical, and pure utopian society, were well received by readers across the globe. The genre and contents of the stories that Mutahhari used in his book resemble, to a large extent, those of traditional Malay folk tales, *hikayat*, and are full of ethical lessons. Not surprisingly, Malay-Indonesians who had read classical stories such as *Hikayat Ali kawin dengan Fatimah* ("The Story of the Marriage of 'Ali and Fatimah"), *Hikayat Nabi mengajar Ali* ("The Story of the Prophet Teaching 'Ali"), and *Hikayat Nabi dan orang miskin* ("The Story of the Prophet and a Poor Man"), had believed them to be true and it is therefore likely that they would have been influenced by Mutahhari's stories *Masihi va zirih-e hazrat-e Ali* ("A

Christian and ʿAliʾs Armor"), and *Aʿrabi va Rasul-e Akram* ("The Bedouin and the Prophet").[44]

III. Reception and Marginalization of Minorities

The Indonesian Academic Context and the Reception of Shiʿism[45]

Indonesia, with its motto "unity in diversity," was at the forefront of promoting and welcoming Shiʿi teachings in Southeast Asia. Although in the New Order period Shiʿa believers were labeled as deviant Muslims, the Islamic Revolution in Iran prompted many to travel from Indonesia to Iran and other parts of the Middle East to acquire Shiʿa Islamic knowledge. Ideological and political works by Mulla Sadra (d. ca. 1640), ʿAli Shariʿati (d. 1977), Murteza Mutahhari, Muhammad Husayn Tabatabaʾi, and other influential Shiʿi figures have all been studied by Indonesian scholars. As Formichi states:

> The works of Shiʿi theologists and philosophers, distributed by Indonesian students returning from Iran and other Middle Eastern countries, have stirred enthusiastic responses on university campuses. The egalitarian messages of Mullah Sadra, Mutahhari and the political views of Ali Shariʿati have been enthusiastically supported by those searching for a "pure" form of Islam.[46]

Although anti-Shiʿa sentiment increased in the 1980s, Indonesian students based in the United States translated Shariʿatiʾs work into English.[47] Many of them already had connections with Iranian revolutionary students based in the United States, and one of their main sources was Shariʿatiʾs work.

The Indonesian Shiʿa were largely free to follow their beliefs after the collapse of Suhartoʾs regime in 1998. As such, the Islamic Republic of Iran, in competition with Saudi Arabia and other Arab countries, has actively supported Southeast Asian students by gifting them numerous scholarship opportunities to study at the international *hawza* in Qum or at *Al-Mustafa International University* (formerly known as *The International Center for Ahl al-Bayt*), which has several international institutes. Indeed, one of the most influential institutes of Al-Mustafa is the Islamic College in Indonesia. Indonesians have spent considerable time studying modern Shi'i figures, and they have become interested in Shi'i Qur'anic exegetical works. The PhD dissertation of Khoirul Imam, for instance, investigates *wilayat al-faqih* (the guardianship of the legist) from Ayatollah Khomeini's perspective, and relates it to the Indonesian context. Ahmad Muhibbin also pursued this religio-political aspect of Shi'a studies and evaluated the concept of *imamah* (leadership) in light of the views of Tabataba'i. Muhibbin introduced the concept of *imamah* in the three chief branches of Shi'ism (i.e. Zaydi, Isma'ili, and Imami) before then analyzing the meaning of the phrases *ulu l-amr* (those in possession of authority), *wilayah* (sovereign power and authority), and *imamah* using Tabataba'i's work. Several other Indonesian researchers have also examined the exegetical approach used by Tabataba'i in his *al-Mizan fi tafsir al-Qur'ān*. Another area of Indonesian research has been Iranian socio-political thought. "The Political Thought of Ali Shari'ati: The Relation between Religion and State" was a PhD dissertation written at the University of Muhammadiyah Yogyakarta in 2007. In this study, following a discussion of the history of religion and Islam, Nugroho comments on the crucial role of Islamic ideology in revolution, from Shari'ati's perspective. Numerous works of and on influential Shi'i figures like Shari'ati, Khomeini, Khamenei, Mutahhari, Muhammad Baqir Shadr (should be read as Sadr), Misbah Yazdi, and Javadi Amuli have been translated and published in Indonesian.[48] Such freedom to explore Shi'ism in Indonesia prompted the establishment of the RausyanFikr institute and publication dedicated to Shi'i philosophy and mysticism, and apparently politics, in accordance with Shi'i teachings in the 1990s, and the *Ikatan Jamaah Ahlulbait Indonesia* (IJABI) (All-Indonesian Assembly of Ahlulbayt Association) in 2000, under the supervision of Jalaluddin Rahmat (b. 1949), to promote Islamic-Shi'i culture in Indonesia.[49]

As will be seen in this image (Figure 3.1), today, Shari'ati's influence is not limited to Iran. Since the 1979 Iranian Revolution, his works have been frequently translated into various Islamic languages, particularly in places where [Persian] Shi'ism has gained a strong foothold, such as Indonesia.[50] This image is the Indonesian translation of Shari'ati's (Syariati in Bahasa Indonesia) on Husayn (the third imam of Shi'is) whose jacket shows the images of Shari'ati as well as the Supreme Leader of Iran, 'Ali Khamenei.

Figure 3.1 The Indonesian translation of Shariʿatiʾs on the third imam of Shiʿis, Husayn

The Malaysian Academic Context and Shiʿi Sources

The story of Malaysians' reception of Shiʿi sources is different. The most important decision regarding Shiʿism in Malaysia was made on May 5, 1996 through reference to the 1984 gathering of the Fatwa Committee of the National Council for Islamic Religious Affairs, Malaysia. According to the new, 1996 declaration, the previous article [Paper No.08.02.1984, article 4.2. (2)], which states "the Zaydiyyah (*Imam lima*) and Jaʿfariyyah (*Imam dua belas*) Shiʿa are known in Malaysia," was revoked, and the instruction of Islamic teachings compatible with the *ahl al-Sunnah wa l-Jamaʿah* (people of the tradition and community; Sunnism) became compulsory in all aspects of social life (e.g., *shariʿa*, faith, and ethics). This declaration restricts freedom of thought and of publication: for example, any *publication* or *distribution* of books, pamphlets, films, and videos pertaining to the teaching of Islam that are contrary to *ahl al-Sunnah wa l-Jamaʿa* was forbidden (*adalah diharamkan*).[51]

The most important organization for monitoring the development of Shi'ism is the Department of Islamic Development Malaysia (Jabatan Kemajuan Islam Malaysia, henceforth JAKIM) which has strong ties with Malaysian academic institutes and faculties of Islam. A book titled *Mengenal Hakikat Syiah* (*Know the Reality of the Shi'a*) was published by Pejabat Mufti Wilayah Persekutuan, in September 2013 at JAKIM amid much celebration.[52] This book was produced in order to prevent the conversion of young Malaysian Muslims to Shi'ism and to make people aware of the "dangers" of Shi'ism. It also draws the attention of readers to the historical development of Shi'ism, the different approaches of Sunnis and Shi'is to the household of Muhammad (*ahl al-bayt*), and the theological conflicts of the Shi'i with the Sunni. Through the support of the Malaysian government, this book, along with many posters, was published and distributed—free of charge—to the public.

The final part of the book ("Terhadap Faham Syiah"; "Understanding the Shi'a") ends by listing the main ideological "deviations" of Shi'ism (*Ciri-ciri penyelewengan yang terdapat dalam ajaran Syiah*):

> (a) all Imams are infallible (*ma'sum*) in everything they do; (b) the Qur'ān as it exists today is distorted; (c) *al-Bada,* which expresses God's knowledge, is changeable and thus suggests God is ignorant; (d) *Raj'a,* according to which the Imam(s) will be resurrected and will punish those, including Abu Bakr, 'Umar, 'Uthman, 'A'ishah, and Mu'awiyah, who oppressed their rights; (e) the concept of *Imamah,* which holds that each Imam is appointed by God. Other issues such as *ghaybah* (occultation), *bara'ah* (adding the name of 'Ali into the *shahadah,* viz. *La ilah illa Allah, Muhammad rasul Allah, 'Ali wali Allah*) (the Muslim profession of faith: "there is no god but God, and Muhammad is the messenger of God, Ali is the vicegerent of God"), *taqiyyah* (dissimulation), and *mut'ah* (temporary marriage) are similarly denounced.[53]

Furthermore, the authors decry the Shi'a because of their visits to the holy shrines (of Husayn in Karbala),[54] their prostration on soil from Karbala while praying (*Sujud di atas batu yang didakwa batu Karbala ketika solat*), and their belief that the Qur'ān was fabricated.[55] The book also warns that whoever follows, supports, or propagates the aforementioned points, anywhere in Malaysia, will be charged under the Laws of Malaysia (Federal Territories) 1997 [Act 559], or another appropriate law.[56]

As with anti-Zionist and anti-Israeli books, red and black are frequently employed on the covers to show the deviation and violations of Shiʿism.[57] Many of these books are displayed every week in university bookshops and exhibitions, as well as during Friday prayers, and there are a number of Malaysian authorities who blame Iran for propagating *Ithna ʿAshari* (the Twelve-Imami) Shiʿism in Malaysia following the triumph of the Islamic Revolution of Iran in 1979.[58]

Reading such government-supported works means Malay students studying in academic contexts only (must) see Islam through the lens of Sunnism, alongside the Arabic language that is often encouraged by the (Arabic-speaking) countries of the Middle East. As such, there is a dearth of studies dealing with non-Sunni Qurʾanic and exegetical studies in Malaysian academic contexts. With the exception of a few Indonesian theses, no Malaysian student has yet comprehensively studied any of the most famous and influential Shiʿi commentators or traditionalists.

Shiʿi Works in Thailand

A travel account narrates the journey of some Persians to Siam (Thailand) in 1685. The work, *Safinih-yi Sulayman* (*The Ship of Sulayman*), was written by Ibn Muhammad Ibrahim, the secretary to the ambassador of the Safavid ruler Shah Sulayman (r. 1666–1694).[59] *Safinih-yi Sulayman* deals with the impact of Shaykh Ahmad al-Qummi (d. ca.1631), a merchant who arrived in Ayutthaya in 1602 and, more generally, the relationship between the Persians and Siamese and the effect of Persian Shiʿism on the Malay Archipelago. Shaykh Ahmad became the first *Shaykh al-Islam* or *chularajmontri* in Siam; his Shiʿi descendants, the Bunnag family,[60] became pillars of the Thai state, and the tomb of this influential politico-cultural figure is still of great significance for some Thais. Part of the inscription on the tombstone of Shaykh Ahmad reads:

> Chao Phya Boworn Rajnayok (Sheikh Aḥmad), Shia-Ithna Ashari (i.e. Twelver Shiʿi) Muslim, was born in 1543 A.D. in the Paeene Shahar district of Qum, the Islamic centre of Iran. Towards the end of King Naresuan the Great's reign [r. 1590–1605], Sheikh Ahmad and his retinue migrated to Ayudhaya and set up their residential and trading quarters in the Ghayee landing district. His business prospered and he became very wealthy. He

married a lady named Chuey, who bore him two sons and a daughter. As a result of his contribution to the development of the port administration during King Songdham's reign, Sheikh Ahmad was appointed by royal command to be Phya Sheikh Ahmad Rattana Rahsethee, Head of "Krom Tha of the Right" in charge of foreign trade and responsible for settling disputes among foreigners other than Chinese. As Chula Rajmontri [i.e., Shaykh al-Islam], leader of the Muslim community, he was the first holder of the "Chula Rajmontri" title and was recognized as the one who introduced the Shia-Ithna Ashari sect [i.e., Twelver Shi'ism] to Thailand. Subsequently, Sheikh Ahmad, together with his devoted friends, helped suppress an uprising in Ayudhya when a group of foreigners seized the Grand Palace. This dangerous deed led to the King promoting him to the title of "Chao Phya." He thus became Chao Phya Sheikh Ahmad Rattana Dhibodi, holding the position of "Principle Minister for Civil Affairs (North)." During the reign of King Prasartthong, when Sheikh Ahmad was 87 years old, the king appointed him "Emeritus Councilor for Civil Affairs" with the new title Chao Phya Boworn Rajnayok." He passed away one year later in 1631 A.D. at the age of 88.[61]

In modern Thailand, links with Shi'ism were significantly developed when Thai Shi'is made official contact with Iranians during the first phase of the 1979 Revolution. A Persian translation of the letter was published by *Darsha'i az Maktab-e Islam* magazine in 1979. The gist of it, titled in translation "A Statement from the Shi'is of Thailand," is as follows:

We are almost two thousand Shi'a in Bangkok and this enormous number of believers only have [*sic*] four mosques throughout Bangkok (Masjid Shahi, Masjid Khushbakht, Masjid Fallah, Masjid al-I'anah al-Islamiyyah) . . . Shaykh Ahmad al-Qummi and his companions left Qum, came here and founded the Shi'a sect in Thailand. Nowadays, these two thousand believers are his descendants. After Shaykh Ahmad passed away, Thai Shi'a do not have a religious leader (*rauhani*), and nobody has yet been to Iraq, Iran, or other Muslim countries to acquire Islamic teachings. Therefore, none of the Thai Shi'a are familiar with Arabic, Perisan, or Urdu, but they use the books of *Jami' 'Abbasi* and *Mafatih al-Jinan* in their ceremonial rituals. Also, in the sacred month of Muharram, mourning for the *ahl al-bayt* (Muhammad's household) is done in Persian but unfortunately we do not have a prayer leader to lead the prayers [...]. We ask that all Shi'a of the world cooperate with the Thai Shi'a in religious affairs.[62]

This letter shows the important role of Shaykh Ahmad al-Qummi in the foundation of Iranian-Thai relations. Following the Iranian Revolution, the new Iranian government started to build upon existing Iran-Thailand links by seeking to strengthen relations with Thailand and its Shi'i communities. In this, the efforts of the Islamic Republic of Iran's embassy in Bangkok have been more focused on cultural and academic initiatives than specifically religious activities, as has also been the case with its embassy in Jakarta. For instance, the Bangkok embassy has held several conferences and launched several books on the scientific and cultural contributions of Persian Shi'i religious thinkers ('ulema') in Southeast Asia. In 1995, *Sheikh Ahmad Qumi and the History of Siam* was published, and some years later, *Measuring the Effect of Iranian Mysticism on Southeast Asia*, edited by Imitiyaz Yusuf, presented thirteen essays dealing with Persian and Shi'i studies in Southeast Asia. These two culturally focused academic publications highlight the influence of Iranian Shi'ism in Southeast Asia and the Malay Archipelago in particularly, although neither of them touch on the contribution of Persian Shi'i Qur'anic exegetical works in Southeast Asia. Through highlighting the role of Persian Shi'ism in Thai history, the contribution of Arabic and other sources in shaping the identity of Muslims in southern Thailand (i.e., Pattani) was ignored in these books.[63]

Also, given that, for example, the College of Islamic Studies at Prince Songkla University (Pattani Campus) is largely Sunni-centric, it is not entirely clear whether these Thai-based Persian Shi'i sources are available in Thai universities.

Indeed, Malay, Indonesian, and Thai academic contexts have been heavily influenced by such unilateral sectarian-focused opinions that were coming from the Middle East.

Malays' Influence on Middle Eastern Exegetical Works

The last few decades have seen an increasing number of attempts to demonstrate the influence of the Middle East on the Malay-Indonesian world.

However, they have only examined the movement from the Middle East to Southeast Asia, and only a few Middle Easterners visit the Malay-Indonesian region to try to objectively explore models of cultural integration. From the first arrival of Islam in the region, Malays were interested in visiting Arabia primarily as pilgrims. In the sixteenth century, the Persian Gulf, Red Sea, and Indian Ocean regions were under the control of the Ottoman Empire, which enabled Malays to travel and strengthened their relationship with the Arab World.[64] Subsequently, many Malay students resided in Arabia in order to acquire Islamic knowledge, including Muhammad Arsyad al-Banjari (d. 1812) and Muhammad al-Nawawi al-Bantani/al-Jawi (d. 1879).[65] Al-Nawawi, originally from Banten in West Java, produced one of the most influential Arabic Qur'ān commentaries of the nineteenth century, titled *Tafsir al-munir li-ma'alim al-tanzil* (also known as *Marah labid li-kashf ma'na al-Qur'ān al-majid*). This two-volume exegesis was first published in Cairo in 1886.[66] It is important for two reasons: (a) al-Nawawi was influenced by the Malay educational context as well as by Middle Eastern classical and modern interpretations of Islam; and (b) many other students, including Shaykh Ahmad al-Hadi (d. 1934) and Mohd Yusof Ahmad (d. 1933),[67] were influenced by his exegesis and lauded his opinions in mosques and religious schools where Malays studied Islam.

As well as influencing Malay scholars, al-Nawawi's exegetical work has also influenced modern Middle Eastern commentaries and educational books. He was interested in the modern debates on reformism conducted in Egypt by Persian activist Sayyid Jamal al-Din [al-Afghani] (d. 1897) and, later, by Muhammad 'Abduh (d. 1905). He opposed the existence of the Dutch East Indies and the colonization of Indonesia, and became so famous in Arabia that he was chosen to be the *imam* of the Sacred Mosque (*al-Masjid al-Haram*) in Mecca, as well as being known as *Sayyid 'Ulama' al-Hijaz* (The Master of the Religious Thinkers of the Hijaz).[68] Al-Nawawi also taught Islamic and Qur'anic exegesis in Mecca.[69] However, there have been no studies written in academic institutes of the Middle East that discuss in detail the contribution of al-Nawawi's or other Malays' works to contemporary exegetical trends, as this requires basic knowledge of the history and literature of Southeast Asia, neither of which are studied by students or academics in the Middle East. This is despite the fact that many of his commentaries on the Qur'ān were and still are examined and cited by Arabs, Persian and Indo-Pakistani exegetes, and scholars.[70]

IV. Forgetting the Language and Culture of Everywhere/Always

Reviewing the publications and dissertations produced in Muslim academic contexts shows that there are a few scholars working on pre-Islamic Arabia and Persia, too, which certainly needs a good command of various languages like Pahlavi, Syriac, Hebrew, and Coptic, among others. Rippin's *Muslims: Their Religious Beliefs and Practices* shows how the non-Muslim powers of the Byzantine and Sassanid empires confronted each other in southern Arabia through their support of various groups of Ethiopian and Nestorian Christians. Current knowledge of pre-Islamic Arabia tells us that there were two main Arabian tribes, the Ghassanids and Lakhmids, who played the role of agents or proxies for the two empires.[71] The sectarian study of Islam grants Muslim researchers only the limited view of an insider, one that does not allow them to survey the history of religion outside particular Islamic traditions (*manqulat*) and the particular Islamic context (*muhit*). It does not permit, for example, a Malay scholar of Islam to write about the link between pre-Islamic Malaya and Buddhist traditions. It also prevents the reception of reports and observations by European travelers of other geographical contexts. For instance, there are very few studies in Iranian, Pakistani, and Indian Islamic academic institutes addressing the importance of O. L. Helfrich and other officers in illustrating the *Tabut Feast*, related to the commemoration of the household of Muhammad (mainly Husayn) in Southeast Asia.[72] It is assumed that this custom, practiced by the Shiʿa, arrived in Sumatra from India. This is also the case in Arabian and Malay-Indonesian academic contexts, where there may be no study of Edward G. Browne's (d. 1926) report on the Constitutional Revolution of Iran, in which he provides a fully developed and unique report on the biography and contribution of Sayyid Jamal al-Din, whose thought led Muslims in general and Muhammad ʿAbduh in particular toward the idea of pan-Islamism. This veil also does not allow an Iranian scholar to explore the importance of King Faisal of Arabia in modernizing the Middle East, and the Islamization of knowledge.

The sectarian study of Islam has led to a "de-Orientalizing" of Muslim academic contexts, too. Other civilizations are alien for students, and they do not see the cultures of the many other Asian communities as relevant to their work. Therefore, South Asian and East Asian languages and religions and Asian religious studies are not taught in Muslim academic contexts.[73]

For instance, Iran is important for a Malaysian student not because of its culture, history, literature, and civilization, but due to the dominant state religion of Shi'ism. Likewise, an Iranian scholar of Islam primarily views the country of Pakistan through the lens of its Sunni population and institutions rather than with its commonalities through Persian culture and language.

Moving toward Africa, the situation becomes still more barren. With the exception of the northern part of the continent (e.g., Egypt, Morocco), places that have been studied by Europeans, there is a serious dearth of research on Islamic and Qur'anic studies in other African countries, such as Niger, Nigeria, Sudan, South Africa, etc. Many scholars of Islam and religious thinkers in these countries are alumni of universities or religious schools in Saudi Arabia, Egypt, Iran, Pakistan, Malaysia, and so forth. Not surprisingly, the tension between political powers in the Middle East (e.g., Saudi Arabia vs. Iran) has affected "local and national power struggles in sub-Saharan Africa."[74] Thus, it is not surprising that the departments of Islam and the Qur'ān in African countries are influenced by Middle Easterners' approaches to Islam and the study of the religion. As such, although there are secular universities in Nigeria, the so-called Islamic studies departments try to preserve the religious languages (esp. Arabic) and ideas deemed important.[75] African universities have become more closely linked to Arab countries since the 1960s. For instance, the Ahmadu Bello University's Arabic and Islamic Studies department was established in 1962–1963. Since then, much effort has been made by Gulf states, particularly Saudi Arabia, to spread Arabic Islamic teachings in African countries:

> Under King Faisal, however, Africa became an ideological battleground between Egypt and Saudi Arabia. Saudi Arabian ulama fought al-Azhar's influence outside the Arab world, the Islamic University in Medina trained missionaries to send abroad, and the Muslim World League . . . brought African Muslim leaders like Bello and Ibrahim Niasse into contact with the Saudi Leadership.[76]

Similarly, post-Revolution activities by Iranian embassies in Africa led to the emergence of new magazines and increased support for Nigerian students interested in Shi'ism.[77] As a result, it is not only Malay-Indonesian *akadmie pengagian Islam* or *ponpes* but Africans' colleges for the study of

Islam, too, that are significantly influenced by the tension between political and religious spheres in the Middle East. The greater the connection with political and sectarian Islam, the greater the ignorance of other cultures and civilizations and their importance.

4

Hatred of Inferiority and Confrontation with the West

Forgetting Some, Remembering Others

From the time I was a BA student, I wondered why *some* Muslims' works on the Qur'ān (in Muslim academic contexts) are often replete with references to Western scientists rather than Western scholars of the Qur'ān. I was personally very impressed with and influenced by such an approach, and had published a Persian apologetic article using the names and works of Einstein, Bucaille, and other physicians and scientists in order to prove the inimitability of the Qur'ān.[1] Later, after starting my PhD, I published a self-critical piece in English in order to correct my earlier work, one which said that ascribing Western scientists' comments to the Qur'ān might not be historically accurate. Although I wanted to publish the critical piece in Persian, too, it has never been accepted by any Muslim journal editor.

Nonetheless, the important thing for me was, and still is, the question of why some Muslim scholars prefer to ignore the works produced by Schacht, Crone, Rippin, and others, and instead to reference works by writers who were not Qur'anic scholars or who were not well qualified to write on the subject, such as Einstein, Bucaille, Moore, etc. In addition, in works by Muslim scholars the names and works of Western Qur'anic scholars are often accompanied by strong criticism with the aim of demonizing, ridiculing, or, politely speaking, rejecting them. In order to explore this, this chapter is divided into two main parts. The first explores how the works of Western scholars of the Qur'ān are often ignored in Muslim academic contexts. The main focus will be on the book *Orientalism* by Edward W. Said (d. 2003), and the way it has caused Muslim scholars and students to be critical of every piece of work from the West. The second part unpacks how Muslims have replaced the works of Western Qur'ān scholars with those of Western scientists. It also explains how some supportive comments about the Qur'ān

Studying the Qur'ān in the Muslim Academy. Majid Daneshgar, Oxford University Press (2020).
© Oxford University Press.
DOI: 10.1093/oso/9780190067540.001.0001

ascribed to Western scientists are the result of misunderstandings and consequently are inaccurate.

I. Forgetting Western Scholars of the Qur'ān: Origins

- "Did you take the Orientalism course?"
- "No, I did not."
- "You should take this course before completing your BA!"

Such was a conversation between me and a university lecturer twelve years ago in Iran. The lecturer, who was a *hujjat al-Islam* (i.e., a member of the clergy) and had a PhD in Qur'anic studies, strongly recommended that I become familiar with the *mustashriqin* or "Orientalists," those who, according to him, talked about Islam a lot. He named many Westerners who, he said, distorted Islamic teachings. The sources for studying Orientalism at that time were those works written post-2000 that had a very critical view of Qur'anic studies as practiced by Western scholars, or the so-called Orientalists. It was the writings of Edward W. Said that formed the backbone of many of these works. Although Said was a professor of comparative literature and a famous literary critic from Colombia University in New York, not a politician or a historian of Islam, hundreds of books on Orientalists' Islamic and Qur'anic studies have been published by Muslims in which references to Edward Said's discourse are clear.[2]

Before Edward Said's *Orientalism*

Muslims have had a generally negative view of Westerners for several centuries.[3] Many important modern works have been written by Muslim scholars in which the status of Muslims vis-à-vis the West is discussed, such as those by Jalal Al-e Ahmad (d. 1969) in Iran, Cemil Meriç (d. 1987) in Turkey, and Abu l-Hasan 'Ali Hasani Nadwi (d. 1999) in India, among others. Each of them directly or indirectly discussed (Western) civilization, power, and authority from different perspectives. Al-e Ahmad, whose followers are still to be found in Iran, for instance, said:

To follow the West—the Western states and the oil companies—is the supreme manifestation of occidentosis in our time. This is how Western industry plunders us, how it rules us, how it holds our destiny.[4]

However, this view was not the dominant one among elites until the first
half of the twentieth century. For instance, in 1317/1938 Abu l-Qasim Sahab
published a glossary of Orientalists in which he discussed the ideas of various
European scholars. On behalf of the Iranian Ministry of Ma'arif (Religious
Teachings), the introduction to the book presented it as an appreciation and
celebration of the works of Orientalists and Western scholars. For Sahab,
unlike Edward Said, both Ignác Goldziher and Theodor Nöldeke provided
Muslims with extremely valuable writings on the history and literature of
Islam.[5] In another similar example, Aboebakar, who was the first scholar to
write on the history of the Qur'ān in Malay, simply defined the Orientalists,
including Nöldeke, Friedrich Schwally, and Gotthelf Bergsträsser, as being
people who were experts on the East (*ahli-ahli ketimuran*), after which he included the names of Muslim scholars who had made valuable contributions
to the history of the Qur'ān (*ta'rikh al-Qur'ān*), such as Abu 'Abdallah al-
Zanjani.[6] Yet such views have been rarely seen in Muslims' writings after the
1970s, since they now unthinkingly accept the view of Edward Said.

II. E. W. Said's *Orientalism*

Said was successful both inside and outside the Middle East. He was a critic at
Columbia University, in New York—a city where many Jews and Arabs had
been living for decades—where he talked about Palestine and either directly
or indirectly supported Palestinians by criticizing the United States and Israel
by means of Western, rather than Arab, scientists and philosophers.[7] He was
able to preserve both his Arab and his American background. According to
my senior colleagues at the Freiburg Institute for Advanced Studies, he was a
pioneer of his time, someone who challenged the imperial-centric role of the
West in the Middle East, at a time in 1960s and 1970s when the United States
and various other Western powers were seen as the symbols of knowledge,
enlightenment, and peace. In such a situation, Said emerged as a corrective, showing the public and academics that history, civilization, and power
are [not] the result of people sharing a particular community, religion, culture, etc. Despite some Westerners' criticism of his approach to Europeans,[8]

Said is still famous for his 1978 masterpiece *Orientalism*, initially published by Pantheon Books in New York, which has encouraged some (Muslim) scholars to write diatribes against Westerners. Although it was a corrective to the previous, one-sided perspective, he did not discuss both sides of the debate. He was focused purely on European narratives on the Orient. For Said, the terms "colonialism" and "imperialism" are selective; they are purely Western phenomena, in the form of those colonists who invaded Muslims lands. He totally ignores rulers of the Orient, such as the Ottoman and Japanese, who were not merely the victims of colonialism but who were themselves colonizers interested in expanding their imperial territory. Had he also highlighted Oriental imperialists he would no longer have been able to only criticize Western powers such as Britain and America.[9]

In *Orientalism*, he positioned all European narrators of the Orient under "the canopy of racism, imperialism, and ethnocentrism." Through scrutinizing European literature and political agendas, Said partly argued that the imagined Orient is a *toy* in the hands of European super-powers:

Yet the Orientalist makes it his work to be always converting the Orient from something into something else: he does this for himself, for the sake of his culture, in some cases for what he believes is the sake of the Oriental. This process of conversion is a disciplined one: it is taught, it has its own societies, periodicals, traditions, vocabulary, rhetoric, all in basic ways connected to and supplied by the prevailing cultural and political norms of the West.[10]

Demonization of Western scholars, culture, and achievements, as seen in Said's *Orientalism*,[11] were and still are—I believe—psychologically and geographically threatening to the Muslim identity. While such mocking of Orientals is only rarely found in literary works nowadays, it is clearly displayed both on social networks and in movies.

For instance, in the movie *Transformers: Revenge of the Fallen* (2009), everybody and everything *inside* the United States is seen as highly advanced and systematic but *outside* of it, viz., in the Middle East, where the Americans head to in order to complete their mission, is backwards. The Americans, who have among them a Redeemer, are to be based in Egypt. The Egypt displayed in this movie is shown as a benighted and ignorant land. The movie does not show Egypt as a land that, in ages past, was often influenced by the ideas of Europeans such as "Homer, Lycurgus, Solon, and Pythagoras, and conquered by Alexander the Great." At that time, Europeans saw Egypt as the jewel of the Orient, a land which "was the focal point of the relationship between Africa and Asia, between Europe and the East, between memory and actuality."[12] It has been known as a land of mystery, the Pyramids of Giza, and the Sphinx (called by Abu l-Hawl, "the Terrifying One"), whose greatness and importance has long been mentioned in ancient folk tales and traditions.[13] For centuries, Egyptians shared their history with the Greek community and inhabitants (Egyptiotes) of Alexandria. Yet in this movie, Egypt is presented as a Bedouin land where autobots climb the pyramids and Americans shoot their enemies. Neither Americans nor autobots know how many Europeans, for centuries, dreamed about the land of Egypt. Instead, the Americans' actions seem to say: *See how I sacrifice myself for my country*; however, they do not die *inside* New York but *inside* America's self-defined global territory, the Middle East. The movie also fails to show how, technologically, Egypt has been one of the advanced Arab countries through the founding of a "smart village" in Cairo.

Such movies, which primarily mythologize the United States and Americans, may raise a (surprising) question in the viewers' mind: To what extent (not *why*) are the people of Egypt benighted? This question psychologically downgrades the image of the Egyptian in the viewers' mind. Thus, the Egyptian sees himself as inferior to an American or, to put it more simply, the American sees himself as superior to an Arab. Here, though, it must be admitted that suggesting a director's approach to the Muslim world is the same as all Americans' does not make sense when it is obvious that there are many Westerners who do not like nor watch such movies; ascribing political approaches and decisions like those presented in some parts of Said's *Orientalism* to all Westerners merely serves to heighten the antagonism between Muslims and Western scholars of Islam, and Westerners in general.

Whether Said was fair or unfair to Westerners in his *Orientalism*, the reflection of his arguments in Muslim media, books, and theses are broadly similar to the following thesis, put forward by one Palestinian student:

The main theses of the book, concerning Orientalism in its imaginative, academic and dominative forms, are: The "Orient" was a European invention; Europe built its self-image in contrast with the image it had of the East in itself; the East was considered essentially inactive, irrational and incapable of governing itself; Orientalism—a consistent, self-sustained, growing discourse—played an important role in justifying and consolidating Western imperialism in the East.[14]

This student then states:

> It was no surprise that *Orientalism*, with such a revealing thought and its author, being of Palestinian-Arab origin, was met with ferocious hostility, disguised in the form of critique, by advocates of imperialism and anti-Arab feelings (e.g. Bernard Lewis); the surprise was that the revelations of Said were not met with due consideration by Arab academics and Arabic academic institutions, let alone becoming part and parcel of the political consciousness of these academics and institutions.[15]

Orientalism, rather than his supplementary work, *Culture and Imperialism*, became Said's *chef d'oeuvre* among Muslims of the late twentieth and early twenty-first centuries not only because it challenged Western policies and presented a new approach to literary criticism, but also because it was able to echo the habitual concerns of Muslims that Europeans have plundered Islamic civilization and identity over the course of history. While earlier Muslim and non-Muslim scholars had used the notions of Orientalism and Western imperialism (seen as having dismembered the unity of Muslims),[16] Said's connection of this notion to European literary works, replete with references to Islamic elements, gained the attention of Muslim academics. It was Said who has directed Muslims' academic discourse about the West through his political and intellectual analysis. During the early years of the Iranian Revolution, when Muslim media and publications from North Africa to the Malay-Indonesian world were analyzing the "truthness" of the revolution[17] and when some Western media tried to critique Khomeini (the leader of the Iranian Revolution),[18] Edward Said took a different stance and "criticized the negative coverage of Khomeini."[19] In line with many Iranian thinkers, he agreed that Khomeini, along with ʿAli Shariʿati, who was influenced by Frantz Fanon, had a significant impact on the revolution's outcome.[20] Indeed, Said emphasized the concern of these revolutionary figures with blotting out the traces of Western imperialism throughout the colonial and imperial regions. Because of this, many Muslims became interested in Said's works and statements, and so those were widely echoed in the media, which itself paid no attention to what various scholars were saying about Said's approaches, especially that taken in *Orientalism*. For example,

Malcolm H. Kerr (d. 1984) an American thinker who was born, grew up, and killed in Lebanon, and who produced several influential works dealing with the politics of Islam and the history of the Middle East, stated that Said's book

> contains many excellent sections and scores many telling points, but it is spoiled by overzealous prosecutorial argument in which Professor Said, in his eagerness to spin too large a web, leaps at conclusions and tries to throw everything but the kitchen sink into a preconceived frame of analysis. In charging the entire tradition of European and American Oriental studies with the sins of reductionism and caricature, he commits precisely the same error.[21]

Similarly, William Montgomery Watt (d. 2006), whose works on the history of Islam are more admired in Muslim academic contexts than those of many other Westerners, believed that:

> Edward Said tried to link up . . . nineteenth-century stereotype of the Orient with previous European perception of the Islamic world. He realizes some of the important differences, but there is one central question which he omits. How can it be that the previous European perception of the Muslim as a warrior spreading his faith by violence and the sword was transformed into a perception of the Oriental as a pusillanimous, weak and ineffectual person. It would surely be better to see the nineteenth-century perception of the Oriental as something new which became possible after the western European powers had ceased to regard the Ottoman Empire as a military threat. Edward Said works out his thesis in great detail, but at many points his interpretations of the motives of those involved seem to be questionable.[22]

In addition, a review by James Clifford raises many questions regarding Said's serious misunderstanding of the West, in which he writes:

> Its author's complex critical posture may, in this sense, be taken as representative. A Palestinian nationalist educated in Egypt and America, a scholar deeply imbued with the European humanities and now Professor of English and Comparative Literature at Columbia, Said writes as "an Oriental," but only to dissolve the category. He writes as a Palestinian, but takes no support from a specifically Palestinian culture or identity,

turning to European poets for his expressions of essential values and to French philosophy for his analytical tools. A radical critic of a major component of the Western cultural tradition, Said derives most of his standards from that tradition. The point in saying this is to suggest something of the situation within which books like Orientalism must inevitably be written.[23]

However, such claims by important thinkers were not well-received in Muslim academic contexts. Said's *Orientalism* had been given a central position since it had systematically blamed Europeans and their literature for all the misery and chaos in the Middle East. As an English-language work that critiqued Western political traditions based on European literature, it had the potential to meet the expectations of Muslim revolutionary thinkers who, in the 1970s, wanted to de-Westernize their culture and Islamicize their educational system. Along with Said, these revolutionaries saw a large portion of the Middle East's challenges as emanating from *inside* the Western colonizers. The "Orient," as defined by European powers, was no longer somewhere "out there" but "a place of extraordinarily urgent and precise details, a place of subdivisions."[24] Said's and many 1970s revolutionaries' (e.g., Khomeini's and Mutahhari's) main concern was oppressed peoples (*mustad'afin*) in general and the Palestinians in particular, and the latter, according to Said, "played a special role in the imagination and in the political will of the West, which is where by common agreement modern Zionism also generated."[25] He published his book on Palestine[26] one year after *Orientalism*, as "Orientals" needed some degree of warm-up before realizing that the conquest of Palestine was not "a pretty thing when you look into it too much."[27] He himself commented that Golda Meir's note on the history of Palestine, of "there being no Palestinian people," woke his "extremely concrete history of personal loss and national disintegration,"[28] which may be termed a sense of inferiority, and so he wrote *Orientalism*.

Taken together, these factors led Muslims to ignore the importance of other American literary critics, such as Toni Morrison, who were also critical of Western imperialism. She also addressed the works that had influenced Said, such as those of Joseph Conrad (d. 1942). Morrison, as a self-declared representative of oppressed people, was also disappointed with the way European authors censored Africa and Africans. She explicitly says how Africa both is and is not their land at the same time:

Although the sound of the name, Africa, was beautiful, it was freighted with the complicated emotions with which it was associated. Unlike starving China, Africa was both ours and theirs, intimately connected to us and profoundly foreign. A huge needy homeland to which we were said to belong but which none of us had seen or cared to see, inhabited by people with whom we maintained a delicate relationship of mutual ignorance and disdain, and with whom we shared a mythology of passive, traumatized Otherness cultivated by textbooks, film, cartoons, and the hostile name-calling children learn to love.[29]

She also says,

In Western novels published through the 1950s, Africa, like Albert Camus' novel, might be called "The Stranger," offering the occasion for knowledge but its unknowableness intact.[30]

Both Morrison and Said display the inferiority imposed on them, as part of a suppressed community. For both of them, their lands, Africa and Palestine, respectively, are suitable sites of discovery for white Christian Europeans and Americans. However, Said's references to the Oriental Arabs in the controversial decade of the 1970s (which saw the war between Israel and Arab states, the American invasion of Vietnam, the Camp David meeting on the "Framework for Peace" between Egypt and Israel, etc.), helped him to have much more of an impact than did other literary critics of the West among Muslims in Africa, Asia, and Europe.

As well as being translated into various European languages, *Orientalism* was translated into Arabic by Kamal Abu Deeb and Mohamed Enani in 1981 and 2006, respectively. Similarly, Asghar ʿAskari and Hamid Fuladvand in 1982, ʿAbdul-Rahim Gavahi in 1992, and Lotf ʿAli Khunji in 2007 translated *Orientalism* into Persian, each of which were published by state publishers. It was also translated into Indonesian by Asep Hikmat in 1984. The Turkish translations (from French) by Nezih Uzel in 1982 and by Selahattin Ayaz in 1989 were published by the conservative publisher Pinar, based in Istanbul. Later on, another Turkish translation by Berna Yıldırım was produced in 1999. The latest translation of Said's *Orientalism* into an Islamic language was done by Pakistanis; its Urdu version by Muhammad ʿAbbas, Nazar Thani, et al. was published by the nationalist publisher Muqtadirah-yi Qaumi Zaban in Islamabad in 2005. Indeed, all these translations were indirectly or directly supported by a particular political, state, or religious party. Such publishers (particularly those in Iran and Turkey), as well as being concerned with how many books they sold, wanted to stick to the mottos and values that are to be found in Said's works. 'Abdul-Rahim Gavahi, the translator of *Orientalism*, who was a diplomat of the Islamic Republic of Iran in years following the 1979 Revolution, became acquainted with Said's *Orientalism* and *The Question of Palestine* through the *Charge d'affaires* of the Palestinian embassy in Sweden. The way he describes Said's works in his preface demonstrates how and why he enjoyed reading and translating Said's works:

> It can be strongly said that this work [viz., *Orientalism*] is one of the best works ever, one which confronts the nonsense and cheap [claims of] Goldziher (and with its domestic equivalence: *Twenty Three Years* [by A. Dashti (1974)]) against the entire East, the Arabs and the Muslim world. And this is the only way that we Muslims have before ourselves: preserving our Islamic principles and values by means of a knowledgeable and virtuous language and being compatible with Islamic *adab*/ethics . . . the statement of the author [Said] resembles those of Jalal Al-e Ahmad (God bless his soul) in *Gharb-zadigi*; with same concern and sympathy: love of one's homeland, culture and traditions, and the religion of our ancestors, Islam; or [and it also resembles those of] the dear intellectual and the deceased martyr Dr. Shari'ati . . . .[31]

For revolutionary Muslims, Said was the heir of anti-Westernists such as Al-e Ahmad. Said's *Orientalism* reignited controversial debates over the role of Europeans in distorting Islamic identity, while at the same time, as mentioned earlier, Maurice Bucaille's 1976 work *La Bible, le Coran et la Science*, criticized non-Muslims' Scriptures and elevated Qur'anic values; while questioning the accuracy of the Christian Bible, Bucaille praised the divinity of the Muslim Qur'ān. Taken together, these factors increased negative attitudes toward the works produced in the West on the Qur'ān and other aspects of Islamic studies.

The publication and translation of Said's and Bucaille's works led to a new collective Islamic consciousness, one that believed, and continues to believe, that: (a) the Muslims' Holy Book, unlike those of non-Muslims, is accurate from a scientific perspective; (b) Muslim identity has been coopted by Europeans; (c) Europeans misinterpret the Qur'ān and Muhammad; and (d) Muslims were mocked and unjustly treated by Europeans for centuries. These two works propagated the message of mid-twentieth-century revolutionaries within academic contexts. For them, Westerners wished to lead Muslims away from the straight path (*sirat al-mustaqim*) and take autonomy (*istiqlal*) away from them:

> [T]he imperialists have propagated foreign laws and alien culture among the Muslims through their agents for the sake of their evil purposes, causing people to be infatuated with the West. It was our lack of a leader, a guardian, and our lack of institutions of leadership that made all this possible. We need righteous and proper organs of government; that much is self-evident.[32]

Both Said's and Bucaille's text-oriented studies seemed to remind Muslims that, and how, an advanced but unfriendly West seized Orientals' knowledge, philology, and philosophy during the medieval period, leaving them at the mercy of European powers who have exploited them for centuries.

Disappeared History in *Orientalism*

Consequences

The terms *Orientalism* and *Orientalist* have negative connotations in the Muslim world in general and the Muslim academic context in particular. With varying levels of regard for their roles, Said called Ernest Renan (d. 1892), Theodor Nöldeke, Ignác Goldziher, Hamilton A. R. Gibb (d. 1971), and Bernard Lewis (d. 2018) Orientalists,[33] thereby suggesting their contributions to modern scholarship within Islamic studies should be ignored and placing them in same arena as colonial officers. Though, admittedly, Lewis is not, according to his critics, the same as someone like Goldziher.

Of course, there were some scholars, colonial officers, and collectors among the so-called "Orientalists" who did ignore and/or look down upon Islamic civilization, or examined it merely for the sake of political and imperial authority.

Said was concerned with the underlying cultural dynamics of West-East relations and suggested there is a common cultural vocabulary that has the effect of belittling the East, and that the caretakers of this vocabulary think that they are merely engaged in a technical, effectively philological endeavor while actually they are securing the power of that common cultural vocabulary, which itself enables and authorizes Western military and economic domination. However, his placing of essentially any Arabist, philologist, and philosopher—many of whom had only a minimal level of dependency on or relations with Western politics—within the category of *Les ennemis de l'Islam* led Muslim academics to view all Europeans as distorters of Islam. He also said that modern studies of Islam produced in England do not present an accurate picture of the religion of Islam and distort the important role of the ʿAbbasid period in history, a time that, according to Muslim thinkers, Sufis, and reformists, was the period of Islamic enlightenment, a "Golden Age."[34]

He also said that "Ignaz Goldziher's appreciation of Islam's tolerance toward other religions was undercut by his dislike of Mohammad's anthropomorphism and Islam's too-exterior theology and jurisprudence."[35] However, he failed to mention that many modern scholars, among others Goldziher, had frequently praised the important contribution of Muslims to Islamic studies; Goldziher referred, for example, to "the Egyptian polymath Jalāl al-Dīn al-Suyūṭī (d. 910/1505), to whom we are indebted for an excellent isagogic work on the science of the Koran."[36] One may wonder if Said would reinterpret his opinions about Goldziher if he had read such quotations about important Islamic figures.

Upon reading Said's work, it is easy to overlook the subtlety of his argument about the underlying cultural dynamics and the Foucauldian philosophical background, and instead to view his book as demonizing all individual Westerners. As such, Muslims are taught to consider all Europeans as either the descendants of medieval Christians, enemies, or the inheritors of Dante who, according to Said, positioned Muhammad in Hell:

> "Maometto"—Mohammed—turns up in canto 28 of the *Inferno*. He is located in the eighth of the nine circles of Hell, in the ninths of the ten Bolgias of the Malebolge, a circle of gloomy ditches surrounding Satan's stronghold in Hell. Thus, before Dante reaches Mohammed, he passes through circles containing people whose sins are of a lesser order: the lustful, the avaricious, the gluttonous, the heretics, the wrathful, the suicidal, the blasphemous . . . .[37]

For Muslims, such sentences are no less provocative than the Muhammad cartoons of the 2000s. It becomes yet more painful for Muslims when they translate it into and understand it within their own language. The translations

of "Muhammad in Hell" and "Muhammad's sin" encompass a new imagining of Muhammad, one which wholly contradicts everything that a
Muslim has been taught to believe in his mind and heart about the Prophet
of Islam since childhood. This is why the Persian translator of *Orientalism*,
Khunji, added a preface in which he said that "the other point which must
be noted is that there are quotations from different people throughout the
book which defamed (*bi-hurmati*) Islam, Prophet Muhammad (pbuh) or the
Glorious Qur'ān."[38] Therefore, while translating the catastrophic status of
Muhammad, 'Ali and the Qur'ān as outlined in canto 28 of Dante's *Inferno*,
the Persian and Turkish translators included epithets and praise both before
and after these names, such as Hazrat-e, or Hz. Muhammad (pbuh), Hazrat-
e, or Hz. 'Ali (pbuh), and Qur'ān Majīd.[39]

It is certainly true that such images of Muhammad and Islam have been
frequently seen in European works. For example, the *Nuremberg Chronicle*
(1493) by Hartmann Schedel (d. ca. 1514) displays the "Orient," including
Jerusalem, Arabia and Persia, as the land of the Bible, while Ethiopia provides
Christians with a *different* Muhammad to the Islamic one:

> Mohammed called himself the Great Prophet of God, and he deceived
> the people of Asia and Africa by black magic; and by the pronouncement
> of a new faith he so influenced them that they completely extirpated the
> name of the [Byzantine] empire. This false faith now holds the upper hand
> more than before; for all Asia and Africa, and a large part of Europe, has
> been subordinated to Mohammedan princes. Now by land and sea they are
> attempting to drive us out of this small corner of Europe. And in order that
> this Mohammed (as is stated in his book of laws) might lead his followers
> still further away from the Christian faith, he emulated certain heretics,
> chiefly the Nestorians, in the interpretation and description of his own
> laws; and he gathered together many things against the Mosaic laws and the
> Gospels, and assembled these in one book. And to increase the grip of his
> laws, he ordained that a man might take four wives of his own race, as many
> concubines as he could support, and as many purchased wives as he wished.
> However, he ordered his followers not to drink wine; and those who obeyed
> his laws he promised the Garden of Eden. Those who scorned his laws he
> threatened with hell. He stated that Moses and John the Baptist were the
> great prophets of God; but that Christ was the greatest of all the prophets
> and born of divine power and cooperation, and not of the human seed of
> the Virgin Mary, etc. After he had reigned six years and had attained the age

of 34 years, he died in the Year of the Lord 632, after having indulged himself in adultery, drunkenness and wantonness.[40]

However, critics of Europeans are silent about the flip side, i.e., that many Christians in Europe were, at that time, terrified by the Muslims' conquests and the threat of their religious teachings, as clearly demonstrated by the phrase, "Now by land and sea they are attempting to drive us out of this small corner of Europe."[41]

This point is completely ignored in *Orientalism*. Similarly, Said said nothing about European concern about the loss of Christian holy sites:

> [T]he occasional pilgrim narrative, like those of Arculf in the first/seventh century and St Willibald at the beginning of the second/eighth would [not] give any indication of the existence of the early caliphate to western Europe, and the writers were more concerned with the Christian Holy Places than with the political condition of the country through which they passed.[42]

One-sided, outraged narratives, as best demonstrated by Said, deliberately conceal *what was really going on in Europe*. Said attempted to show how earlier literature and classical narratives about the *Orient* caused Christian Europeans, particularly the French and English, to divide the world into two parts: "us" and "them." However, he ignores the fact that medieval Muslims did exactly the same and classified the world into *Dar al-Islam* (House of Islam) and *Dar al-Harb* (House of War). "Us" is presented as the knowledgeable and powerful one while the latter, the *Orient*, is not "just another colony" but "the vindication of Western imperialism."[43] At this point, the work of Gil Anidjar should be recalled; he declared that Said's *Orientalism* "must be read as a critique of Christianity . . . . Orientalism is secularism, and secularism is Christianity. Said took us on these syllogistic steps . . . ."[44]

A Muslim reader, therefore, experiences a feeling of inferiority, which motivates him to ignore Europeans—as well as other Christians—without even considering how Muslims did precisely the same to Christians—ignoring them and viewing them as inferior—in the early periods of Islam.[45] Without remembering, or perhaps even knowing, that Muslims conquered or invaded the West, they assume that scholars of Islam (who are, in Said's eyes, the same as colonial officers), invaded their identity, culture, religion, family, and ancestors. It was Frantz Fanon (d. 1961), the famous French activist and intellectual, who developed this perspective, which was later taken on by many revolutionary thinkers (e.g., 'Ali Shari'ati)[46] and post-colonial scholars in the 1970s:

> The history of French conquest in Algeria, including the overrunning of villages by the troops, the confiscation of property and raping of women, the pillaging of a country, has contributed to the birth and the crystalli- zation of the same dynamic image. At the level of the psychological strata of the occupier, the evocation of this freedom given to the sadism of the conqueror, to his eroticism, creates faults, fertile gaps through which both dreamlike forms of behaviour and, on certain occasions, criminal acts can emerge. Thus the rape of the Algerian woman in the dream of a European is always preceded by a rendering of the veil. [47]

Such notions of the "raping of women" and the "pillaging" of Algeria were later expanded in and through *Orientalism*, to the extent that all European rulers, literary figures, and thinkers used to degrade Orientals. In this regard, Said says,

> The Oriental woman is an occasion and an opportunity for Flaubert's musings; he is entranced by her self-sufficiency, by her emotional careless- ness, and also by what, lying next to him, she allows him to think.[48]

Thus, for Muslims, everything *Western*, including *education*, could poten- tially threaten their identity, face, and dignity. As such, as mentioned earlier, Muslims have, for decades, been trying to create specifically indigenous (Ar. *ahli*; Pers. *bumi*; Malay: *asli*) academic syllabi, through which a Muslim en- gineer or physician can also be a religious thinker and supporter of Islamic teachings.

The bipolar world [re-]created by Said does not allow the reader to think about the evolution of human rationality through which people's depend- ency on traditions was oriented toward intellectual and cognitive science. As mentioned earlier, the figures of Muhammad and Muslims in Dante's *Inferno* and Schedel's *Nuremberg Chronicle*, as well as the declaration by the Christian polemist Embrico that "God struck Muhammad dead as punish- ment for his sins, and pigs began to devour his corpse . . ."[49] gradually waned and were replaced with objective and more scholarly understandings of re- ligion. For many nineteenth-century scholars, Islam, following Christianity and Judaism in becoming a wider academic discipline and *not* a faith, had the potential to be examined through the lens of science and history. The majority of European scholars of Islam do not question the significance for Muslims of, for example, the *hajj*, or fasting during Ramadan, but, using both religious and nonreligious sources, mainly debate over why and how these practices took shape in Islamic culture.

Following the politicizing of Goldziher by Said, other post-Enlightenment scholars of Europe, such as Kant and Ranke were directly or indirectly rejected by Muslims. Said's *Orientalism* mentally put these scholars inside the "Orient," as being people who expressed this "cultural, temporal, and geographical distance . . . in metaphors of depth, secrecy, and sexual promise."[50]

Rejection of Europeans' Contribution: A Historical Culture

The lack of references to European intellectual movements and literary works and their impact on Orientals (i.e., Muslims), as well as Said's overwhelming urge to display how the idea of the *Orient* became distorted in European literature, are obvious throughout his work. As such, Said's work is read in a specific way in Muslim academic contexts. Consequently,

> there is a failure to acknowledge Orientalist discourse as capable of self-criticism in order to protest an aspect of Western society or contest inaccurate understandings of the Oriental others. It is an odd, almost theological, position to assume that resistance to a distorted image of the Orient, or of the imperialist goals as such, was structurally impossible from within the European intellectual community.[51]

For example, Said did not explain how Sayyid Jamal al-Din, one of the most influential figures in modern Islam and the promoter of the Pan-Islamic movement, could have had more than a basic understanding of religious and intellectual reformism if he had never communicated with Ernest Renan, the famous French thinker of the nineteenth century. These two figures met each other in France and shared a "commitment to religious reform."[52] Sayyid Jamal al-Din himself said:

> M. [viz., Monsieur] Renan wanted to clarify a point of the history of the Arabs that had remained unclear until now and to throw a living light on their past, a light that may be somewhat troubling for those who venerate

these people, though one cannot say that he has usurped the place and rank that they formerly occupied in the world. M. Renan has not at all tried, we believe, to destroy the glory of Arabs, which is indestructible; he has applied himself to discovering historical truth and making it known to those who do not know it, as well as to those who study the influence of religions on the history of nations, and in particular on that of civilization.[53]

In addition to Sayyid Jamal al-Din, there is also no reference to other such examples, such as Muhammad ʿAbduh's interest in translating Spencer's *On Education*[54] and Tantawi Jawhari's (d. 1940) translation of Kant's *Education* and his interest in John Lubbock's (who was a friend of Darwin) *The Beauty of Nature*. Jawhari, along with many other nineteenth- and twentieth-century Muslims, divided Europeans into three categories: (a) followers of a religion, viz., Christians; (b) scientists and philosophers, i.e., Aristotle, Rousseau, Kant, Darwin, Einstein, etc.; and (c) colonial officers and Orientalists.[55] It is clear from their writings that the aforementioned Muslims were, for a period of time, extremely interested in interacting with European scholars and philosophers. By contrast, Said's definition of *Orientalists* as being those who are *aliens* in Muslim lands—both mental and physical—caused his readers to neglect the important contributions of Europeans to science and civilization. Yet history tells us that Muslims, although impressed by Greco-Egyptian treatises,[56] have neglected non-Islamic sources and rejected Westerners' important contributions from the very earliest period of Islam.

III. Muslim Study of the Qurʾān in Light of *Orientalism*

It is clear that Muslim traditionalists ignored the contribution that Greek philosophy and literature made to their culture, particularly those sources of knowledge (either biblical or non-biblical) that were produced before the emergence of Islam. As a reader of Joseph Lumbard's polemical work on Western Islamic Studies, it seems clear to me, and other readers of such material, that if someone wants to examine the Qurʾān in light of pre-Islamic literature, his approach will be labeled as "colonialist epistemological,"[57] an approach which, according to Lumbard, has penetrated other areas. He claims that Gabriel S. Reynolds, Andrew Rippin, John Wansbrough, and anyone else who wants to situate historical contexts prior to Islamic exeget-ical works in order to study the Qur'ān, are "colonialists."

Through the works of Said, as well as those of Bucaille and other post-1980s works, a reader in a Muslim academic context may be "certain" that the works of an *Orientalist*, who is also a "non-Muslim," contradict Islamic teachings and beliefs in general, and those related to the Qur'ān in partic-ular. It is hard for a Muslim reader to distinguish between the approaches of a European scholar and those of a European colonial officer. The boundary between post-Enlightenment European academia and the European polit-ical, ideological, and military domains is blurred, and a Muslim reader may see all kinds of European studies of the *Orient* and his religion through the lens of a conspiracy. As one such example, S. Parvez Manzoor, whose work "Method against Truth: Orientalism and Qur'anic Studies" is widely circu-lated via Islamic networks, says:

> The Orientalist enterprise of Qur'anic studies, whatever its other merits and services, was a project born of spite, bred in frustration and nourished by vengeance: the spite of the powerful for the powerless, the frustration of the "rational" towards the "superstitious" and the vengeance of the "orthodox" against the "non-conformist". At the greatest hour of his worldly-triumph, the Western man, coordinating the powers of the State, Church and Academia, launched his most determined assault on the citadel of Muslim faith. All the aberrant streaks of his arrogant personality—its reckless ra-tionalism, its world-domineering fantasy and its sectarian fanaticism—joined in an unholy conspiracy to dislodge the Muslim Scripture from its firmly entrenched position as the epitome of historic authenticity and moral unassailability.[58]

Similarly, Muzaffar Iqbal takes an anti-Orientalist viewpoint on Western scholars of Qur'anic studies:

> The *Encyclopaedia of the Qur'ān* [published by Brill in 2001–2006] carries the stamp of the Academy; its editors and contributors are trained in the Academy; most of its articles build upon the previous academic scholarship on the Qur'ān. This academic pedigree can be traced back to the work of the nineteenth Orientalists and, through them, to the five centuries of discourse on the Qur'ān by Christian polemicists-cum-philologists who appeared on the Western academic scene in the fourteenth century . . . it is the vast store of

Orientalism from which most of the articles of EQ draw their material, although "[t]oday an Orientalist is less likely to call himself an Orientalist than he was almost any time up to World War II," as Edward Said noted in 1978.[59]

Iqbal, influenced by Said, is here limiting philology to Western academia where, he claims, the anti-Islamic slogans of the medieval period are still (in)directly promoted, not only by scholars but also by publishers. A rejection of what has been discovered through philology ("the discipline of making sense of texts . . . the theory of textuality as well as the history of textuality itself"[60]) ignores not only what has been argued and discovered by Western intellectuals including, among others, Friedrich Nietzsche (d. 1900), Ulrich von Wilamowitz-Mollendorrf (d. 1931), and Sheldon Pollock (b. 1948), but also and more importantly what was practiced by Muslim commentators of the Qur'ān. As Bruce Fudge has underlined, both the Europeans' Qur'anic studies and the Muslims' Qur'anic exegesis (*tafsīr*) did, and still do, utilize philology. For example, to decode the identity of "the Companion of the Trench" in Q 85:4, Fudge compared the methodologies used by various Muslim exegetes. Unlike Iqbal, but in line with Pollock, Fudge emphasized the global aspect and use of philology from the earliest period of Islam:

> There are many similarities between the Orientalist and *tafsīr* traditions: despite fundamentally different goals and methodological constraints, their methods remain quite similar. That Orientalists betrayed the text with their arrogant philology is not an uncommon complaint; what is less well known but no less valid is that the same accusation can be, and has been, levelled at the *tafsīr* genre as well. The commentarial tradition sought to limit and control the potential of the text. Rather than dwell on the thematic possibilities and rhetorical potential of the revelation, commentators tended to go in the opposite direction, deeper and deeper into lexical and morphological minutiae.[61]

Yet, as mentioned earlier, Muslim academic contexts have not accepted philology as a discipline because they believed that Europeans developed their control over the Islamic world by means of philology. Today, Middle Eastern Qur'ān scholars, by referring to Said's critique of "Westerners' inhuman view of the Orient,"[62] deem that the *Orientalism* project, maintaining its domineering and ruling spirit, has entered a new phase, called "post-modern Orientalism."[63] As such, they take a dim view of European works published in all *places* and at all *times*.

Another problem with Said's approach is that he failed to separate the approaches of Nöldeke from those of various openly polemical figures. Thus, by using *Orientalism* as their reference point, Muslims ignore the contribution of Western scholars to modern Qur'anic studies, and by interpreting Said's statement that Europeans consider "their civilization, community and religion (Christianity) superior than those of Orientals," Muslim scholars have rejected the Qur'anic works of Nöldeke, Wansbrough, and Rippin with the conclusion that:

> There have been various approaches used by Orientalists, including colonialism, conversion, and truth-seeking. However, rejection of the Qur'ān has been the common feature in all these approaches; [. . .] through the course of Orientalists' Qur'anic studies, it became apparent that many people have produced works with the sole purpose of rejecting and proscribing the Qur'ān, in every century.[64]

Many Muslim scholars see in Western Qur'anic studies the notions that "Islam is a heresy of Christianity, Muhammad is a fake and unethical prophet, and the Qur'ān is the combination of both Old and New Testaments." One of the main sources used by these scholars is Said's *Orientalism*.[65]

IV. Misunderstanding of Europeans in *Orientalism*

The first impression I had upon reading *Orientalism* was that it emphasized the *inferiority* of Orientals displayed in European literature. But did all Occidentals downgrade Orientals and Muslims? The inaccuracy of this criticism of the West in *Orientalism* becomes clearer when a number of important gaps within the text related to the status of Muslims are examined. It may have been possible to reorient the harsh criticism of Europeans by Oriental academics if these had been filled within the pages of *Orientalism*.

Social Criticism of the West by Means of Fictional Muslims

The first point, as Daniel Martin Varisco (b. 1951) also has noted, is that Said ignored a specific genre of fiction that was popular in eighteenth-century Europe. This is the genre constituted by the many works collectively known as *Lettres Persanes* or *Persian Letters*, some of which were produced pseudonymously or anonymously with the purpose of social (self-)criticism of the Western context in which they were written.[66] It has been said that Montesquieu's work in this genre tried to reject imperialism and defend "radical individualism":

> Although *Lettres persanes* is a light work, Montesquieu proposes through the dilettante [alizing] dialogue of two Persian travellers many of the arguments that are later solidified in the political philosophy of his 1748 *Esprit des lois* . . . Montesquieu offers a disjointed series of some 161 letters exchanged by various combinations of the two main travellers, their friends at home, the eunuchs and women of Usbek's harem, Usbek's nephew, a mullah, and a Jew. Commentators generally view Usbek as a reflection of the more conservative, graver, and reflective side of Montesquieu, whereas Rica [a young man recently arrived in Paris who has yet to taste the delights of the Oriental harem but is confronted with the exotic civilization of eighteenth-century Parisian society] is a sarcastic and delightfully harlequinesque. Ironically, as the letters coming from Persia described the destruction of Usbek's harem in his absence, the Parisian letters playfully deconstruct French social mores, philosophical speculation, and politics.[67]

Along with Mostesquieu's work, another fictional piece, *Letters from an Armenian in Ireland to His Friends at Trebisons*, was published in Dublin in 1756. In this, the letters are sent to fictional figures including Abdallah, his daughter Zelima, and his friends Ali Izra and Osman. These letters display the comprehension of a *fictional* Oriental traveler, residing in Western Europe, of a foreign context.[68]

I also came across an old printed book, dated 1735, in the University of Otago's Special Collections, titled *The Persian Letters, continued: or; The Second Volume of Letters from Selim at London, to Mirza at Ispahan*, whose author's name has not been definitively established, although it has been argued that it was George Lyttleton (d. 1773). It is believed that fictions written against Robert Walpole (the first Prime Minister of Great Britain) were popular in the 1730s and 1740s in England, and that "George Lyttelton's *Letters from a Persian in England to His Friend at Ispahan* (1735), [was] an epistolary novel satirizing many of Walpole's economic politics."[69] In this book, Selim is a fictional Muslim who is searching for liberty and "his censures upon Vice and Corruption are not abated; but rather increased."[70] The book includes thirty-six letters on various topics, including: "The Reasons of Selim's stay at London"; "The News-Papers"; "The Numidian History"; "Charity"; "King Charles I"; "Punishing Crimes"; "The Abuses of Toleration"; "Justice"; etc.

However, three of the letters are not addressed to Isfahan but to Houli Mollack, one of the [fictional] Holy Ministers of the Tomb of the Great Prophet, in which the topics of "Religion," "Religion and Morals," and "Fornication" are discussed. In contrast to what Said stated in *Orientalism* regarding the dark and distorted image of Islam and Muhammad in Europe, these fictional letters, published in books that were widely read by European intellectuals and the wider public, present a brighter and kinder picture of Muslims and their culture. The letters move from describing the study of the Qur'ān in Muslim academic contexts as it actually is to showing how it could be different if various other histories of East-West interaction were to come to the fore, as well. Excerpts from each of these letters, textually edited/modernized by myself, follow:

Letter VI. To Houli Mollack, one of the Holy Ministers of the Tomb of the
   Great Prophet

"On Religion" (pp. 34–38)

What I wrote to you, venerable Mollack! Some moons ago, that the true Religion was by degrees introducing itself among these infidels, I can now with great pleasure and more certainty, give to you ground to believe. The great obstacle which hindered the English hitherto from being true Muslims (*Mussulmen*), was their reverence for Jesus Christ, whose life and miracles we likewise have great regard for, next to those of Muhammad (*Mahomet*), our great Prophet. But that respect for Christ is wearing off apace. Would not you believe it, Holy Servant of the venerable Tomb, there is scarce a week passes without some scandalous pamphlet against their Messiah. And which is more pleasing to me, as I know it will be to you likewise, many of the priests of that religion laugh at the veneration paid to him . . . And one great advantage those priests have above others is that they are much in favor with some great ladies of the kingdom, especially such as set up for polite learning . . . These books and pamphlets against the Church of England make way for our Prophet's religion; and our Holy Qur'ān (*Alcoran*) is not so ill spoken of here as formerly; and I have seen a good vindication of our Holy Prophet and his doctrine, which has not been ill received, and a fine edition of the Qur'ān is published, and dedicated to a great Lord . . . But let the unbelievers, of one and the other Church, deal blows at one another in the dark, whilst we Muslims wait a fair opportunity to propagate the Truth by means of their divisions. For although our holy religion is chiefly to be maintained by the sword, yet surely we are not forbidden to introduce it by other means, till we have an opportunity of doing it by force . . .

Letter XIV . . .*of Religion and Morals* (pp. 83–87):

Venerable guardian of the Tomb! I should not presume to trespass upon your commands to me, to give you an exact account . . . of my observations upon religion in England. There will not be a memory of Christianity left in England shortly, at least not in this city. One cannot go into any company of fashion, but they are entertained with what the few zealots call blasphemy . . . But I know the holiness makes you think that they who do go to the mosques (viz., churches) here, go to pray to Allah (*Alla*) and his Prophet the Messiah. No, venerable Mollack, prayers are out of the question. It is true they do worship there, but few mind it except the priests and clerks, or perhaps some old people; the rest of the audience are curtsying and bowing to their acquaintances all round the church, or ogling one another . . .

Letter XIV. . . *of Fornication* (pp. 109–112)

Fornication has been long practiced in this country, in place of plurality of wives, and the lords and great people have lived as avowedly with their mistresses, as they are very properly called here, as any Mussulman. And what is more, some ladies of good quality and fortunes have, just as openly, entertained their gallants, and born children to them; and some of those ladies have turned them off, when they had made them thin-chopped, as they would do another servant . . . But what I would observe to you (thee), holy Mollack, is, that we cannot choose but hope for good success to our Qur'ān from such a public attempt in a Christian country. And what pity it was that Mr. Goat did not believe in the resurrection, that he might have introduced whoring as the chief ingredient of the happiness of the next life. But what he has broached may be mended by some fellow of better sense: and his performance may set nature at work; however stupidly he has treated reason and judgement . . .

Despite these letters' ironic highlighting of concerns about the international and national affairs of England, it does not show any *superiority* or *inferiority* of either Europeans or Muslims. The letters also refer to the Qur'ān and Muhammad, but they do not display a particularly dark or cruel image of Islam. Instead, Muhammad's holiness is noted and his followers, Muslims, despite being capable of using the sword, are displayed as kind and patient people who are able to find other, peaceful ways of spreading their religion. The letters, of course, warn English people about the depravity of the English governmental system and the loss of their identities; however, they in no way reflect what Said refers to as Scott's *Saracens* being "the redoubtable Orient."[71]

Orientals Viewed Positively by Europeans

Translations of Oriental Works

It has been suggested that there was some negligence in Said's work since it does not explore all the literary and cultural contexts of Europe and ignores the fact there was an "imaginative and enlightenment Orientalism"[72] in post-sixteenth-century Europe. According to Aravamudan, *Enlightenment Orientalism* was

> a fictional mode for dreaming with the Orient—dreaming with it by constructing and translating fictions about it, pluralizing views of it, inventing it, by reimagining it, unsettling its meaning, brooding over it ... enlightenment Orientalism was a Western style for translating, anatomizing, and desiring the Orient.[73]

Europeans became interested in translating Arabic tales, particularly *The Thousand and One Nights*, also known as *The Arabian Nights*, in the eighteenth century. As such, Antoine Galland translated it into French as *Mille et Une Nuits*, helping European intellectuals pave the way for the eighteenth-century enlightenment:

> At the beginning of the 18th century, the European literary traditions had not yet crystallized into clearly defined, modern, generic forms, and the Arabic tales presented a treasury of literary material and models which invited experiment.[74]

The French version of *The Arabian Nights* was first published, in 1704, for the general population by a bookshop interested in fairy tales and other stories.[75] It was later translated into other languages and has kept its prestige and reputation in Europe ever since.[76] Apart from the specific content of the tale (e.g., the "unbound imagination"), it was its literary aspect that

> fostered the interest in the work and stimulated writers and intellectuals to experiment with the various models it provided and seek inspiration from its narrative wealth. Since especially in the 18th century new literary forms emerged which defined the modern European literary tradition, the *Thousand and one nights*, as a source of inspiration and emulation, penetrated into the capillaries of European literature.[77]

Furthermore, there were always other various Middle Eastern, Asian, and African stories, often dreaming/imagining/searching for a utopia wherein wise, honest, patient, and beautiful people were living, which, unsurprisingly, stimulated Europeans to translate those works, too.[78] However, Said's work only concentrates on his own as well as Europeans' views of the *Orient* and *Orientalism* in which the inferiority of Orientals and superiority of the Occidentals are clearly displayed. Said's work fails to mention that Europeans had read many other, different types of works on the Orient and Orientals, many of which were supportive rather than polemic in nature.

Unreal but Optimistic

A point seemingly passed over in silence in Said's *Orientalism* is that a significant proportion of global literature and subsequent cultural understanding is based on unreal reports and stories. Raymond J. Howgego has produced many reference work on *Exploration*, the final volume of which deals with *invented and apocryphal travel narratives*. Many people in the seventeenth, eighteenth, and nineteenth centuries, some of whom were colonial officers, intellectuals, and literary figures, read these anonymous or pseudonymous Oriental and Occidental stories and exploration reports. According to Howgego, the "literature of the imaginary or contentious journey" can be divided into eight categories:

1. The apocryphal narrative
2. The invented narrative
3. The plagiarized narrative
4. The utopian narrative
5. The spoof narrative
6. The Robinsonade ("inspired by Defoe's *Robinson Crusoe*")

7. The extra-terrestrial voyage
8. The futuristic narrative[79]

These reports tell us about human aspirations, dreams, and even fame-seeking.[80] Some exploration stories are not set on earth but in the heavens and on other planets (such as the Moon, Mars, and Venus). For instance, Sir Humphrey Lunatick's (pseud. of Francis Gentelman) *A Trip to the Moon* (1764) sketches an imaginary island on the moon called Noibla, where people have their own customs, religion, and ideology.[81] This story clearly depicts the intellectual, religious, and political concerns of some Europeans during the eighteenth century and the Enlightenment:

> So much of the ceremony being over, the twelve virgins circling round me, dancing all the time with very odd gestures, and singing a Hymn of Exultation, gave me so plentiful an ablution, that I began to be weary. Having finished these rites, they all prostrated themselves before me, and retired to their places on each side of the well . . . I intended to have made a pecuniary acknowledgement; but my host perceiving the design, hold, Son of Earth, says he, the works of religion and hospitality are not sold here; nor have we any coin but social intercourse and mutual regard; aid I not tell thee (to you) we had no envy or discord among us . . . Behold, my friends and brothers of the Island of Noibla, the most favoured spot of all this lunar world, behold, ye Sons of natural and untainted liberty, the Fiend who, having got a footing on the terrestrial globe, rulers every government, any every individual, of all sexes, ages, and degrees . . . [82]

European concerns surrounding religion in general and Christianity in particular during the Enlightenment period are also seen throughout the first German work of science fiction, which was written by Eberhard Christian Kindermann in 1744. His *Die Geschwinde Reise auf dem lufft-Schiff nach der obern Welt* provides readers with a short story of five travelers (who are "representative of the five senses") who visit the Moon and Mars. They come across a religious utopia on the latter planet "where the people converse directly with God, rather than through the medium of the Holy Bible."[83]

In a similar manner, many stories present imaginary cities, peoples, and cultures of the Orient. One such is *Usong: Eine Morgenländische Geschichte* ("Usong: An Eastern Tale/An Oriental Story") by Albrecht von Haller (d. 1777), which was published in Bern in 1771. It tells the story of Uson, a

Persian king acquainted with virtues and wisdom.[84] The depiction of a *merciful* image of the Orient is also apparent in *The Travels of Cyrus*, by Andrew Michael Ramsay (d. 1743). Cyrus, in this story, is the son of the Persian king Cambyses and of Mandana, the daughter of Astyages of Media. Persia is introduced as a land of wise people, who learn constructive, not destructive, science:

> They [Persians] were not versed in those Arts and Sciences which polish the mind and manner. But they were great masters of the sublime Science of being content with simple nature, of despising death for the love of their country . . . [85]

Ignoring People in *Orientalism*

A number of early-modern European scholars spoke in support of Islam and the Qur'ān. Henry Stubbe (1632–1676), known as the "defender of Islam," wrote *An Account of the Rise and Progress of Mahometanism, with the Life of Mahomet and Vindication of Him and His Religion from the Calumnies of the Christians* (ca. 1670). Stubbe, a pioneering European scholar, declared that the name of the Prophet of Islam should be rendered in accordance with his own spelling and not, as Europeans used to, as "Magmed," or "Machomet."[86] Stubbe also believed that the statement "Muhammad himself, with the help of a Jew or a Nestorian Christian, assembled the Qur'ān" was a rumor. He declared that the Qur'ān was compiled in Arabia not by ordinary people but by the owners of "the eyes of the faithful" who were well acquainted with faithfulness.[87] Stubbe agreed with the concept of *occasions of revelation* and stated that the Qur'ān was disclosed on different occasions in Muhammad's life. The literal aspect of the Qur'ān caught Stubbe's attention and he was convinced of its literary or *adabi* inimitability (*i'jaz*).[88] He described Muhammad as a wise prophet who did not believe in omens and superstitions:

> Whether it were his great prudence, or care for the worship of the true God, I shall not determine, but certainly his legislative care extended far when he prohibited all observation of omens and all divination by Lotts, as debated to do or forebear an action, by opening of Alcoran (the Qur'ān) (as the Romans did Virgil), or shooting an Arrow into the air, or drawing an arrow out of the sheaf, whereon should be written it is not the pleasure of God. This great Prophet would not suffer his Moslemin to employ anything but reason in their debates.[89]

Undoubtedly, there was a desire among some Europeans to discover the Holy Land and biblical cities, but there were many people studying Oriental religions in general, and Islam in particular, not for any political purpose but simply the sake of knowledge. Yet *Orientalism* did not even attempt to distinguish between academic figures and colonial officers; both are, according to Said, the product of one imperial system. Conflating colonialism with European literary and scientific movements led to important neutral and supportive reports, stories, and works being completely ignored in Said's project.[90]

I partially sympathize with Said over how hard it was when some readers found alleged anti-Westernism in *Orientalism*.[91] While reading it, the *inferiority* of Orientals through the lens of the European is obvious. Although Said classified the [bookish] Orientalism into personal and particularly professional categories, he deemed that "they are not so separate from each other as one would image. Nor does each category contain 'pure' representative types."[92] Yet he failed to point out that some colonial officers and rulers (a) were not readers of polemical works; (b) were lovers of the *Oriental* world, not conquerors; and (c) were keen to learn about the *Orient*. He also failed to note that many scholars of Islam were *not* colonial officers, nor were they interested in converting Muslims to Christianity. Furthermore, if he had pointed out how Muslims themselves had attempted to ruin historical monuments in the Orient, such as the Sphinx in the fourteenth century, a monument which was subsequently preserved by European travelers and scholars,[93] Said could have changed the view of *Oriental* readers about the role of non-Muslims in the Orient and Orientalism.

Translations of *Orientalism* are read and cited in many Muslim academic contexts, and any such translation "inevitably domesticates foreign texts, inscribing them with linguistic and cultural values that are intelligible to specific domestic constituencies."[94] The rendition of "Mohammed explains his punishment to Dante, pointing as well to Ali, who precedes him in the line of sinners whom the attendant devil is splitting in two . . . Even though the Koran specifies Jesus as a prophet, Dante chooses to consider the great Muslim philosopher and king as having been fundamentally ignorant of Christianity,"[95] alongside the singular failure to refer to Stubbe's *defense* of Islam, Ramsay's *depiction* of Oriental power, Europeans' *support* of Egyptian history, and *Muslim invasions* of Europe, shows an image of the West (and the Westerner) simply as cruel, partisan, and rapacious, always considering itself superior to and uncaring about the Orient.

V. Remembering Scientists

Imaginative Reports on the Qur'ān

The presentation of an inferior or a superior *Orient* is also seen in some classical and modern Muslim works. A common reference is to the Muslims'
so-called *Golden Age* (eighth to the thirteenth century) and the Europeans'
so-called *Dark Ages* (fifth to the fifteenth century), after which Muslims lent
their knowledge to *Occidentals*, as a result of which Europeans became advanced in science and industry. The disparaging of European achievements
in order to highlight the superiority of Muslims peaked in the late nineteenth
century and coincided with the emergence of new scientific disciplines in the
West. Following the view of Muhammad 'Abduh, Tantawi Jawhari agonized
over the Muslims' backwardness and decline, and this was one of the main
reasons he wrote his Qur'anic exegesis, in which he highlighted scientific
matters for so-called benighted Muslims by addressing important points regarding the backwardness of the Muslim world as well as Western advances.

He suggested that Europeans had made such technological progress recently mainly due to their contact with Muslims during and following the
period of the Crusades, and had originally acquired knowledge and scientific ideas from them. Jawhari's scientific views about various Qur'anic verses
are not only rooted in Muslim backwardness in modern times but also in
theological-jurisprudential notions as to why Muslims—those whom, according to the Qur'ān "Your blessings are upon"—could assess only non-
Muslim (i.e., Jewish or Christian) discoveries of the divine wonders. Jawhari
assumed that Muslims were totally ignorant of and unschooled in the science of nature and empirical knowledge. For this reason, he felt he ought to
write or compile a fully developed exegesis in which all verses of the Qur'ān
are explained according to the situation of the world in which Muslims were
then living. Egyptians were aware of the (re-)emergence of different philosophical, literary, and political movements in the West in the eighteenth
and nineteenth centuries, such as idealism and transcendentalism. In addition, Tantawi Jawhari included scientific matters in line with the familiarity of Muslims with modern science and Western discoveries. It is well
documented that the advances in technology and medicine and their various sub-branches in the nineteenth century, which were reported in Arab
journals, had led to higher survival rates in the West than in Muslim communities. For instance, while diseases like cholera were widespread, medical

science had helped prevent deaths from it, but no such cures were to be found among Muslim populations. It must surely have been disgraceful for the Muslim reformists and nationalists who trumpeted having Avicennaean and Averroesean knowledge in their history to bear witness to such progress in non-Muslim societies.

This feeling remained and continued to develop in the Orient. Since the nineteenth century, Orientals have tried to ignore or explain away the originality of the theories expressed by Western scientists and have often ascribed modern (Western) discoveries to their own religion and culture. For instance, some Hebrew works had connected the notions outlined in Darwin's *Origin of Species* (1859) to ideas found in the Old Testament.[96] Similarly, Jawhari contended that explanations about living beings, and even the way plants and minerals build chains that ascend from a lower to a higher order, were expressed by Ibn Khaldun (d. ca. 1406), Ibn Miskawayh (d. ca. 1030) (in *Tahdhib al-akhlaq*), al-Razi, and others; as such, Darwin's theory of evolution by natural selection would be nothing new.[97]

This was not the end of this trend in the Muslim world. As much as a European figure could be viewed as a great thinker, the desire to connect him to the teachings of Islam was greater still. To counter their feelings of backwardness and humiliation, late-nineteenth- and some twentieth-century Muslim scholars attempted to find a relationship between important Western figures and the Qur'ān. This was not an attempt to reject Orientalism but to show how Orientalists (i.e., European scholars of Islam) were unaware of Islamic and Qur'anic teachings. Indeed, they wanted to prove that European scientists and thinkers, whose interests lay in nonreligious studies and were not affected by Christian polemics and the Orientalists' attacks, were just and free of bias when speaking about the Qur'ān, Islam, and Muhammad. Many of them examined the empirical science found within the Qur'ān in order to prove the superiority of Islamic teachings. As mentioned previously, some Muslims, impressed by Said's and Bucaille's approaches, established a number of academic institutes in the 1980s (either independent or attached to universities) through which they announced Qur'anic inimitabilities, whether scientific, literal, or numerical, etc. As such, by referring to the statements of Western scientists, including those made in Bucaille's book, Muslims have tried to prove that, while Europe feels itself superior to the Orient and Muslims, it is Islam and the Qur'ān that are *superior* to any other religion and scripture, and the latter is the source of all forms of knowledge used by Europeans. As such, and despite having few reliable sources, various positive statements regarding the Qur'ān supposedly made by European thinkers were and still are widely disseminated throughout the Muslim world, and are remarkably popular. In addition, a number of books dealing with the Qur'ān and Muhammad from the perspectives of Europeans were published in the 1980s and 1990s.[98] However, none of these works discussed the originality and occasions of such positive statements. As such, I prepared an article, which was also a piece of self-criticism, in which I examined whether such supportive comments made by Western scientists and figures regarding the Qur'ān are reliable or not. Despite a huge amount of effort on my part since 2013, no Islamic journal has agreed to publish it as, according to them, doing so would "damage Islam"; in one of my last attempts, the journal manager told me that "*maqali-yi shuma dar marhala naha'i baray-e chap az suy-e sardabir ta'id nashudih ast/* at the final pre-publication level [i.e., at the last minute] your essay has been denied by the editor in chief."[99] In this article, I had tried to demonstrate some political issues and misunderstandings within Muslims' references to Western scientists and literary figures, something that I was influenced by some years ago. In what follows, I will discuss one such example.

Situating Einstein in Islam[100]

An important figure was Albert Einstein (d. 1955), whose famous paraphrase of Kant's quip about concepts and intuitions, that "science without religion is lame, religion without science is blind,"[101] attracted the attention of various religious communities. However, Muslim scholars have presented another image of Einstein's approach toward religion, Islam, and the Qur'ān. Various blogs, websites, publishers, and journals in the Muslim academic context have all promoted various statements ascribed to Einstein, of which the most important shows that he (probably) said, "The Quran is not a book of algebra or geometry but is a collection of rules which guides human beings to the right way, the way which the greatest philosophers are unable to decline."[102] The main source for this statement is unclear, but numerous Muslim scholars have repeated it in their works. Before this, in 1927, Subhi Raghib had written a poem in the book *Haqaiq majhulah 'an al-kawn* (*Unknown Facts about the Universe*), when Einstein was at the pinnacle of his success, which presented Einstein as a wise man and put him on the same level as a mosque's imam.[103] According to Max Jammer, in support of Einstein's theory, Raghib referred to various Qur'anic verses and opined that Einstein could only prove small parts of what God has revealed in the Qur'ān.[104] In 1929, 'Abbas Mahmud al-'Aqqad wrote an article in *al-Muqtataf* magazine in which he declared that:

> a fourth dimension or the bounds of the universe and the reality of time and space [*al-bu'd al-rabi' wa hudud al-kawn wa haqiqa al-zaman wa l-makan*] can only be described by a mathematician's hypothesis [*bi l-fard 'ala tariqa al-riyadiyyin*] or by religious faith that is followed by worshipers [*aw bi l-iman 'ala tariqa al-muta'abbidin*]. There is really no difference between the alternatives, because mathematical assumptions and religious faith are both based on surrender and acceptance [*asasahu al-taslim*].[105]

Jawhari himself produced a short report, titled "The Theory of Relativity: Einstein," which was published in a monthly review of *Humayun* in 1935. He stated:

> Therefore, what we see as creatures [beings] are nothing more than oscillations that depend on the frequency of vibrations and appear in various forms: "And you see the mountains, thinking them rigid, while they will pass as the passing of clouds. [It is] the work of Allah, who perfected all things" (Q 27:88). We comprehensively described this notion in the commentary of *al-Jawahir* [*fi tafsir al-Qur'ān al-Karim*] on *surat al-Nur* (Q 24) and *sura Maryam* (Q 19). This theory was not that of Einstein; in reality, he borrowed it from others and built other principles upon it.[106]

Declarations linking Einstein's theory and Qur'anic/Islamic statements have continued to this day. For example, Zakir Kapadia delivered a talk in which he attempted to show several Qur'anic verses that prove the existence of the theory of relativity in the Qur'ān, 1,000 years before Einstein. Kapadia said: "He showed that time is dependent on mass and velocity. In the history of humanity, no one had expressed this fact clearly before. With one exception though: the Holy Qur'ān included information about time being relative!" he referred to Q 22:47; 23:112–114; 32:5; 70:4, among others.[107] As well as various Middle Eastern scholars, a number of Malay-Indonesians have argued that Einstein's theory had already been discussed, in Q 18 (*surat al-Kahf*).[108]

It should be noted that such discussions took place in the Christian church as well. The Archbishop of Canterbury, Randall Davidson (1848–1930), was informed by Lord Haldane that "relativity was going to have a great effect on theology, and that it was his duty as head of the English Church to make him-self acquainted with it." Davidson, therefore, asked Einstein "what effect rel-ativity would have on religion." "None. Relativity is a purely scientific matter and has nothing to do with religion," Einstein confidently replied.[109]

For some Muslim communities, these statements have the potential to demonstrate that Einstein's thoughts and innovations are compatible with God's will and Islamic teachings; thus, Einstein knows both Islam and the Qur'ān. It came to my attention that some people tried to connect Einstein with the famous Shiʻi cleric Ayatollah Brujirdi (d. 1961). I was unable to find any authentic publication by Einstein with the title *Die Erklärung*, so-called *deceleration*, in which he corresponded with Brujirdi in the final years of his life. One of the adherents of this claim has stated that:

> In this secret correspondence between Ayatollah Boroujerdi and Einstein, which was clandestinely translated by a select number of translators ap-pointed by the Shah, Einstein confirms his relativity theory is mentioned in the holy Koran and some of the Hadith from the Shiite holy book, Nahjolbalagheh and the writings of the 16th century Shiite cleric, Alameh Majlisi. Einstein admits in his letters that only Shiite Islam provides the the-ological proof for relativity and no other religion does so.[110]

I found another version of such claims in a Malay blogpost titled *Masa Sih Albert Einstein Seorang Syiah?* (*Was Albert Einstein really a Shiʻa believer?*),[111] and in some accredited Shiʻi news agencies and databases (e.g., rasadnews,[112] taghribnews,[113] brujirdi[114]) contacts between Einstein and Burujirdi are mentioned. These databases all mention that Einstein's letter was written around 1954.

The Accuracy of Such Reports

However, I went through the digital letters and communications of Einstein. Among his works, there is only one document titled *Erklärung*, dated January 26, 1926. This document refers to the "recent defamation in the newspapers of the pacifist writer and courageous fighter of his beliefs, Prof. Nicolai" and to the fact that "teachers at high-schools therefore expressed their regret and signed a statement [saying] that he did not harm German esteem."[115]

Furthermore, the *Guardian* newspaper published a report showing that Einstein wrote about his nonreligious faith to a Jewish philosopher, Eric Gutkind (d. 1956), in 1954. It should be noted that I found some letters showing that these two thinkers were in contact from at least 1944, when they discussed relations between workers and intellectuals.[116] The *Guardian* article, indeed, altered ideas surrounding various controversial issues regarding Einstein, science, and religion by revealing that Einstein called religions "childish superstitions."[117] Gutkind shared his book, titled "Choose Life: The Biblical Call to Revolt," with Einstein. In 1954, a year before his death, Einstein explicitly expressed his stance on religious beliefs in the German "God letter," which begins with the indisputable comment:

> The word God is for me nothing more than the expression and product of human weaknesses, the Bible a collection of honorable but still primitive legends which are nevertheless pretty childish. No interpretation no matter how subtle can (for me) change this. These subtilized interpretations are highly manifold according to their nature and have almost nothing to do with the original text. For me the Jewish religion like all other religions is an incarnation of the most childish superstitions. And the Jewish people to whom I gladly belong and with whose mentality I have a deep affinity have no different quality for me than all other people. As far as my experience goes, they are also no better than other human groups, although they are protected from the worst cancers by a lack of power. Otherwise I cannot see anything "chosen" about them.[118]

This statement highlights that he said nothing about the differences or priorities of each religion, and suggests that Islam was, for Einstein, something akin to Judaism or Christianity. Furthermore, the *Guardian* article ended with the statement: "Despite his categorical rejection of conventional religion, Brooke said that Einstein became angry when his views were appropriated by evangelists for atheism. He was offended by their lack of humility and once wrote 'The eternal mystery of the world is its comprehensibility.'"[119] Moreover, there is another letter by Einstein in the Science Museum of Jerusalem, dated August 21, 1952 to Mr. Jacob Rapp, in which he positioned religion and religious beliefs, without grading them, into the two groups of reasonable and non-reasonable. The first of these is classed as "justified and necessary" while the latter is "unjustified and injurious."

As should be clear, all these statements by Einstein himself contradict the imaginary Einstein concocted in the Muslim world, the one who supposedly admired Qur'anic teachings. Although many Europeans have praised Islam, references to Western scientists and literary figures and non-Islamic studies scholars are the most obvious in the Muslim world. The Islamization, Qur'anization, or Shi'itization of Western theories or statements in order to display the authority of Islamic teachings has, therefore, been practised by Muslims for decades. These strategies have helped them in their attempts to overcome an *imaginary* (literary) and a *proven* (industrial/scientific) inferiority. Thus, the Qur'ān has not only played a scriptural role but is also a vehicle by which Muslims seek to take ownership of anything of which they had been deprived. In order to deny Western critical analysis of religion in general, and Islam in particular, Muslims have thus made use of seemingly every single positive phrase of Western scientists, including some falsely ascribed to them, about the Qur'ān and Islamic teachings, and more besides. As such, it can be convincingly argued that the economic and industrial/scientific gap between Muslims and Western powers has and continues to influence the way Islam is studied in Muslim academic contexts.

5

Final Remarks

I. Conclusions

It may be truly said that studying the Qurʾān in the Muslim academy is more political than other disciplines. In the Muslim world both state and religious politics routinely affect the trajectory of the study of Islam. Universities, institutes, and academic journals are largely supervised by both government and religious parties. In addition, whether writing or publishing in the Middle East, Southeast Asia, or the West, journals and research activities are confronted with Muslim groups whose main concern is to preserve their particular traditional Islamic orthodoxy against those of rival sects as well as against Christian, secular, and/or critical readings of Islam.

Today academic attacks on a scholar's race, religion, and methodology often play a big role in the defense of Islamic beliefs by a raft of religious groups who have appointed themselves guardians of Islamic "orthodoxy."

The personal attack phenomenon was amply illustrated in the question period following Peter G. Riddell's 2014 lecture on Malay Qurʾān interpretations in Kuala Lumpur. Riddell, who has worked for more than thirty years on Islamic topics with Muslim colleagues and friends and is widely recognized for his work to "decolonize" Malay Islamic studies was peppered with personal questions in the wake of his talk.

Questioners wished to know, for example, whether studying Islam influenced Riddell's perspective toward Islam and if he conducted his research for "personal satisfaction" or if there were, perhaps, "other purposes" behind his work? When the questions were not underhanded accusations, they were sly leading ones intended to trip this scholar into a response which could then later be used to prove a moral hostility to Islamic [Sunni] teachings: From his, Riddell's perspective, one questioner demanded, what are Muslim weaknesses?[1]

Muslims religious parties also control what work may be published and how. And not just in such bastions of Muslim sectarianism and illiberalism

Studying the Qurʾān in the Muslim Academy. Majid Daneshgar, Oxford University Press (2020).
© Oxford University Press.
DOI: 10.1093/oso/9780190067540.001.0001

as Iran or Arabia, either. The rules for publication are simple, as my personal experience, which follows, illustrates.

I was asked by a very famous and old Islamic studies journal at one of the most reputed universities in the British Isles, which is led by traditional Muslim scholars, to write a review of Massimo Campanini's 2016 *Philosophical Perspectives on Modern Qur'anic Exegesis*. On the basis of earlier issues of the journal, I guessed that this journal would probably not publish a critical review of the book. All the same, rather than decline outright, I decided to write a strong critical review. Truth will out, right? I sent the celebrated British review my critical commentary, writing:

> If I were asked to introduce an apologetic work on modern Qur'an commentaries to my colleagues and students, one of my first choices would be Campanini's. Although he insists on saying that modern (German) philosophy is behind his reasoning, he writes as a theologian or missionary whose argument is based on the notion that "being in Islam is God and God discloses Himself in the Qur'an". Such a basis simply cannot be considered as the backbone of a scholarly volume. The author seeks to find "the door of the secrets of Being," and so it would be asking too much to expect any critical discussion of modern quranic exegetical works . . . Campanini attempts to direct philosophical arguments towards the conclusions he wants to reach, but in fact the philosophers he cites do not follow his approach. For him, Nietzsche is a nihilist; as such, Heidegger is the appropriate philosopher.[2]

To my utter lack of surprise, the celebrated British journal decided not to publish the review, which appeared later in *Reading Religion*, a publication of the American Academy of Religion. If nothing else does, this personal experience should make crystal clear that as long as the approach to Islam and Islamic theology (as long as it is Sunni or Shiʿi) is not critical, a scholar's work may be widely received in today's Muslim academy.

Also, methodological and bibliographical disagreements crop up frequently in the Muslim academy but are usually ignored because of the sectarian rivalry of Sunni and Shiʿi Islam. While many Shiʿi sources in Sunni institutes are usually just slipped up on the top shelf where you will not notice them, unless you are looking hard and can get them with the tips of your finger, among Shiʿi scholars, Sunni exegetical and theological treatises are welcome as the object of one-sided criticism. Ignoring the other culture and civilization led scholars in Qum, Mashhad, and Tehran to be incurious to what is going on in Indian, Pakistani, Nigerian, or Emirati academic contexts.

My personal experience illustrates the state of inter-sect communication and exchange.

To obtain my master of arts in Qur'ān and Hadith at Qum, I worked on the contribution of Indian scholar of Islam, tele-imam, and preacher Zakir Naik, in the area of religion and science. Naik, it must be said, is "arguably the most popular Muslim televangelist in English, has been promoting [his] narratives on digital media since the mid-1990s," and, as such, both Muslim and non-Muslim scholars, including Vika Gardner, E. Carolina Mayes, Salman Hameed, and Raoof Mir, have been investigating and publicly discussing his influence in the physical and digital world since his appearance on the scene.[3]

Confident of the pertinence of my thesis, therefore, and, perhaps, in pleasurable anticipation of kudos from my elders and tutors, I personally translated, then analyzed, *Qur'ān and Modern Science: Compatible or Incompatible?* It is one of Naik's most celebrated works.[4]

One may well imagine my discomfiture when, as my defense session opened, one of my judges underlined the unimportance of Zakir Naik's work in the world and among Islamic scholars. He had been hoping, he added, that I would translate and subject to critical analysis work by European Islamic scholars. It seemed that he was not aware how Naik influences current trends in "Islam and science" in South Asia.

It is often the case that Islamic studies experts in Muslim academia are both sectarian critics and religious thinkers ('ulema) who are not interested in critical reading of Islamic texts. While examining a classical Qur'ān commentary produced centuries ago, a Sunni or Shi'i scholar of Islam based in Qum, Mecca, or Ankara, using his own theological sources, measures the "correctness" of the classical commentator's interpretation.

In the modern academy, where studies are supposed to be as rationally objective as possible, one of course does the opposite of what a 'ulema-commentator does. A critical historical scholar tries to assess the quality of the approach and method in light of critical rigor and history, utilizing previous commentaries on a text in an attempt to gauge its scope and subsequent influence on religious, philosophical, social, and political movements within Islam. None of this is especially welcome for someone used to working in so-called 'ulematic mode.

Just as scholarly tradition is biased toward the use of an obsolescent critical method, the traditional tension between the Shi'i and Sunni academies tends to constrict space for potential domestic and foreign contributions to Islam and Islamic studies. As a result, critical study of mystical (Sufi) figures and traditions with respect to the Qur'ān and their contribution to the study of Qur'ān and *tafsir* are still in their infancy. Too, the role of Chinese, Indian, African, and other non-Muslim communities in the study of the Qur'ān and Islam remains greatly under-researched.

At the same time that there are praiseworthy efforts by a new generation of Islamic scholars such as Mehrdad 'Abbasi (in Iran) and Yusuf Rahman (in Indonesia) to promote academic reading of Islam outside the Muslim academy, there are huge numbers of traditionalists, supported by Islamic governments and religious groups, that have gained significant influence in terms of suppressing academic and critical approaches to Islam and the Qur'ān. These groups have been moving into the West, where they are establishing Islamic colleges, departments, and centers that are attached to reputable Western, secular, liberal, universities.

II. Islamic Apologetics Everywhere

Monitoring of university lecturers, particularly young ones, who teach any subject in which Islam is a focal point is a common occurrence in the Muslim academy. In addition to such monitoring, lecturers are not normally permitted to invite students to critically challenge Islamic beliefs or to accept outsider views on issues such as the origin of the Qur'ān or the life of the Prophet Muhammad.

This suppression of non-orthodox knowledge (using a narrow and politicized understanding of "orthodoxy") and ideas has developed and shaped a type of reflexive academic censorship. This censorship encourages substitution of apologetics or forceful but beside-the-point argument for critical analysis, most often with the purported goal of protecting "Islamic identity": This is Islamic Apologetics. However, my personal experience, as well as the experiences of some of my colleagues, as a lecturer in a very liberal context allows me to imagine the emergence of Islamic Apologetics in the West, in which the Qur'ān is not allowed to be critically analyzed. Indeed, as will be seen, a naïvely liberal context might produce illiberal results.

Before starting to teach classes on the Qur'ān and *Hadith* in the University of Otago (in New Zealand), where I was the lecturer (teaching fellow) of Islamic studies, I was advised to teach some tutorials on monotheistic religions so that I would become familiar with the students, teaching culture, and the, for me unfamiliar, academic context.

During the first session, the students asked about some Qur'anic verses dealing with non-Muslims, *jihad*, Islamic sectarianism, and the historical figures of Abraham and Muhammad. At this point, I drew their attention to works on Islamic civilization by such renowned scholars as Abdelwahab Meddeb. In the final minutes of the first class, a stranger with a long black beard and seemingly of Middle Eastern/Central Asian origin, appeared and started observing the proceedings.

Once class was over, the visitor expressed his strong opposition to what had been taught in the class and, to my surprise, then went to the head of the department to demand that my contract not be renewed. It eventually became clear that a female Muslim student in the class had texted a member of a religious party, called the Muslim University Students' Association, which then sent this representative to monitor this class.

My experience of monitoring and harassment by a conservative or fundamentalist-oriented Islamic group in a Western classroom is not by any means unique to me or to New Zealand. Lecturers in North American universities have reported that they have been monitored, sometimes still are monitored, by Muslim Students' Association representatives.[5]

Such people fulfill or are forced into the role of Muslim theologians (*mutakallimun*), preserving and defending the foundations of Islam against challengers and critics. Upon encountering "falsehoods" spread by so-called enemies of Islam, these "theologians" are meant to act as determined defenders of their religion. Their primary responsibility is to revise those accounts and stop the circulation of such arguments in society. It becomes a duty (*farida*) under Islamic practical law: "commanding good" (*al-amr bi l ma'ruf*) and "forbidding evil" (*al-nahy 'an al-munkar*), which is associated with *Irshadic* Power.

What my monitor and his associates wanted from me—and what they presumably wanted from my North American peers—was that I stop using the sources that I had been suggesting that my students consult. Young students, they told me, should not read such works.

More interestingly, the Muslim Students' Association in New Zealand used to organize "Islam and Modern Science" exhibitions spiced with references to Maurice Bucaille, Keith Moore, Zakir Naik, and so on, to show how Islam is a comprehensive religion. While speaking with Rippin in 2015, I called these students "academic warriors," although he suggested "academic activists" as a proper phrase. For these academic warriors/activists, showing the greatness of their belief is so crucial so they try to stop critical analysis about their Islam, and promote apologetic views about it. But it is interesting that they do not try to engage and show how it is true; they merely shut down opposition. It may suggest they themselves feel truly threatened, on a personal level, as if they will hear something that causes them to doubt their own faith.

I will never forget the answers of two students in New Zealand (one from South Asia, the other from the Middle East) to one of the final exam's questions about the contribution of Muslim women to society in light of Qur'anic verses and the Night Ascension of Muhammad. The first student critically suggested that Muslim women should not contribute in any way to society and should instead, as recommended in traditions (though without providing any reference), stay at home to care for children, otherwise she would become obsessed with fashion and breast enlargement. I used to hear such answers among traditionalists in the Muslim academy, yet I was rather surprised by his answering this question without any reference to Qur'anic verses or other scholarly sources; he was influenced purely by his traditional concerns. The other student, by referring to some *hadith* compendia, but without providing any discussion, apologetically described the story of Muhammad's journey as well as the greatness of "Rasul Allah" (God's messenger). While I definitely respect their approach, neither the textbook (Rippin's *Muslims: Their Religious Beliefs and Practices*) nor I taught them this. Both students were trying to preserve their Islamic identity while in the West. For them, the Western scholarly understanding of Islam contradicts their traditional teachings. They Islamicized *Islamic studies*, thereby modifying it to Islamic Apologetics, an apologetic version compatible with what they had been taught in their original educational contexts. They grew up with the notion of *Irshadic* Power, and so, while studying in the West, they had to consider where their final destination (*anjam*) in the hereafter (in heaven or hell) would be. For many of them, being impressed by Wansbrough's, Rippin's, Powers', and Shoemaker's approach is no different from being atheist.

On another occasion, to connect colonialism with the emergence of modern Islamic exegetical works I suggested further reading to students, including Fanon's *A Dying Colonialism*, Said's *Orientalism* and *Culture and Imperialism*, and Huntington's *The Clash of Civilizations*. The only MA student in the class objected to the suggestion of Huntington, saying that one lecturer in politics identifying as "Muslim" had characterized it as "crap."

Unsurprisingly, perhaps, such unscholarly and dismissive reviews of Huntington's works by traditionalists are not unusual; unsurprising, perhaps, too, is that Edward W. Said, also on my list of consultable experts, had harshly criticized *The Clash of Civilizations*, calling Huntington a polemicist whose work was neither neutral, descriptive, nor objective.[6]

It has become clear to me that over the years what Edward Said has said or written is better-considered by traditionalist, nationalist, and anti-imperialist Muslims than by the run of intellectuals, historians, and philosophers. For the former group, as well as for some Muslims in the West, as well as many Western liberals, Huntington's central thesis of a " . . . centuries-old military interaction between the West and Islam [that] is unlikely to decline,"[7] is not a comfortable read. Traditionalist, nationalist, anti-imperialist and some Western-based Muslims, at least, have concluded that Huntington's work, if studied at all, should therefore be confined to political science and international affairs students and surely not trouble the tender consciences of students of religion and Islam. Because of this, they feel duty-bound to select some and to censor other sources that they make available for their students.

My own experience—and the reported experience of other colleagues working in the West—of monitoring by [self-appointed] guardians of Islamic orthodoxy and their efforts to defend Islam from so-called enemies in the West, suggests to me that Islamic Apologetics will soon appear *everywhere*— shades of Michel Houellebecq's *Soumission*—wherever and whenever scholars or students apply any type of religious/traditionalist pressure in the liberal Western environment.[8]

The way people "reject" Huntington and "support" Said, or vice versa, is not particularly important for this study. The way they interpret and use their approaches is, I believe, crucial and essential. Indeed, just as Huntington's more recent *Clash* thesis seems to have provided grist to anti-Islamic mills in the West and anti-imperialist ones in the Islamic world, Said's misunderstanding of Western motives combined with the centrality of Said's thesis for Muslim scholars and current Muslim misinterpretation of and hostile views toward the West and Westerners are no accident; both have had a significant influence on the Muslim academy.

It has become apparent to me that there is, at least in terms of methodology and objectives, a *clash of studying Islam* within the Muslim and Western academies. In light of Said's work and as it is echoed by Muslims such as Muzzafar Iqbal and Fouad Haddad, for some Muslim scholars getting on board with the critical historical approaches to methodology involved in Western *Islamic studies* seems equal to an admission of Muslim *inferiority*.

Scholars within Muslim academic contexts, where nationalism, politics, and religion are all mixed together, are expected to produce descriptive, neutral, and apologetic studies of the Qur'ān and its exegesis rather than anything controversial, and to do so with only limited mentions of the modern theories presented by scholars such as Wansbrough, Crone, McCauliff, etc. Any reference to Western Qur'anic studies is strictly subject to the latter's compatibility with (traditional) Islamic teachings. Even translations of Western Qur'anic studies works in the Muslim world are selective and only occur if the text in question is neutral in tone or is accompanied by a critical review.

Islamic studies in the West will, it seems, be reshaped so that is not itself anymore—it will be domesticated and sectarianized and become a vehicle by which Islam is examined indigenously and thus become an apologetic tool; it will be Islamic Apologetics, with the potential to translate, interpret, or employ an *Islamic studies* piece in a very restricted manner. For example, as mentioned previously, Walid A. Saleh's review of David S. Powers' work was translated, but the methodology expounded by Saleh, among others, regarding the textual and intertextual connections between [post-]biblical literature and Qur'anic commentaries was not imported into Muslim academic contexts particularly in Southeast Asia.[9] Similarly, the biography of Qadi 'Abd al-Jabbar (d. ca. 1025) by Gabriel Said Reynolds was translated into Persian,[10] but the methodology Reynolds developed in his book *The Qur'ān and its Biblical Subtext* was not imported by Iranian scholars, instead being openly criticized.[11] It will remain restricted to a particular environment, isolated from other civilizations and cultures.

Many scholars, including Edward Said (though after the publication of *Orientalism*), tried to promote de-nationalization of education and bring democratic and liberal notions into the Muslim academy. Said wrote,

> And surely there can be nothing more important in the long run of Egypt's life than education, and the life of the mind, especially here in our part of the world, where, alas, we lag behind in democracy, the freedoms of expression, opinion, and the press, and full participation in societies so long dominated by national security concerns, and not the intellectual and civic health of the people.[12]

Today, working on new Qur'ān projects dealing with West Africa is almost impossible in most religious studies departments in the Muslim academy (particularly in the Middle East). However, in a few places, scholars are trying out a new discourse that encourages students to see Western Qur'anic studies in a more positive light.

***

Let's return to the origins of the academic study of Islam. As mentioned previously, it was Ranke who opened up a new approach toward history within European (and American) academic contexts. This approach was, at the outset, the result of a philosophical concern raised by Kant who, according to Foucault and unlike earlier thinkers, asked, "what are we? in a very precise moment of history."[13] This question was not posed simply to find an answer for human origin, race, and nationality, but was, rather, related to a transformational process of *everything* and an evolution of *ours* and *ourselves*. It directly alerts us to how "a historical awareness of our present circumstance" is important. Muslims and other Orientals indirectly resisted this question as they conducted their various anti-authority struggles that occurred widely in the final decades of the twentieth century "not to discover what we are but to refuse what we are."[14] Indeed, some Orientals stood against any type of approach that told them about *who they are* and anything that caused their unique (and imagined) historical identity to pale:

> The main objective of these struggles is to attack not so much "such or such" an institution of power, or group, or elite, or class but rather technique, a form of power.[15]

It should be always kept in mind that in the Muslim academy rejection of Wansbrough's or Powers' critical historical approaches to the history of the Qur'ān and Muslim believer-communities is not just related to the geo-ethnic ("European") origin or non-Muslim religious affiliation of their authors. The rejection is also a rejection of the modern analytical techniques they employ. Anyone, European or not, Muslim or not, who presents or paraphrases any idea that runs contrary to those of the traditional ones and their popularizers is at risk of rejection. Nasr Hamid Abu Zayd, among others, was exiled upon rewording various theories related to the Qur'ān and revelation, while I can well imagine the anger of some students regarding new statements of 'Abdolkarim Soroush about the "Prophetic Dreams."

Such global opposition is tied in with the conversion of "brilliance and daring to caution and fear, from the advancement of knowledge to self-preservation,"[16] and as such will not be restricted to the Muslim academy alone. It may be seen everywhere that such conversions occur. It can also be manifested as new-born *Islamic religious studies*, or the anthropological, sociological, ethnographical, and/or psychological study of Muslim or any other [religious] communities in religious/Islamic studies departments, in which history—and particularly anything deemed controversial or unacceptable to the Muslim community—is hidden behind contemporary political-Muslim traditional interests. In fact, the stronger the connection with politics and traditionalism, the more diminished is the academic approach toward religion and the greater the conservative presentation of religious studies, in both the Western and the Muslim academic contexts. This trend can be seriously destructive. The terrible and sad mass shootings at mosques in the New Zealand city of Christchurch was done by an Australian citizen. This is despite the fact that huge amount of money has been allocated to the anthropology, sociology, psychology, and ethnography of Muslim communities (e.g., refugees) in both Australia and New Zealand. Thus, one may wonder why such financial and academic investments did not work properly and not help people to get thoroughly familiar with the notions of otherness and integration. I had previously observed the conversion of "the advancement of knowledge to self-preservation" in New Zealand. Following the incident of Charlie Hebdo in France in 2015, I published a report titled "New Zealand and Islam deserve deeper joint study" in the *Otago Daily Times* (ODT), in which I said "[. . .] to not have terrors, blasphemy, harassments and social violence in the future—like the incidents of France, Denmark and so on—New Zealand needs something more than security, freedom, justice and police and that would be education."[17] Upon its publication, I received several anonymous and pseudonymous letters from non-Muslim Australians and New Zealanders who raised their objections to Muslims immigration and integration:

Dr. Daneshgar, University of Otago . . . Sir 2nd and 3rd generation Lebanese Muslims living in Australia no intention of being Australian; enclosed are some attachments. We the infidels can live with Muslims, they can't live with us [. . .] dated 16-3-2015.[18]

The enclosed document titled "The Sword of Islam" says:

> [. . .] Islam is the fastest growing religion in the World, not for the love
> of Allah, but for the fear of the Sword. ("Time International June 1992")
> [. . .] Us infidels beware of the Sword of Islam [. . .] Past and present
> governments have failed to Govern New Zealand in New Zealand's best in-
> terest as a Nation, the welfare and security of its Citizens . . .[19]

Later on, some of my colleagues conservatively advised me not to publish such notes in newspapers again. However, I decided to contact the New
Zealand Police (in Dunedin) helping them to prevent and counter extremism
and radicalization by means of history and philology. After several meetings
and rounds of discussions, I did not hear any news from them about our
collaboration.

Ignorance of and resistance to the history of religion indicate that the
conservative presentation of religious studies can be considered as a serious
threat to academic and public freedom and scholars should be aware of and
try to counter it using philological, philosophical, and more importantly
critical instruments.

Notes

Preface

1. E. B. White, *Here Is New York* (New York: The Little Bookroom, 1999), 26.
2. Ibid.
3. In Islamic tradition a dream may be considered a part of prophecy.
4. Roy Mottahedeh, *The Mantle of the Prophet: Religion and Politics in Iran* (New York: Simon and Schuster, 1985), 179.
5. In some cases, Sunnis only referred to Shiʿi sources, and vice versa, when they want to write an essay critical of the other.
6. See Marwa Elshakry, *Reading Darwin in Arabic, 1860–1950* (Chicago: University of Chicago Press, 2014).
7. White, *Here Is New York*, 27.
8. History suggests this, too. Archives and reports suggest that the visitors to the so-called Orient and Occident seem to have been divisible into these categories. Only a small number of travelers and visitors, among the thousands of them, were in search of the type of mutual understanding that could help future generations. It seems that many modern studies (e.g., in geography) could not have been done if travelers and scholars such as Marco Polo (d. ca. 1324), Ibn Battuta (d. ca. 1377), Henry Salt (d. 1827), and Edward G. Browne (d. 1926) had not provided us with their observations and reports. Indeed, regardless of their nationality, religion, or race, reports and geographical maps from such travelers have assisted humans in building their future.
9. I completed the first draft of this book in early 2017, before my move to Germany. It does not take account of my academic experience in Europe.
10. Ruqayya Rabiʿi Navidehi and Mahdi Bakuyi, "Naqd va Barrisi-yi Barjam va Pasa-barjam az Didgah-e Qurʾan-e Karim," in *Conference-e Melli-yi ruykard-ha-yi nuvin –e ʿUlum Insani dar Qarn-e 21* (Rasht, 1396/2017), 33 pp.
11. Khosrow Sobhe, "Education in Revolution: Is Iran Duplicating the Chinese Cultural Revolution?" *Comparative Education* 18.3 (1982): 271–280.
12. Bill Readings, *The University in Ruins* (Cambridge, MA: Harvard University Press, 1996), 4.
13. Ibid., and Khosrow Sobhe, "Education in Revolution: Is Iran Duplicating the Chinese Cultural Revolution?," 271–280.
14. Professor Barnes was the president of this center from 1975 to 1977. See "Harvard Business School Professor Emeritus Louis 'By' Barnes Dies at 81" [online source].
15. "Imam Sadiq University" [online source].
16. Muhammad Iqbal, "First World Conference on Muslim Education and Its Possible Implications for British Muslims," *Learning for Living* 17.3 (1978): 123–125.

17. Ibid.
18. SAW: *sall^a Allah 'alayh wa-sallam*; AS: *'alayhi/ha/him al-salam*; and RA: *radiy^a allah^u 'anh^u*.
19. Akeel Bilgrami, *Secularism, Identity, and Enchantment* (Cambridge, MA and London: Harvard University Press, 2014), 76.
20. Paul Morris, et al., eds., *The Teaching and Study of Islam in Western Universities* (London: Routledge, 2013), i.
21. Robert W. Hefner and Muhammad Qasim Zaman, eds. *Schooling Islam: The Culture and Politics of Modern Muslim Education* (Princeton, NJ: Princeton University Press, 2007).
22. Feryal Salem, "Introduction to the Muslim World: The Challenges and Opportunities of Teaching Islam in Theological Seminaries," special issue, *The Muslim World* 108.2 (2018): 211. Recent fieldwork have been conducted by Ervan Nurtawab in Indonesia and Andreas Dürr in Afghanistan. I was informed by Abdullah Saeed (on 26.02.2018) that he has changed the direction of his joint project with Andrew Rippin a bit, "after Andrew passed away just at the time when [they] were starting [their] fieldwork."

Introduction

1. For example, see Devin Stewart and Gabriel Said Reynolds, "Afterword: The Academic Study of The Qur'ān—Achievements, Challenges, and Prospects," *Journal of the International Qur'ān Studies Association* 1 (2016): 173–183.
2. See Majid Daneshgar, "'Father of Ignorance': How and Why Marginal Figures within Islam Remain Marginal," FRIAS Lunch Lecture 2018, Ignorance—What We Don't Know (Freiburg: Freiburg Institute for Advanced Studies, University of Freiburg, June 2018).
3. See Edward W. Said, *Orientalism* (New York: Vintage, 1978), 106–107.
4. On the other hand, connecting various types of violence to religious studies topics will not permit an exploration of any possible mental and psychological disorders of an attacker. For instance, a report published by the BBC revealed that Khalid Masoud, who killed and injured several people in London in March 2017, had been detained several times due to violence before converting to Islam in 2004, as he also was after that date when working in the Middle East. See *Who Was Khalid Masoud?* (*Khalid Mas'ud ki bud?*) [online source].
5. On this subject, see Aaron W. Hughes, *Situating Islam: The Past and Future of an Academic Discipline* (Sheffield: Equinox Publishing Ltd, 2007).
6. Recently, a center and library for Islamic studies in European languages has been established in Qum, attached to hawza 'ilmiyya. However, the available sources are selective. It should be noted that, unlike Muslim academic contexts, there is some evidence suggesting that the Chinese have organized debates and programs for the study of Marxism indirectly. See David Kotz, "The State of Official Marxism in China Today," *Monthly Review* 4.59 (2007): 58–64.

7. Edward W. Said, "On the University," *Alif: Journal of Comparative Poetics* 25 (2005): 26–36 (based on Said's lecture at AUC in 1999).

8. Toni Morrison, *The Origin of Others* (Cambridge, MA: Harvard University Press, 2017), 48.

9. Ibid., 99–100.

10. Ibid., 3–4.

Chapter 1

1. Edward W. Said, "On the University," *Alif: Journal of Comparative Poetics* 25 (2005): 26–36.

2. E.g., Nancy G. Siraisi, *Avicenna in Renaissance Italy: The Canon and Medical Teaching in Italian Universities after 1500* (Princeton, NJ: Princeton University Press, 2014).

3. For instance, Murteza Aghatehrani moved to Canada (McGill University) and then the United States (Binghamton University, the State University of New York) to pursue graduate studies. He was also in charge of the Islamic Institute of New York and its mosque dedicated to Shiʻi teachings. Upon his return to Iran, he actively participated in academic and political discourses. He was also elected as the member of the Islamic Parliament of Iran. He was chosen as the teacher of Islamic ethics in the cabinet of former President of Iran Mahmoud Ahmadijejad, *Daftar-e Nashr-e Athar-e Ustad Murteza Aghatehrani*: http://aghatehrani.ir/119/%D8%B2%D9%86%D8%AF%DA%AF%DB%8C-%D9%86%D8%A7%D9%85%D9%87/ [online source].

4. Majid Daneshgar, "al-Mizan Pazhuhi bi Zaban-ha-yi Uruppa-yi va Asiya-yi." Center and Library for Islamic Studies in European Languages (2015). *Center and Library for Islamic Studies in European Languages (2015)* [online source].

5. See Michel Foucault, "The Subject and Power," *Critical Inquiry* 8.4 (1982): 777–795.

6. Ibid.

7. Mohsen Jan Nezhad and Jalal-e-Din Jalali, *English for the Students of Qurʾanic Sciences and Tradition* (Tehran: SAMT, 2014), 25.

8. *Mushakhkhassat-e Kulli, Barnama va Sar-fasl-e Durus* (Department of Qurʾān and Hadith), University of Isfahan (2014), 2.

9. Ibid.

10. Ibid.

11. Foucault, "The Subject and Power."

12. These are explored in some detail in the following chapters.

13. Mohsen Alviri, *Mutaliʻat-e Islami dar Gharb*, 7th ed. (Tehran: SAMT, 1393/2014).

14. Also, this volume does not address the works of American or European scholars working in Muslim academic contexts.

15. Said, "On the University."

16. Some Iranian journals who criticize Western Islamic studies have also been translated into Urdu to be studied by the Shiʻis of India and Pakistan.

17. Aaron W. Hughes, *Theorizing Islam: Disciplinary Deconstruction and Reconstruction* (London and New York: Routledge, 2014), 1, 3, and 5. I also thank Tracy Danison and Aaron W. Hughes for commenting on rhetorical strength of the term "Islamic Apologetics" in this study.

18. Edward W. Said, *Reflections on Exile* (Cambridge, MA: Harvard University Press, 2000), 190.

19. These are, primarily, accepting God's unity, the Qur'ān's divine origin, Muhammad's prophecy and sinlessness, as well as accepting, on the Shi'i side, 'Ali and his descendants as the best successors of God on earth.

20. Muslih al-Din Sa'di Al-Shirazi, *Gulistan: Taman Mawar* (Kuala Lumpur: Islamic Book Trust, 2017)

21. Nazmi Yaakub, "Gulistan karya Sa'di bukan hanya warisan Parsi, Iran," *Bharian*, September 2017 [online source].

22. There are always some exceptions. Some Arab departments hired American or European scholars of Islam whose works will be considered in the near future.

23. William A. Graham, "Those Who Study and Teach the Qur'ān," Proceedings of the International Congress for the Study of the Qur'ān, Australian National University, Canberra, May 8–13, 1980 (Canberra: Australian National University, 1981), 9–28.

24. However, the translators' preface of many translated volumes produced by the British empire show that the purpose of the translation was not learning and increasing knowledge in order to develop their colonialism but to expand their knowledge about the greatness of Eastern civilizations. See the English translations of texts produced in Fort William College, Kolkata, India.

25. Vrolijk and van Leeuwen, *Arabic Studies in the Netherlands*, 105.

26. Charles J. Adams, "Reflections on the Work of John Wansbrough," *Method & Theory in the Study of Religion* 9.1 (1997): 75–90.

27. Edward Gaylord Bourne, "Leopold von Ranke," *The Sewanee Review* 4.4 (1896): 385–401.

28. Michael E. Pregill, "Some Reflections on Borrowing, Influence, and the Entwining of Jewish and Islamic Traditions; or, What the Image of a Calf Might Do," in *Islamic Studies Today: Essays in Honor of Andrew Rippin*, ed. Majid Daneshgar and Walid A. Saleh (Leiden and Boston: Brill, 2016), 167.

29. I agree with Wokoeck that Islamic Studies was established by Martin Hartmann and Becker in Germany, although my emphasis is on the shaping of a modern approach to the study of Islam in scholarly works. See Ursula Wokoeck, *German Orientalism: The Study of the Middle East and Islam from 1800 to 1945* (New York: Routledge, 2009), 177.

30. Theodor Nöldeke, *Geschichte des Qorāns* (Gottingen: Verlag der Dieterichschen Buchhandlung, 1860); Marco Schöller, "Post-Enlightenment Academic Study of the Qur'ān," in *Encyclopaedia of the Qur'ān*, ed. Jane Dammen McAuliffe (Leiden and Boston: Brill, 2004), 187–208; Peter G. Riddell, "Reading the Qur'ān Chronologically," in *Islamic Studies Today: Essays in Honor of Andrew Rippin*, ed. Majid Daneshgar and Walid A. Saleh (Leiden and Boston: Brill, 2016), 297–316.

31. John Wansbrough, *Qurʾānic Studies: Sources and Methods of Scriptural Interpretation*, edited with a foreword, translation, and expanded notes by Andrew Rippin (Amherst, NY: Prometheus, 2004), x.

32. A note dedicated to King William IV in the preface of a Persian-English book published in London, preserved in the Otago University Special Collection.

33. William A. Graham, "Those Who Study and Teach the Qurʾān."

34. Ibid.

35. Ignaz Goldziher, *Schools of Koranic Commentators*, ed. and trans. Wolfgang H. Behn (Weisbaden: Harrassowitz, 2006), 58.

36. Ibid., 197–232.

37. Ibid., 198.

38. Schöller, "Post-Enlightenment Academic Study of the Qurʾān."

39. Ibid. Also see Jane D. McAuliffe, "A Concluding Appreciation," in *Islamic Studies Today: Essays in Honor of Andrew Rippin*, ed. Majid Daneshgar and Walid A. Saleh (Leiden: Brill, 2016), 386–395.

40. Giuseppe Gabrieli, "Fakhr-al-din al-Razi," *Isis* 7.1 (1925): 9–13.

41. Harald Motzki, "Alternatives Accounts of the Qurʾān's Formation," in *The Cambridge Companion to the Qurʾān*, ed. Jane Dammen McAuliffe (Cambridge: Cambridge University Press, 2006), 60.

42. It should be noted that Gerald R. Hawting (b. 1944), the emeritus professor of at the School of Orietnal and African Studies, London, is positioned in the category of (b) and (c).

43. Wansbrough, "Qurʾānic Studies," xi.

44. Schöller, "Post-Enlightenment Academic Study of the Qurʾān."

45. Ian Brown, *The School of Oriental and African Studies* (Cambridge: Cambridge University Press, 2016), 314.

46. Adams, "Reflections on the Work of John Wansbrough," 75–90.

47. Ibid.

48. Ibid.

49. Ibid.

50. Ibid.

51. Fred M. Donner, *Narratives of Islamic Origins: The Beginnings of Islamic Historical Writing* (Princeton, NJ: The Darwin Press Inc., 1998), 37.

52. Ibid., 37–38. See also Rippin's foreword to Wansbrough's *Qurʾānic Studies*.

53. Donner, *Narratives of Islamic Origins*, 39.

54. David S. Powers, *Muḥammad Is Not the Father of Any of Your Men: The Making of the Last Prophet* (Philadelphia: University of Pennsylvania Press, 2009), 171.

55. Ibid., 196.

56. Parts of this section has been published in the journal of *Der Islam*. I thank *Der Islam* (De Gruyter) for granting me permission to re-use parts of my review here. Majid Daneshgar, "David S. Powers, *Zayd*," *Der Islam* 94.1 (2017): 299–304.

57. Mohammad Ali Amir-Moezzi, *The Silent Qurʾān and the Speaking Qurʾān: Scriptural Sources of Islam Between History and Fervor*, trans. Eric Ormsby (New York: Columbia University Press, 2016), 48.

58. Alphonse Mingana, "The Transmission of the Kur'an," *The Muslim World* 7.3 (1917): 223-232. See also Crone and Cook, *Hagarism*.

59. Amir-Moezzi, *Silent Qur'ān*.

60. Ibid., 60.

61. Mohammad Ali Amir-Moezzi, "Powers David S., Zayd: The Little Known Story of Muḥammad's Adopted Son, Philadelphia, University of Pennsylvania Press, 2014, 175 p.," *Revue des mondes musulmans et de la Méditerranée*, 139 [online source].

62. Brett Wilson also published various works dealing with the history of the Qur'ān translations in Turkey, e.g., M. Brett Wilson, *Translating the Qur'an in an Age of Nationalism: Print Culture and Modern Islam in Turkey* (Oxford: Oxford University Press in association with the Institute of Ismaili Studies, 2014).

63. It is a commonplace belief that Winstedt's works are largely considered the backbone of Malay cultural studies.

64. An excerpt from his PhD thesis can be found in Peter G. Riddell, "The Sources of Abd al-Ra'ūf's *Tarjumān al-mustafīd*," *Journal of the Malaysian Branch of the Royal Asiatic Society* 57.2 (247) (1984): 113–118.

65. Roman Loimeier, "Translating the Qur'ān in Sub-Saharan Africa: Dynamics and Disputes," *Journal of Religion in Africa* 35.4 (2005): 403–423.

66. Hassan Ma'ayergi, "Translations of the Meanings of the Holy Qur'an into Minority Languages: The Case of Africa," *Institute of Muslim Minority Affairs Journal* 14.1–2 (1993): 156–180.

67. Touraj Daryaee, "The Study of Ancient Iran in the Twentieth Century," *Iranian Studies* 42.4 (2009): 579–589.

Chapter 2

1. This issue needs further assessment, which will be done in the future.

2. Wael Hallaq, *An Introduction to Islamic Law* (Cambridge: Cambridge University Press, 2009), 104.

3. Ibid.

4. Malay-Indonesian governments used to provide their students with scholarships in order to study religious studies in Western institutes.

5. Nonetheless, some Iranian institutes that belong to *hawza* (Islamic Shi'i seminary), not the ministry of research, science and technology such as The Imam Khomeini Educational Research Institute in Qum, send their *tullab* or students, who have already firm basis of Islam, to North American universities such as McGill, Concordia, and Toronto.

6. 'Isq Muttaqi-zadeh et al., "Barrisi jam' Qur'ān-e Payambar (SAW) va Imam 'Ali (AS) az Nigah-e Mustashriqan va Ahl-e Sunnat," *Qur'ān Pazhuhi-yi Khavar-shinasan* 11 (1390/2011): 31–44.

7. Nasrullah Sulaymani, "Nishast-e 'ilmi-yi Qur'ān va Mustashriqan: Jam'i az Asatid ba Hudur-e Hazrat-e Ayatollah al-'Uzma Makarim Shirazi," *Qur'ān va Mustashriqan* 2 (1386/2007): 15.

8. See Bensalem Himmich, *al-'Arab wa l-Islam fi Maraya al-Istishraq* (Cairo: Dar al-Shuruq, 2011).

9. Hassan Rezaei Haftadur, "Barrisi-e Kitab-e Jam' Avari-yi Qur'an-e John Burton," *Qur'an Pazhuhi Khavar-shinasan* 7 (1388/2009): 103–132.

10. Abu Ammar Yasir Qadhi, *An Introduction to the Sciences of the Qur'an* (Birmingham, AL: al-Hidayah, 1999), 388.

11. Ibid. See also John Burton, *The Collection of the Qur'an* (Cambridge: Cambridge University Press, 1977/1979), 234.

12. Richard Bell, *Introduction to the Qur'an*, ed. William Montgomery Watt, trans. Baha'iddin Khurramshahi (Qum: Markaz-e Tarjuma Qur'an Majid bi Zaban-ha-ye Khareji, 1382/2003); trans. Lilian D. Tedjasudhana as *Pengantar Quran* (Jakarta: INIS, 1998).

13. This book was translated as *al-Mustashriq al-injilizi William Montgomery Watt, Muhammad Salli Allah alayh wa alih wa salam fi Mecca*, trans. 'Abdulrahman 'Abdallah al-Shaykh (Cairo: al-Hay'a al-Masriyya al-'amma lil-Kitab, 1415/1994).

14. "Dar Sayeh-yi Aftab: Guft-u-gu-yi Qur'an Pazhuhana ba Ustad Baha'iddin Khurramshahi," *Ma'arif* 56 (1387/2008) [online source].

15. Baha'iddin Khurramshahi, "Muqaddama bar Tarjuma-yi Qur'an-e Richard Bell, edited/revised by Montgomery Watt," *Tarjuman-e Wahy* 1 (1376/1997): 83–103.

16. Stephen J. Shoemaker, *The Death of a Prophet: The End of Muhammad's Life and the Beginnings of Islam* (Philadelphia: University of Pennsylvania Press, 2011), 7–8.

17. Sent by the editor on September 28, 2016.

18. Walid A. Saleh, "Review of *Muhammad Is Not the Father of Any of Your Men: The Making of the Last Prophet*, by David S. Powers," along with the preface to *Muhammad Is Not the Father of Any of Your Men*, trans. 'Ali Aghaei, *Kitab-e Din* 10.193 (1392/2013): 10–18.

19. Walid A. Saleh, "Review of *Muhammad Is Not the Father of Any of Your Men: The Making of the Last Prophet*, by David S. Powers," *Comparative Islamic Studies* 6.1–2 (2010): 251–264.

20. "Gharb talash mikunad marja'iyyat-e 'ilmi dar Qur'an ra az ma bigirad" [online source].

21. Muzaffar Iqbal, *The Qur'an, Orientalism and the Encyclopaedia of the Qur'an* (Selangor: Islamic Book Trust, 2009).

22. Although he had planned to co-edit several volumes on the way is Qur'an and its commentaries examined in the four countries of Qatar, Turkey, Indonesia, and Iran.

23. "Andiru Ribin, Biritaniy" [online source].

24. Following French scholars of Qur'anic manuscripts, very few Arab and Iranian scholars of Islam paid attention to different fragments of the Qur'an preserved in different libraries. However, such fields of study in the Muslim world are still in their infancy. For example, see Bashir B. Hassan al-Himyari, "Mushaf of Tübingen University No (MaVI165): Descriptive and Analytical Study," *Journal of al-Imam al-Shatibi Institute for Quranic Studies* 20 (1436/2015): 13–84; Morteza Karimi-nia, "The Qur'an supposedly handwritten by Imam Reza, kept at the Astan-e Quds Library

(Mashhad) and its supplements: a comparison between MS 1586 and MS 4354a, and a few Qur'anic folios at London's auctions," *Ayene-ye Miras* 60 (1396/2017): 31–70.

25. Muzaffar Iqbal, *The Qur'an, Orientalism and the Encyclopaedia of the Qur'an* (Selangor: Islamic Book Trust, 2009), 46. I purchased this book at the University of Malaya Bookshop.

26. Hossein Bahri, "The Role of Translation Movements in the Cultural Maintenance of Iran from the Era of Cyrus the Great up to the Constitutional Revolution," *Translaiton Journal* 15 (2011) [online source].

27. It should be noted that, unlike other Muslim communities, the Iranian public's general unfamiliarity with the English language has been another factor in its eagerness to read the translated works of Western scholars.

28. "Kitab-e *Da'ira al-Ma'arif-e Qur'an* bar rushd-e Qur'ān-pazhuhi dar Iran athar guzasht," *Mehr News* (khurdad 1396/June 2017) [online source].

29. Heller and Rippin, "Yāfit̲h̲," EI2.

30. Parviz Azadi and Majid Ma'arif, "Tahlil va naqd-e mutali'at-e Qur'āni-yi mustashriqan," *Qur'ān-shinakht* 5.1 (2012): 125–154.

31. Parviz Azadi, "Arzyabi Azad Andishi dar ravish-e mutala'at-e Qur'āni-yi Andrew Rippin," *Bonyan-e Marsus-Iran Ministry of Science, Research and Technology* 8.2 (1393/2014): 52–55.

32. Muhammad 'Ali Mahdavi Rad and Nusrat Nilsaz, "Tarikhgudhari-ye tafsir-e mansub bi Ibn 'Abbas. Naqd-e ravish-e tahlil-e adabi-yi Wansbrough va Rippin," *Taaqiqat-e 'ulum-e Qur'an va hadith* 3.6 (1385/2006): 27–64.

33. See, for example, Hafiz Muhammad Ajmal et al., "Qur'ānic diacritical marks and dot-system and the Orientalists. A Critical Study," *Hazara Islamicus* 4.1 (2015): 1–18.

34. Tauseef Ahmad Parry, "Western Scholarship on Qur'anic Studies in 21st Century: A Brief Study of the Contribution of Jane D. McAuliffe and Andrew Rippin," *Hazara Islamicus* 1.2 (2012): 1–10. See also his report titled "West Knows How to Honor Their Academicians," *KashmirReader* (June 2018), 9.

35. 'Abd al-Rahman Badawi, *Mawsu'a al-mustashriqin*, 2nd ed. (Beirut, 1993).

36. 'Abd al-Rahmān Badawi, *Ensiklopedi tokoh orientalis*, trans. Amroeni Drajat (Yogyakarta, 2003).

37. Mohammad Khalifa, *The Sublime Quran and Orientalism*, 2nd ed. (Karachi: International Islamic Publisher, 1989). For the Malay version see Mohammad Khalifa, *Al-Quran dan Orientalisme*, trans. Zakaria Stapa and Mohamad Asin Dollah (Kuala Lumpur: Dewan Bahasa dan Pustaka, 1993).

38. "Why Are Some Books Banned in Malay but Allowed in English?" [online source].

39. E.g., The original version of Robert Spencer's *Onward Muslim Soldiers* is banned across Malaysia.

40. Andrew Rippin, "Analisis Sastra Terhadap al-Qur'ān, Tafsir, dan Sirah. Metodologi John Wansbrough," in *Pendekatan Kajian Islam Dalam Studi Agama*, ed. Richard C. Martin, trans. Zakiyuddin Bhaidhawy (Surakarta: Muhammadiyah University Press, 2001), 201.

41. Syamsuddin Arif, *Orientalis dan Diabolisme Pemikiran* (Jakarta: Gema Insani, 2008), 45.

42. Mehmet Akif Koç, "The Influence of Western Qur'ānic Scholarship in Turkey," *Journal of Qur'ānic Studies* 14.1 (2012): 9–44.

43. See Selahattin Sönmezsoy, *Kur'an ve Oryantalistler* (Ankara: Fecr Yayınevi, 1998).

44. Muhammad A. Chaudhary, "Orientalism on Variant Readings of the Qur'an: The Case of Arthur Jeffery," *The American Journal of Islamic Social Sciences* 12.2 (1995): 170–184.

45. E.g., Mesut Okumuş, "Arthur Jeffery ve Kur'an Çalışmaları Üzerine," *Ankara Üniversitesi İlahiyat Fakültesi Dergisi* 43.2 (2002): 121–150.

46. Muhammad A. Chaudhary "Oryantalizmin Kıraat Farklılıklarına Bakışının Tenkidi-Arthur Jeffery Örneği," çeviren Mahmut Ay, *İstanbul Üniversitesi İlahiyat Fakültesi Dergisi* 25 (2011), 189–204.

47. Andrew Rippin, "Kur'ân 7/40: Deve İğnenin Deliğinden Geçinceye Kadar," çeviren Mehmet Dağ, *Dinbilimleri Akademik Araştırma Dergisi* II.4 Samsun (2002): 1–7; "Tefsir Çalışmalarının Bugünkü Durumu," çeviren İsmail Albayrak, *Sakarya Üniversitesi İlahiyat Fakültesi Dergisi* 8 (2003): 139–156; "Tefsir Çalışmalarının Mevcut Durumu," çeviren Erdoğan Baş, *İslâmi Araştırmalar Dergisi* 16.3 (2003): 454–461.

48. To read about the growth in science in the Middle East, see, for example, Andy Coghlan, "Iran Is Top of the World in Science Growth," *New Scientist/Daily News*, March 28, 2011 [online source]. Today, the apparent competition is the result of four different events: (a) the post-1979 revolution of Iran [re-]creating a Neo-Sunnism-Shi'ism Muslim world; (b) the post-Cold War industrial and constructiveness movement based on relations to [one or some] Western powers; (c) the post-9/11 [and post-War on Terror] attempt of Muslims to unite; and (d) the oil-free but profitable industrial technology. King Faisal's attempt to create a brotherly bond between Islam and advanced development as well Muhammad Reza Shah Pahlavi's desire to bring both the culture and technology of the West to Iran were influential but not comparable with each other; however, the revolution of 1979 changed the context by introducing the motto *Sadirat-e Inqilab* (Exporting the Revolution). It was to be expected that an Islamic revolution built upon Shi'i-Imam Husayni teachings and anti-Westernization would not be warmly received by other Islamic nations. Subsequently, due to the media, the separation and competition between Sunnis and Shi'is has become more apparent than ever.

49. L. Gardet, "'Ilm al-Kalām" [online source].

50. Andrew Rippin, et al., "Arabic Software for the IBM," Courseware Reviews (*Journal of Compute and the Humanities*) 25.6 (1991): 445–465; "The Qur'ān on the Internet: Implications and Future Possibilities," in *Muslims and the New Information and Communication Technologies*, ed. Göran Larsson and Thomas Hoffman, Muslims in Global Societies Series, vol. 7 (Dordrecht: Springer, 2013), 113–126.

51. Andrew Rippin, *Muslims: Their Religious Beliefs and Practices*, 4th ed. (London and New York: Routledge, 2012), 278–280.

52. 'Ali Ma'muri, "Danish-e Zaban Shinasi va Karburd-ha-yi an dar mutali'at-e Qur'āni," *Qur'ān va 'ilm* 1 (1386/2007): 161–176.

53. Abolghasim Ali-Dust et al., "Tahlil hamsani-yi Zaban-e Qur'ān va Qaum va Pay-amad-ha-yi an," *Dhihn* 54 (1392/2013): 5–38.

54. Sakina Haqqani, "Barrasi-yi Ara-yi Duktur Bucaille va Professor Arberry Piramun-e Masuniyyat-e Qur'ān az Tahrif," *Bayinnat* 69 (1390/2011): 89–96.

55. Maurice Bucaille, *The Bible, the Qur'ān and Science*, trans. Alastair D. Pannell and Maurice Bucaille (Tripoli: Islamic Call Society, 1978), 90.

56. Stefano Bigliardi, "The Strange Case of Dr. Bucaille: Notes for a Re-examination," *The Muslim World*, 102.2 (2012): 248–263.

57. Bucaille, *The Bible, The Qur'ān and Science*, 7.

58. Ibid., 8–9.

59. Leif Stenberg, *The Islamization of Science: Four Muslim Positions Developing an Islamic Modernity* (Stockholm: Almqvist & Wiksell International, 1996), 228–233. I thank Brill Academic Publishers for granting permission to reuse a few parts of my forthcoming *EQ*'s entry on "Maurice Bucaille."

60. Ibid.

61. Christopher A. Furlow, "Intersections of the Qur'ān and Science in Contemporary Malaysia," in *The Qur'ān in the Malay-Indonesian World: Context and Interpretation*, ed. Majid Daneshgar, Peter G. Riddell, and Andrew Rippin (London: Routledge, 2016), 229–250.

62. Keith L. Moore, "A Scientist's Interpretation of References to Embryology in the Qur'ān," *Journal of the Islamic Medical Association of North America* 18.1 (1986): 15–17; M. Daneshgar, "The Qur'ān, Orientalists and Western Scholars," *al-Bayan Journal of Qur'ān and Hadith Studies* 10.2 (2012): 4–9.

63. Keith L. Moore, "A Scientist's Interpretation," 15–17.

64. Keith L. Moore and 'A.M. Azzindani, *The Developing Human with Islamic Additions*, 3rd ed. (Jeddah: Abul Qasim Publishing House, 1982–1983), viii.

65. *Dr. William W. Hay's Comments about the Holy Koran* [online source].

66. The main references in this regard are extracts from the video "This Is the Truth" by Shaykh Azzindani.

67. See also Raoul Keller, *Virale Verbreitung einer Ideologie: Islamistische Fundamentalisten nutzen die Wissenschaft* [online source].

68. The University of Malaya (UM) in Malaysia is a pioneer in organizing international conferences on the numerical inimitability of the Qur'ān.

69. For more information, see the works of Zaghloul el-Naggar, Zakir Na'ik, Harun Yahya, etc.

70. Many such studies are published in the *Interdisciplinary Qur'anic Studies Journal* [online source].

71. *al-Majistir al-tanfidhi fi l-tamwil al-Islami* (Riyadh: Jami'a al-Malik 'Abd al-Aziz, n.d.).

72. Walid A. Saleh, "A Fifteenth-Century Muslim Hebraist: Al-Biqā'ī and His Defense of Using the Bible to Interpret the Qur'ān," *Speculum* 83.3 (2008): 629–654.

73. Yousef Casewit, "A Muslim Scholar of the Bible: Prooftexts from Genesis and Matthew in the Qur'ān Commentary of Ibn Barrajān of Seville (d. 536/1141)," *Journal of Qur'ānic Studies* 18.1 (2016): 1–48.

74. Elliott A. Bazzano "Ibn Taymiyya, Radical Polymath, Part 2: Intellectual Contributions" *Religion Compass* 9.4 (2015): 117–139.

75. Roberto Tottoli, "Origin and Use of the Term Isrāʾīliyyāt in Muslim Literature," *Arabica* 46.2 (1999): 193–210.

76. For more, see Majid Daneshgar, *Ṭanṭāwī Jawharī and the Qurʾān*; I thank Taylor & Francis (Routledge) for granting permission to reuse a few parts my earlier work about Tawfiq Sidqi.

77. Oddbjørn Leirvik, "History as a Literary Weapon: The Gospel of Barnabas in Muslim-Christian Polemics," *Studia Theologica* 56.1 (2002): 4–26.

78. Ibid.

79. Tantawi Jawhari, *al-Jawahir fi tafsir al-Qurʾān al-Karim* (Cairo: Matbaʿa Mustafa al-Babi al-Halabi, 1923–1935), 2:122.

80. Leirvik, "History as a Literary Weapon"; Tantawi Jawhari, *al-Jawahir* 2:122.

81. Walid A. Saleh, "Sublime in Its Style, Exquisite in Its Tenderness: The Hebrew Bible Quotations in al-Biqāʿī's Qurʾān commentary," in *Adaptions and Innovations. Studies on the Interaction between Jewish and Islamic Thought and Literature from the Early Middle Ages to the Late Twentieth Century, Dedicated to Professor Joel L. Kraemer*, ed. Y. Tzvi Langermann and Joseph Stern (Leuven: Peeters, 2007), 331–347.

82. For instance, Nik Hasan bin Nik Muhammad (d. 1944), a Malay interpreter of the Qurʾān who has been significantly influenced by al-Qurtubi, Ibn Kathir, al-Shawkani, and Sayyid Qutb, put Shiʿis, Qadiyanis, Christians and Jews in same bracket as heretics. See Mustafa Abdullah, "Qurʾanic Interpretation in Thailand," in *The Qurʾān in the Malay-Indonesian World: Context and Interpretation*, ed. Majid Daneshgar, Peter G. Riddell, and Andrew Rippin (London and New York: Routledge, 2016), 61–82.

83. Christine Schirrmacher, *Mit den Waffen des Gegners* (Berlin: Klaus Schwarz, 1992), 353.

84. Oddbjørn, "History as a Literary Weapon."

85. See the works by Ayatollah Ahmad Bihishti and Aʿzam Puya in the late 1990s.

86. "The Comprehensive Muslim e-Library" and "DFAJ" [online source].

87. See Noor Specialized Magazines website. According to its page, there are seventy active Qurʾān and *Hadith* journals in Iran [online source].

88. See "Malaysia Citation Centre" [online source].

89. Navid Kermani, "From Revelation to Interpretation: Nasr Hamid Abu Zayd and the Literary Study of the Qurʾān," in *Modern Muslim Intellectuals and the Qurʾān*, ed. Suha Taji-Farouki (Oxford and London: Oxford University Press in association with the Institute of Ismaili Studies, 2004), 173.

90. Ibid., 175.

91. John R. Stone, "Reflections on the Craft of Religious Studies," in *The Next Step in Studying Religion: A Graduate Guide*, ed. Mathieu E. Courville (London and New York: Continuum, 2007), 174.

92. See "Islamic World Science Citation Center (ISC)" [online source].

93. Islamic World Science Citation Center (ISC), *Policy Plan* (Tehran: The Supreme Council for Cultural Revolution, 2008), 1. Other objectives can be obtained from ISC's website.

94. Muhammad Baqir Khurramshad, *Danishgah-e Tamaddun-saz: Tamaddun-e Nuvin-e Islami-Irani*, ed. Mustafa ʿAbbasi Muqaddam (Tehran: Ministry of Research, Science and Technology, 1386/2007), introduction.

95. Being the leader of other Muslim universities, while being the only Shiʿi government in the world, will be a challenge for forthcoming generations.

96. A. K. Brohi, "Islamization of Knowledge: A First Step to Integrate and Develop the Muslim Personality and Outlook," in *Conference Proceeding on Islam: Source and Purpose of Knowledge* (Herndon, VA: International Institute of Islamic Thought, 1988), 11.

97. Ibid.

98. Ibid., 12.

99. Christopher A. Furlow, "Intersections of the Qurʾān and Science in Contemporary Malaysia," in *The Qurʾān in the Malay-Indonesian World: Context and Interpretation*, ed. Majid Daneshgar et al. (London and New York: Routledge, 2016), 236.

100. Ismaʿil Raji al Faruqi, "Islamization of Knowledge: Problems, Principles and Prospective," in *Conference Proceeding on Islam: Source and Purpose of Knowledge* (Herndon, VA: International Institute of Islamic Thought, 1988), 21.

101. Saeid Edalatnejad, "Books of Scholars of the Time of Nāṣir al-Dīn Shāh," in *Encyclopaedias about Muslim Civilizations*, ed. Aptin Khanbaghi (Edinburgh: Edinburgh University Press in association with the Aga Khan University, 2009), 138.

102. A. Teyfur Erdogdu, "Osmanli Devrinde Son Sadrazamlar," in *Encyclopaedias about Muslim Civilizations*, 141.

103. Rizwanur Rahman, "Urdu daʾirah-yi maʿarif-e Islamiyya," in *Encyclopaedias about Muslim Civilizations*, 174.

104. Western publishers such as Brill digitize some of them, including the *Encyclopaedia Islamica*, which is the abridged English version of the Persian *Daʾirat al-maʿarif-e buzurg-e Islami*.

105. "Ayin-e Ru-namai az Danishnama-yi ʿUlum-e Qurʾān dar Qum Surat Girift," *News* No. 5318 (Esfand 21, 1395/February 2017) [online source].

106. Andrew Rippin, "Review: *The Integrated Encyclopedia of the Qurʾān, vol. 1: Allah, Ahmad, A—Beautiful Names of Allah by Muzaffar Iqbal*" *Journal of the American Oriental Society* 136.1 (2016): 222–225.

107. Gibril Fouad Haddad, "A Response to Andrew Rippin's Review of *The Integrated Encyclopedia of Qurʾān, Volume I*," *Islamic Sciences* 14.1 (2016): 91–94.

108. Thanks to social networks, foundations of *academic associations*, and connections of young Muslim scholars with Western academic contexts, there are new movements in the Muslim world encouraging researchers to read, but not follow, modern Qurʾanic scholarship. However, there are domestic debates on the study of Islam between two groups: traditionalists and revivalists. For traditionalists, highlighting the greatness of Islam is the purpose of studying Islam. The latter group is more complex. Some

revivalists, using translations of Western scholarly works or inviting western Qur'anic scholars, want to make their people review their approaches. They want Muslims, of course, not to argue about the origin of Islam or the accuracy of Muhammad's prophecy but to produce indigenous works. If they translate, the preference would be neutral works, e.g., addressing exegetical figures, not those by Crone (*Hagarism*) or Power (*Zayd*). As the prevailing voice in academic institutes belongs to governments, whose legitimacy is built upon Islamic traditions, academic journals will continue to publish material that, to a large extent, follows Islamic tradition.

109. Yadullah Nasiriyan, "Tahqiqi darbara-yi Tabanni va Zayd b. Haritha," *Maqalat va Barrisi-ha* 57.58 (1374/1995): 51–70.
110. Mahmud Sh. Khattab, "Zayd b. Haritha al-Kalbi: al-Qa'id al-Shahid," *al-Buhuth al-Islamiyya* 15 (1406/1985): 205–236.
111. 'Abd al-Maqsud Habib, "Fakhr al-Shabab al-Muslim: Zayd b. Haritha," *Minbar al-Islam* 42.2 (1404/1983): 70–72.
112. See, for example, Nasir Makarim Shirazi, *Tafsir nemuna* (Tehran: Dar al-kutub al-Islamiyya, 1995), 17:325.
113. Al-Zamakhshari, *al-Kashshaf* (Beirut: Dar al-Kutub al-'Arabi, 1986), 3:540.
114. Fadl b. Hassan al-Tabrisi, *Jawami' al-jami'* (Tehran: Intisharat Danishgah Tehran va Mudiriyyat-e Hawza 'Ilmiyya Qum, 1377/1998), 3:317.

Chapter 3

1. Sheldon Pollock, "Future Philology? The Fate of a Soft Science in a Hard World," *Critical Inquiry* 35.4 (2009): 931–961.
2. Sidney Griffith, *The Bible in Arabic: The Scriptures of the People of the Book* (Princeton, NJ: Princeton University Press, 2015), 177.
3. See Majid Daneshgar and Donald J. Kerr, *Middle Eastern and Islamic Materials in Special Collections University of Otago* (Dunedin: University of Otago Special Collections, 2017)>, 20.
4. Rippin, *Muslims*, 35.
5. Saleh, *In Defense of the Bible*, 14.
6. Sidney Griffith, *The Bible in Arabic: The Scriptures of the People of the Book* (Princeton, NJ: Princeton University Press, 2015), 177, 177.
7. Ibid., 176.
8. Ibid., 4.
9. http://biblehub.com/commentaries/gill/genesis/20.htm.
10. Ahmad Shah, *Miftah-ul-Quran* (Lahore: The Book House, 1906), 2:39.
11. Tustari's commentary also refers to this *Raqim*, as the land of the People of the Cave (the Seven Sleepers). Tustari, *Tafsir al-Tustari* (Beirut: Dar al-kutub al-'ilmiyyah, 1423), 1:97.
12. *Tafsir Ibn 'Abbas*, trans. Mokrane Guezzou [online source]. For more information about this Qur'an manuscript kept at the University of Otago, see my article "A 'Baptized' Qur'an?" in the the *Mizan Project*.

13. See "Genesis 19," Gill's Exposition [online source].
14. Moezzi, *Silent Qur'ān*, 35.
15. Ibid., 15.
16. Shahab Ahmed, *What Is Islam?: The Importance of Being Islamic* (Princeton, NJ and Oxford: Princeton University Press, 2016), 32.
17. Michael E. Pregill, "I Hear Islam Singing: Shahab Ahmed's What Is Islam? The Importance of Being Islamic," *Harvard Theological Review* 110.1 (2017): 149–165.
18. Hussain Othman, "Conceptual Understanding of Myths and Legends in Malay History," *SARI: Jurnal Alam dan Tamadun Melayu* 26 (2008): 91–110.
19. Majid Daneshgar, "Dhū l-Qarnayn in Modern Malay Commentaries and other Literature on Qur'anic Themes," in *The Qur'ān in the Malay-Indonesian World: Context and Interpretation*, ed. Majid Daneshgar et al. (London and New York: Routledge, 2016), 212–228. I thank Taylor & Francis (Routledge) for granting permission to reuse a few parts of this chapter in this book.
20. Personal communication via email, September 15, 2014.
21. It recalls "The misuse of mut'a, or 'temporary marriage,' for instance—mostly by individuals who were actually Sunni—led to severe accusations against the local Shi'i community as a whole" Christoph Marcinkowski, "The Iranian Shi'i Diaspora in Malaysia," *Middle East-Asia Project at the Middle East Institute*: https://www.mei.edu/publications/iranian-shii-diaspora-malaysia [online source].
22. See Majid Daneshgar, "The Study of Qur'ān Interpretation in the Malay-Indonesian World: A Select Bibliography," in *The Qur'ān in the Malay-Indonesian World: Context and Interpretation*, ed. Majid Daneshgar, Peter G. Riddell, and Andrew Rippin (London and New York: Routledge, 2016), 7–22.
23. Fathullah Najjar-zadegan, *Tafsir-e Tatbiqi: Barrisi-yi Tatbiqi-yi Mabani-yi tafsir-e Qur'ān va Ma'arifi az Ayat dar didgah-e Fariqayn* (Qum: Markaz-e Jahani-yi 'Ulum-e Islami, 1388/2009), 367.
24. Ibid., 373.
25. For one of the most comprehensive studies on Persian-Malay literature, see Alessandro Bausani, *Note sui Vocaboli Persiani in Malese-Indonesiano* (Naples: Istituto Universitario Orientale, 1964).
26. See Majid Daneshgar and Donald J. Kerr, *Middle Eastern and Islamic Materials in Special Collections University of Otago* (Dunedin: University of Otago Special Collections, 2017).
27. Ibid.
28. Claire Kramsch, *Language and Culture* (Oxford: Oxford University Press, 1998), 10.
29. Said, "On the University."
30. Jennifer W. Nourse, "The Meaning of Dukun and Allure of Sufi Healers: How Persian Cosmopolitans Transformed Malay–Indonesian History," *Journal of Southeast Asian Studies* 44.3 (2013): 400–422.
31. Syed Muhammad Naguib Al-Attas, *The Mysticism of Hamzah Fansuri* (Kuala Lumpur: University of Malaya, 1970), 468.
32. Marcinkowski, *Shi'ite Identities*.

33. Karel A. Steenbrink, "Jesus and the Holy Spirit in the Writings of Nūr al-Dīn al-Ranīrī," *Islam and Christian-Muslim Relations* 1.2 (1990): 192–207.

34. Nourse, "The Meaning of Dukun," 400–422.

35. Although less so, Malays were still the recipients of translations of foreign-language works, translations of Urdu, Persian (e.g., *Gul Bakawali*), and German (*Robinson Crusoe*) stories sold out in Malaya. Holger Warnk, "The Role of Translations in the Development of Modern Malay Literature, 1850–1950," *Journal of the Malaysian Branch of the Royal Asiatic Society* 80.1 (292) (June 2007): 91–113.

36. Ibid.

37. Daneshgar, "Dhū l-Qarnayn in Modern Malay Commentaries and other Literature on Qur'anic Themes."

38. Martin van Bruinessen, "Genealogies of Islamic Radicalism in Post-Suharto Indonesia," *South East Asia Research* 10.2 (2002): 117–154.

39. A. Bausani, "Ta'thir-e Farhang va Zaban-e Farsi dar Adabiyyat-e Andunizi" ("The Influence of Persian Culture and Language on the Literature of Indonesia"), *Danishkadih Adabiyyat va 'Ulum-i Insani Danishgah Tehran* 53 (1345/1966): 4–15. The shah of Iran also intervened by helping to reestablish the "relations [of Malaysia] with Pakistan." Chandran Jeshurun, *Malaysia: Fifty Years of Diplomacy, 1957–2007* (Kuala Lumpur: The Other Press, 2007), 97.

40. Philip Mathews, ed., *Chronicle of Malaysia: Fifty Years of Headline News, 1963–2013* (Kuala Lumpur: Editions Didier Millet, 2007), 84.

41. See Majid Daneshgar, "The Study of Persian Shi'ism in the Malay-Indonesian World: A Review of Literature from the Nineteenth Century Onwards," *Journal of Shi'a Islamic Studies* 7.2 (2014): 191–229.

42. Ibid.

43. Ori Goldberg, *Shi'i Theology in Iran: The Challenge of Religious Experience* (London and New York: Routledge, 2012), 34.

44. Murtaza Mutahhari, *Dastan-e Rastan* (Tehran: Sadra, 1980).

45. I thank *Journal of Shi'a Islamic Studies*, Islamic College of London, for granting me permission to reuse parts of my essay in this part. The original publications is Majid Daneshgar, "The Study of Persian Shi'ism in the Malay-Indonesian world: A Review of Literature from the Nineteenth Century Onwards," *Journal of Shi'a Islamic Studies* 7.2 (2014): 191–229.

46. Chiara Formichi, "Lovers of the Ahl al-Bayt: Indonesia's Shi'ism from the Keratin to Qum," *Inside Indonesia CV* (July–September 2011), accessed March 2, 2014, available at http://www.insideindonesia.org/weekly-articles/lovers-of-the-ahl-al-bayt/.

47. Van Bruinessen, "Genealogies of Islamic Radicalism in Post-Suharto Indonesia," 117–154.

48. Refer to the publications of Penerbit Sadra Press and RausyanFikr Institute.

49. The Indonesian Consortium for Religious Studies and the Cultural Center of the Iranian Embassy in Yogyakarta organized the International Conference on Historical and Cultural Presence of Shias in Southeast Asia: "Looking at Future Trajectories" in February 2013 at the Auditorium of University Club, Universitas Gadjah Mada, Yogyakarta, Indonesia. The conference proceedings, 336 pages long, have apparently

since been published in Indonesia. The main panels of the conference were: (a) "Dynamic Presence of Shias in Nusantara," with contributions by Jalaluddin Rakhmat, Siti Maryam, Yance Zadrak Rumahuru, and Kamaruzzaman Bustaman Ahmad; (b) "Dynamic Presence of Shias in Southeast Asia," with contributions by Syed Farid Alatas, Julispong Chularatana, Qasem Kakaei, Rabitah Mohamad Ghazali, and Yusuf Roque Santos Morales.

50. Although his works were read by Indonesians before the Iranian revolution, Indonesian scholars paid more attention to his works after the revolution.

51. "Syiah di Malaysia," *Portal Rasmi Fatwa Malaysia* (1996).

52. Pelancaran Buku, "Mengenal Hakikat Syiah" [online source].

53. Ibid., 140.

54. This recalls how Middle Eastern Shi'is, on the other hand, reject the statements of Sunnis regarding visiting shrines.

55. This is one of the oldest controversies between Sunnis and Shi'is; see Amir-Moezzi, *Silent Qur'an*.

56. Datuk Wan Zahidi, *Mengenal Hakikat Syiah*, 141.

57. See the book *Protokol-Protok Mesyuarat Para Pemimpin Ilmuwan Zions: Dengan Prakata dan Nota-Nota Penjelasan* (2014).

58. This was published in an article titled "Shi'as Are Not Muslims, Claims JAKIM."

59. Ibn Muhammad Ibrahim, *The Ship of Sulaiman*, ed. J. O'Kane (London: Routledge and Kegan Paul, 1972).

60. In Persian: *khandan-e bunnag*; in Arabic: *bunnag 'ashirah*. For more information on the Bunnag family, see "The Second Lineage – Sheikh Ahmad Qumi" [online source].

61. Marcinkowski Christopher, "The Safavid Presence in the Indian Ocean: A Reappraisal of the Ship of Solayman, A Seventeenth-Century Travel Account to Siam," in *Iran and the World in the Safavid Age*, ed. Willem Floor and Edmund Herzig (London: I. B. Tauris, 2012), 379–406; Mas'ud Taraqqi Jah, "Istita Mihwar: al-Islam fi Tayland wa-duwar al-Shaykh Ahmad al-Qummi," *al-Tawhid* 83 (1375/1996): 130–142.

62. "Sukhani az Shi'ayan-i Thailand," trans. Muhammad Ali Muhammadi, *Darsha'i az Maktab-e Islam* 11 (1357/1979): 59–60.

63. Mustaffa Abdullah discussed how many Thai and Malay Thai Qur'anic exegetical works were influenced by Sayyid Qutb. Abdullah, *Qur'anic Interpretation in Thailand*.

64. Azyumardi Azra, *Islam in the Indonesian World: An Account of Institutional Formation* (Jakarta: Mizan Pustaka, 2006), 164.

65. Haziya Hussein, "Qur'ānic Exegesis in Malaysia," in *The Qur'ān in the Malay-Indonesian World*, ed. Majid Daneshgar et al. (London: Routledge, 2016), 140–141.

66. Peter G. Riddell, *Islam and the Malay-Indonesian World: Transmission and Responses* (Honolulu: University of Hawaii Press, 2001), 193–194.

67. Haziya Hussein, "Qur'ānic Exegesis in Malaysia," 140–141.

68. Peter G. Riddell, *Islam and the Malay-Indonesian World*, 196.

69. Muhammad Thohir Aruf, "Tarjama al-Shaykh Nawawī al-Bantānī wa Tafsīruh" *Journal of Indonesian Islam* 4.1 (2010): 151–175.

70. See Muhammad Ali Ayyazi, *al-Mufassirun: Hayatuhum wa Manhajahum* (Tehran: Wizara al-Thaqafa wa l-Irshad al-Islami, 1373/1414/1994), 639–640.

71. Rippin, *Muslims*, introduction.

72. O. L. Helfrich, W. R. Winter, and D. M. J. Schiff, "Het Hasan-Hosein of Taboet-feest te Bengkoelen" ("The Hasan-Husayn or Tabut Celebration in Benkoelen"), *Internationales Archivfür Ethnographie* 1 (1888): 191–196.

73. Among East Asian Islamic studies, only the works by Toshihiko Izutsu, who was influenced, by Leo Weisgerber (d. 1985) and Henry Corbin (d. 1978), including *God and Man in the Koran: Semantics of the Koranic Weltanschauung*, which were different compared with those of Western scholars of the Qurʾān, have been examined in the Muslim academic context. Takeshita Masataka, "Toshihiko Izutsu's Contribution to Islamic Studies," *Journal of International Philosophy* 7 (2016): 78–81.

74. Alexander Thurston, "Interactions between Northern Nigeria and the Arab World in the Twentieth Century" (MA thesis, Georgetown University, 2009), 2.

75. Alex Thurston, "Nigerian Universities: Islamic Studies in Secular Universities," *The Revealer: A Review of Religion and Media* (2012) [online source].

76. Thurston, "Interactions between Northern Nigeria and the Arab World," 35.

77. Ibid., 59.

Chapter 4

1. For example, see Ahsan bu l-Filfil, *Nashʾat al-Kawn wa Hayrat al-ʿUlamaʾ* (Beirut: Dar al-Kutub al-ʿilmiyya, 2010); Kamal Rouhani, *Din-suzi-yi Muʿasir* (Sanandaj: Aras, 1390/2011).

2. Some of them are listed at Kutub wa Dirasat ʿan al–Istishraq [online source].

3. One of the harshest views is outlined in Jalal Al-e Ahmad's (d. 1969) *Occidentosis* (*Gharb-zadigi*). Parts of this chapter were also presented at academic symposiums in Kuala Lumpur and Frankfurt in 2013 and 2018 respectively.

4. Jalal Al-e Ahmad, *Occidentosis: A Plague from the West (Gharbzadegi)*, trans. R. Campbell and introduction by Hamid Algar (Berkeley, CA: Mizan Press, 1984).

5. Abu l-Qasim Sahab, *Farhang-i Khavar-shinasan dar Sharh-e Hal va Khadamat-e Danishmandan-e Iran-shinas va Mustashriqin* (Tehran: Shirkat-e Tabʿ-e Kitab, 1317/1938), 147 and 248.

6. H. Aboebakar, *Sedjarah al-Qurān*, 3rd ed. (Jakarta: Sinar Pudjangga, 1952), 9.

7. See James Clifford, "*Orientalism* by Edward W. Said," *History and Theory* 19.2 (1980): 204–223.

8. It is said that he deliberately concentrated on French and British literature and removed those of other colonial powers, including the Germans, Russians, Dutch, Greeks, and so on, meaning that he concluded that "Orientalism was a product of empire." Suzanne L. Marchand, *German Orientalism in the Age of Empire: Religion, Race, and Scholarship* (Cambridge: Cambridge University Press, 2009), xix. However, some Muslim scholars including Arkoun and Sadiq Jalal al-Aʿzam critiqued Said's approach towards the origin of the Orient as well as the Greek knowledge and civilization. See Hasan Ansari's blog "Kateban" [online source].

9. Daisuke Nishihara, "Said, Orientalism, and Japan," *Alif: Journal of Comparative Poetics* (2005): 241–253.
10. Said, *Orientalism*, 68.
11. I do agree with Traboulsi that Said's *Culture and Imperialism* published in 2004, "corrected and complemented Orientalism." Through this book, Said critiqued "Occidentosis—the tendency to blame all ills on the West—and rejected conspiracy theories." Fawwaz Traboulsi, "Edward Said's *Orientalism* Revisited," *The Translator* 15.1 (2009): 179–183.
12. Said, *Orientalism*, 84.
13. See C. E. Bosworth, *Eastward Ho! Diplomats, Travellers and Interpreters of the Middle East and Beyond, 1600–1940* (London: East & West Publishing, 2012), 60.
14. Nadia ʿAli Khalil Hamad, *Abu-Dib's Translation of Orientalism: A Critical Study* (MA thesis, an-Najah National University, 2006), 1.
15. Ibid.
16. Syed Abdul Vahid Muʿini, ed., *Maqalat-i Iqbal* (Lahore: Al–Qamar Enterprises, 1963), 222. See also S. Razi Wasti, "Dr Muhammad Iqbal from Nationalism to Universalism," *Iqbal Review* 1.19 (1978): 35–45.
17. For instance, see Yusuf Abdullah Puar, *Perjuangan Ayatullah Khomeini* (Jakarta: Pustaka Antara Jakarta, 1979).
18. See William B. Quandt, "The Middle East Crises," *Foreign Affairs* 58.3 (1979): 540–562.
19. See Edward W. Said, "Iran and the Press: Whose Holy War?," *Columbia Journalism Review* 18 (1980): 23–33. Read an analysis at David Zarnett, "Edward Said and the Iranian Revolution," *Democratiya* 3.9 (2007): 43–53.
20. Said, "Iran and the Press."
21. Malcolm H. Kerr, "Said Edward W., Orientalism (New York: Pantheon Books, 1978). Pp. xiii+ 368," *International Journal of Middle East Studies* 12.4 (1980): 544–547.
22. William Montgomery Watt, *Muslim-Christian Encounters: Perceptions and Misperception* (London: Routledge, 1991), 109.
23. James Clifford, "*Orientalism* by Edward W. Said," 204–223.
24. Edward W. Said, "Zionism from the Standpoint of Its Victims," *Social Text* 1 (1979): 7–58.
25. Ibid.
26. Edward W. Said, The *Question of Palestine* (New York: Vintage, 1979).
27. This was a statement by Joseph Conard, whose ideas were examined by Said as part of his Harvard PhD thesis. Said used this note when he started writing the article Edward W. Said, "The Idea of Palestine in the West," *MERIP Reports* 70 (1978): 3–11.
28. Said, *Orientalism*, 337.
29. Morrison, *The Origin of Others*, 101.
30. Ibid., 103.
31. Edward W. Said, *Sharq-shinasi*, trans. ʿAbdul-Rahim Gavahi, 7th ed. (Tehran: Dafter-e Nashr-e Farhang-e Islami, 1395/2016), 4, 6–7.
32. Ruhullah Khomeini, *Islamic Government* (Najaf: n.p., 1971), 47.
33. Said, *Orientalism*, 105.
34. Ibid., 303.

35. Ibid., 209.
36. Goldziher, *Schools of Koranic Commentators*, 42.
37. Said, *Orientalism*, 68.
38. Edward W. Said, *Sharq-shināsi*, trans. Lotf ʿAli Khunji, 3rd ed. (Tehran: Amir Kabir, 1394/2015), 13.
39. Ibid., 112; Edward W. Said, *Şarkiyatçılık: Batının Şark Anlayışları*, trans. Berna Yıldırım, 3rd ed. (Istanbul: Metis, 2017), 78.
40. Hartmann Schedel, *First English Edition of the Nuremberg Chronicle: Being the* Liber Chronicarum *of Dr. Hartmann Schedel* (Madison: University of Wisconsin Digital Collections Center, 2010), folio CLI verso.
41. Ibid.
42. Hugh Kennedy, *The Prophet and the Age of the Caliphates: The Islamic Near East from the Sixth to the Eleventh Century*, 3rd ed. (London: Routledge, 2016), 104.
43. Said, *Orientalism*, 32, 35.
44. Gil Anidjar, "Secularism," *Critical Inquiry* 33.1 (2006): 52–77.
45. See Fanon's works, esp. *Studies in a Dying Colonialism*.
46. Shariʿati, who studied in France, had translated Fanon's works into Persian.
47. Fanon, *Studies in a Dying Colonialism*, 23.
48. Said, *Orientalism*, 187.
49. Quoted in Tolan, *Sons of Ishmael*, xiii.
50. Said, *Orientalism*, 222.
51. Daniel Martin Varisco, *Reading Orientalism: Said and the Unsaid* (Seattle and London: University of Washington Press, 2007), 177–178.
52. Monica M. Ringer and A. Holly Shissler, "The al-Afghani-Renan Debate, Reconsidered," *Iran Nameh* 30.3 (2015): 28–45.
53. Excerpt from Nikki R. Keddie and Hamid Algar, eds., *An Islamic Response to Imperialism: Political and Religious Writings of Sayyid Jamal al-Din al-Afghani* (Berkeley and Los Angeles: University of California Press, 1968), 181–87.
54. Marwa el-Shakry, *Reading Darwin*, 195.
55. Majid Daneshgar, *Ṭanṭāwī Jawharī and the Qurʾān: Tafsīr and Social Concerns* (London: Routledge, 2017), 80–81,
56. Salim Khan, *Islamic Medicine*, 11–12.
57. Joseph E. B. Lumbard, "Decolonizing Qurʾanic Studies," presented at the Ninth Biennial Conference on the Qurʾān (London: SOAS, 2016).
58. Parvez Manzoor, "Method against Truth: Orientalism and Qurʾanic Studies," *Muslim World Book Review* 7 (1987): 33–49. This article has been republished by one of the most important government- and endowment-based Shiʿi networks [online source].
59. Muzzafar Iqbal, *The Qurʾān, Orientalism and the Encyclopaedia of the Qurʾān* (Kuala Lumpur: Islamic Book Trust, 2009), 20. Iqbal also delivered various lectures and published several works on Orientalism in various countries, including Arabia, Iran, Pakistan, Malaysia, etc., that rejected Europeans' Qurʾanic studies. See, for example, *Barrisi va naqd-e Qurʾān-pazhuhi dar sunnat-i daʾirat al-maʿarif-yi gharb (1913–2013) (Assessment and Critique of Qurʾānic Studies in Western Encyclopaedic Movement (1913–2013))* [online source]; other critical works on Orientalists' Islamic

studies that are influenced by Said's *Orientalism* are *Islam Aur Mustashriqin* by Hafiz Muhammad Zubayr in Urdu (2013) and *Islamic Studies in the West* by Mohsen Alviri in Persian (2014). As mentioned earlier, the latter, and due to the closeness of the Iran and Russia relationship, has just been translated into Russian.

60. Sheldon Pollock, "Future Philology?"

61. Bruce Fudge, "Philology and the Meaning of Sūrat al-Burūj," in *Islamic Studies Today: Essays in Honor of Andrew Rippin*, ed. Majid Daneshgar and Walid A. Saleh (Leiden and Boston: Brill, 2016), 239–259.

62. Hamid Parsa-nia and Hadi Beygi Malik Abad, "Sharq-Shinasi-yi Post-Modern: Zamina-ha va Payamad-ha," *Contemporary Islamic Thought Studies* 2.1 (2016): 33–55.

63. Ibid.

64. Parviz Azadi and Majid Ma'arif, "Tahlil va naqd-e mutala'at-e Qur'āni-yi mustasghriqan," *Qur'ān Shinakht* 5.1 (2012): 125–154.

65. 'Abd al-Radi Muhammad 'Abd al-Muhsin, *Madha Yurid al-Gharb min al-Qur'ān* (Riyadh: al-Bayan, 2006), 141–142.

66. Varisco, *Reading Orientalism*, 184.

67. Ibid.

68. Alessandro S. Crisafulli, "A Neglected English Imitation of Montesquieu's *Lettres Persanes*," *Modern Language Quarterly* 14.2 (1953): 209–216.

69. Eliza Haywood, *Adventures of Eovaai Princess of Ijaveo: A Pre-Adamitical History*, ed. Earla Wilputte (Ontario: Broadview Press Ltd., 1999), 20–21.

70. *The Persian Letters, Continued; Or, the Second Volume of Letters from Selim at London, to Mirza at Ispahan* (London: E. Davis, 1735), 1.

71. Said, *Orientalism*, 60.

72. Srinivas Aravamudan, *Enlightenment Orientalism: Resisting the Rise of the Novel* (Chicago: Chicago University Press, 2012), 8.

73. Ibid.

74. University of Kent (UK), "The Arabian Nights in European Literature—An Anthology," in *Encounter with the Orient* [online source].

75. Yuriko Yamanaka and Tetsuo Nishio, eds., *The Arabian Nights and Orientalism: Perspectives from East and West* (New York: I. B. Tauris, 2006), 220.

76. Robert Irwin, *The Arabian Nights: A Companion* (New York: Tauris Paperbacks, 2010).

77. "The Arabian Nights in European Literature—An Anthology."

78. *Ordering the Orient: A History of the Publication of Eastern Texts in Europe and America and the Production of a Cultural Economy of Orientalism, 1850–1939* [online source].

79. Raymond J. Howgego, *Encyclopedia of Exploration: Invented and Apocryphal Narratives of Travel* (New South Wales: Hordern House, 2013), vii–ix.

80. To read a review of Howgego's work, see Danielle Clode, "Review: *Encyclopedia of Exploration: Invented and Apocryphal Narratives of Travel*," *Transnational Literature* 6.1 (2013): 1.

81. See Howgego, *Encyclopedia of Exploration*, 174.

82. Sir Humphery Lunatick (Francis Gentleman), *A Trip to the Moon. Containing an Account of the Island of Noibla. Its Inhabitants, Religious and Political Customs, etc.,* 2nd ed. (London: S Crowder, 1765), 24–27.

83. Howgego, *Encyclopedia of Exploration,* 241.

84. Ibid., 203.

85. Chevalier Ramsay, *The Travels of Cyrus to Which Is Annexed, A Discourse upon the Theology and Mythology of the Ancients* (Dublin: S. Powell, 1728), 2. Such compliments for the Persians recall Browne's preface to *The Persian Revolution* in which he admires the Persians' desire for knowledge and refers to a prophetic statement—whose authenticity is disputed—that "were knowledge in the Pleiades, some of the Persians would reach it" (*law kan^a al-'ilm bi l-thurayya lana lah^u rijal min al-Faris*). Edward G. Browne, *The Persian Revolution of 1905–1909* (Cambridge, MA: Cambridge University Press, 1910), xv.

86. Bosworth, *Eastward Ho!,* 32–33.

87. Ibid.

88. Ibid.

89. Henry Stubbe, *An Account of the Rise and Progress of Mohametanism,* ed. Hafiz Mahmud Khan Shairani (London: Luzac & Co., 1911), 178.

90. There are many works on Asian and Islamic regions and languages produced by Europeans in which the author(s) admires the rich culture and literature of Orientals. For instance, William Jones gives a sympathetic view on Persians and the Persian language in his preface on the book of the Persian grammar. William Jones, *A Grammar of the Persian Language* (London: Printed for J Murray and J Sewell 1797), preface.

91. Said, *Orientalism,* 330.

92. Ibid., 158.

93. Bosworth, *Eastward Ho!,* 60.

94. Lawrence Venuti, *The Scandals of Translation: Towards an Ethics of Difference* (London and New York: Routledge, 1998), 67.

95. Said, *Orientalism,* 68–69.

96. Marwa Elshakry, "Global Darwin: Eastern Enchantment," *Nature* 461 (7268) (2009): 1200–1201.

97. This point was made in a section titled *Laysa madhhab Darwin jadidan* ("Darwin's school of thought/Darwinism is not new").

98. E.g., Muhammad Hilmi, *'Ulama' al-Gharb Yadkhulun al-Islam* (Cairo: Dar al-Nahda al-'Arabiyya, 1994)

99. Email sent to me on November 12, 2016.

100. I thank Brill Academic Publishers for granting permission to reuse a few parts of my essay already published as Majid Daneshgar, "Behind the Scenes: A Review of Western Figure s' Supportive Comments Regarding the Qur'ān," *al-Bayan Journal of Qur'an and Hadith Studies* 11.2 (2013): 131–153.

101. Robert Crawford. *The God/Man/World Triangle: A Dialogue between Science and Religion* (New York: St. Martin's Press, 1997), 67.

102. "Quran from the Point of View of Non-Muslims," *Roshd* [online source].

103. Subhi Raghib, *Haqaiq Majhoulah 'an al-Kawn* (Homs, Syria: n.p., 1927); Max Jammer, *Einstein and Religion: Physics and Theology* (Princeton, NJ: Princeton University Press, 2011), 9.

104. Raghib, *Haqaiq Majhoulah.*

105. 'Abbas Mahmud al-'Aqqad, "Einstein al-Mafhūm," *al-Muqtataf* 1.1 (1929): 16–22. Max Jammer, *Einstein and Religion: Physics and Theology*, 9–10.

106. Tantawi Jawhari, "The Theory of Relativity: Einstein," *Humayun* 8 (1935/ 1314): 13–15.

107. Zakir Kapadia, *Einstein's Theory in the Holy Quran*, http://khutbahbank.org.uk/v2/ ?p=537.

108. Nurul Maghfirah, *99 fakta Menakjubkan dalam al-Qur'ān* (Jakarta: Mizan, 2015), 111–112.

109. Tonči Matulić, "Theology: Einstein's Concept of God with the Theological Implications on the Einstein's Physical View of the World," *Filozofska Istraživanja* 26.3 (2006): 531–557. See also *Relativity and Quantum Physics*, International Catholic University [online source].

110. *Einstein Was a Shiite Muslim* [online source].

111. "Masa Sih Albert Einstein Seorang Syiah" [online source]; see also "Einstein and Islam"; "Did Einstein Write a Letter to the Late Ayatollah Boroujerdi?" [online source].

112. "The Letter of Einstein to Ayatullah Brujirdi" (*matn-i name-ye Einstein bi Ayatollah Brujirdi*) [online source].

113. "Albert Einstein in a letter to Ayatollah Brujirdi: 'I prefer Islam'" (*Albert Einstein dar namei bi Ayatollah Brujirdi*: "Islam ra bar tamami-ye Adyan-e Jahan tarjih midaham") [online source].

114. "Some Notes of Einstein's Final Treatise" (*guzid-ei az akharin risali-yi Einstein*), trans. 'Issa Mahdavi, Iskandar Jahangiri [online source].

115. Felipe Cabello, "El gran europeo Georg Friedrich Nicolai: médico y pacifista. Berlín, Alemania, 1874-Santiago, Chile, 1964," *Revista médica de Chile* 141.4 (2013): 535–539.

116. Einstein's response to Gutkind is preserved in the Einstein Archives, No. 124-379, dated 22.06.1944.

117. James Randerson, "Childish Superstition: Einstein's Letter Makes View of Religion Relatively Clear," *The Guardian* (May 13, 2008) [online source].

118. *Einstein's "God Letter" to Eric B. Gutkind: On the Existence of God* [online source]; see also *Albert Einstein and Religion* [online source].

119. *Einstein's "God Letter" to Eric B. Gutkind.* I thank the Science Museum of Jerusalem for providing me with interesting information about the letters of Einstein.

Chapter 5

1. "Rakaman bagi Tafsir al-Qur'an in the 17th Century Malay World oleh Professor Dr. Peter G Riddle di Balai Ilmu, Akademi Pengajian Islam pada 23 September 2014" [online source].

2. Majid Daneshgar, "Philosophical Perspectives on Modern Qur'anic Exegesis: Key Paradigms and Concepts, by Massimo Campanini," *Reading Religion* (2018) [online source].

3. Vika Gardner, E. Carolina Mayes, and Salman Hameed, "Preaching Science and Islam: Dr. Zakir Naik and Discourses of Science and Islam in Internet Videos," *Die Welt des Islams* 58.3 (2018): 357–391; Vika Gardner, and Salman Hameed, "Creating Meaning through Science: 'The Meaning of Life' Video and Muslim Youth Culture in Australia," *Journal of Media and Religion* 17.2 (2018): 61–73; Raoof Mir, "Zakir Naik and His Audiences: A Case Study of Srinagar, Kashmir," *Journal of Religion, Media and Digital Culture* 7.2 (2018): 203–222.

4. Majid Daneshgar, *Tarjuma, Naqd va Barrisi-yi Kitab-e Qurʾān va ʿilm, Sazigari ya Na-sazigari, Dr. Zakir Naik* (MA thesis, University of Qum, 1389/2010).

5. "Warnings about Potential Muslim Radicalization Went Ignored, Ex-U of C Prof Says," *CBC News*, June 25, 2014 [online source].

6. Edward W. Said, *The Myth of the "Clash of Civilizations": Professor Edward Said in Lecture* (Northampton, MA: Media Education Foundation, 1998).

7. Samuel P. Huntington, "The Clash of Civilizations?," *Foreign Affairs* 72.3 (1993): 31–32.

8. Michel Houellebecq, *Soumission* (Paris: Flammarion, 2015).

9. It should be noted that some Iranians including Mehrdad ʿAbbasi have translated a few *tafsiri* articles of Saleh (but not those related to the importance of the Bible among Muslim commentators).

10. S. Mehdi Husayini, "Faraz va Furud-e Qadi ʿAbd al-Jabbar-e Muʿtazili by Gabriel S. Reynolds," *Ittilaʿat-e Hikmat va Maʿrifat* 28 (1387/2008): 17–25.

11. Mojtaba Zorvani, et al. "A Study of Gabriel Reynolds' Ideas Regarding the Guardianship over Mary in the Quran," *Pajuhash-ha-ye Quran va Hadith* 49/2 (2016–2017), 269–284.

12. Said, "On the University."

13. Michel Foucault, "The Subject and Power."

14. Ibid.

15. Ibid.

16. Said, "On the University."

17. Majid Daneshgar, "New Zealand and Islam Deserve Deeper Joint Study," *Otago Daily Times* (March 2015) [online source].

18. A letter sent to the author (personal archives).

19. Ibid.

Bibliography

I Printed Works

ʿAbd al-Radi Muhammad ʿAbd al-Muhsin. *Madha Yurid al-Gharb min al-Qurʾān.* Riyadh: al-Bayan, 2006.

Abdullah, Mustafa. "Qurʾanic Interpretation in Thailand." In *The Qurʾān in the Malay-Indonesian World: Context and Interpretation*, edited by Majid Daneshgar, Peter G. Riddell, and Andrew Rippin, 61–82. London and New York: Routledge, 2016.

Aboebakar, H. *Sedjarah al–Qurān.* 3rd ed. Jakarta: Sinar Pudjangga, 1952.

Adams, Charles J. "Reflections on the Work of John Wansbrough." *Method & Theory in the Study of Religion* 9.1 (1997): 75–90.

Ahmed, Shahab. *What Is Islam?: The Importance of Being Islamic.* Princeton, NJ and Oxford: Princeton University Press, 2016.

Ajmal, Hafiz Muhammad, et al. "Qurʾanic Diacritical Marks and Dot–System and the Orientalists: A Critical Study." *Hazara Islamicus* 4.1 (2015): 1–18.

ʿAli-Dust, Abolghasim, et al. "Tahlil hamsani–yi Zaban-i Qurʾān va Qawm va Pay–amad–ha–yi an." *Dhihn* 54 (1392/2013): 5–38.

Al-e Ahmad, Jalal. *Occidentosis: A Plague from the West (Gharbzadegi).* Translated by R. Campbell and introduction by Hamid Algar. Berkeley, CA: Mizan Press, 1984.

Alviri, Mohsen. *Mutaliʿat–e Islami dar Gharb.* 7th ed. Tehran: SAMT, 1393/2014.

Amir–Moezzi, Mohammad–Ali. "Powers David S., Zayd: the little known story of Muḥammad's adopted son, Philadelphia, University of Pennsylvania Press, 2014, 175 p." Revue des mondes musulmans et de la Méditerranée [En ligne] (2015): 139.

Amir-Moezzi, Mohammad Ali. *The Silent Qurʾān and the Speaking Qurʾān: Scriptural Sources of Islam Between History and Fervor.* Translated by Eric Ormsby. New York: Columbia University Press, 2016.

Anidjar, Gil. "Secularism." *Critical Inquiry* 33.1 (2006): 52–77.

al-ʿAqqad, ʿAbbas Mahmud. "Einstein al–Mafhūm." *al–Muqtataf* 1.1 (1929): 16–22.

Aravamudan, Srinivas. *Enlightenment Orientalism: Resisting the Rise of the Novel.* Chicago: Chicago University Press, 2012.

Arif, Syamsuddin. *Orientalis dan Diabolisme Pemikiran.* Jakarta: Gema Insani, 2008.

Aruf, Muhammad Thohir. "Tarjama al–Shaykh Nawawī al–Bantānī wa Tafsīruh." *Journal of Indonesian Islam* 4.1 (2010): 151–175.

Al-Attas, Syed Muhammad Naguib. *The Mysticism of Hamzah Fansuri.* Kuala Lumpur: University of Malaya, 1970.

Ayyazi, Muhammad ʿAli. *al–Mufassirun: Hayatuhum wa Manhajahum.* Tehran: Wizara al–Thaqafa wa l–Irshad al–Islami, 1414/1373/1994.

Azadi, Parviz and Majid Maʿarif. "Tahlil va Naqd–e Mutaliʿat–e Qurʾāni–yi Mustashriqan." *Qurʾān–shinakht* 5.1 (1391/2012): 125–154.

Azadi, Parviz. "Arzyabi Azad Andishi dar Ravish–e Mutalaʿat–e Qurʾāni–yi Andrew Rippin." *Bonyan–e Marsus–Iran Ministry of Science, Research and Technology* 8.2 (1393/ 2014): 52–55.

Azra, Azyumardi. *Islam in the Indonesian World: An Account of Institutional Formation.* Jakarta: Mizan Pustaka, 2006.

Badawi, ʿAbd al–Rahman. *Ensiklopedi tokoh orientalis.* Translated by Amroeni Drajat. Yogyakarta: LKIS, 2003.

Badawi, ʿAbd al–Rahman. *Mawsuʿa al–Mustashriqin.* 2nd ed. Beirut: Dar al–Malayin, 1993.

Bahri, Hossein. "The Role of Translation Movements in the Cultural Maintenance of Iran from the Era of Cyrus the Great up to the Constitutional Revolution." *Translation Journal* 15.4 (2011): 1–22.

Bausani, Alessandro. *Note sui Vocaboli Persiani in Malese–Indonesiano.* Naples: Istituto Universitario Orientale, 1964.

Bausani, Alessandro. "Taʾthir–e Farhang va Zaban–e Farsi dar Adabiyyat–e Andunizi." *Danishkadih Adabiyyat va ʿUlum–i Insani Danishgah Tehran* 53 (1345/1966): 4–15.

Bazzano, Elliott A. "Ibn Taymiyya, Radical Polymath, Part 2: Intellectual Contributions." *Religion Compass* 9.4 (2015): 117–139.

Bell, Richard. *Introduction to the Qurʾān.* Edited by William Montgomery Watt. Translated by Bahaʾiddin Khurramshahi. Qum: Markaz–e Tarjuman–e Qurʾān–e Majid bi Zaban– ha–yi Khariji, 1382/2003.

Bell, Richard. *Introduction to the Qurʾān.* Edited by William Montgomery Watt. Translated by Lilian D. Tedjasudhana as Pengantar Quran. Jakarta: INIS, 1998.

Bigliardi, Stefano. "The Strange Case of Dr. Bucaille: Notes for a Re-Examination." *The Muslim World* 102.2 (2012): 248–263.

Bilgrami, Akeel. *Secularism, Identity, and Enchantment.* Cambridge, MA and London: Harvard University Press, 2014.

Bosworth, Clifford Edmund. *Eastward Ho! Diplomats, Travellers and Interpreters of the Middle East and Beyond, 1600–1940.* London: East & West Publishing, 2012.

Bourne, Edward Gaylord. "Leopold von Ranke." *The Sewanee Review* 4.4 (1896): 385–401.

Brohi, A. K. "Islamization of Knowledge: A First Step to Integrate and Develop the Muslim Personality and Outlook." In *Conference Proceeding on Islam: Source and Purpose of Knowledge,* 5–12. Herndon, VA: International Institute of Islamic Thought, 1988.

Brown, Ian. *The School of Oriental and African Studies.* Cambridge: Cambridge University Press, 2016.

Browne, Edward G. *The Persian Revolution of 1905–1909.* Cambridge: Cambridge University Press, 1910.

van Bruinessen, Martin. "Genealogies of Islamic Radicalism in Post-Suharto Indonesia." *South East Asia Research* 10.2 (2002): 117–154.

Bucaille, Maurice. *The Bible, the Qurʾān and Science.* Translated by Alastair D. Pannell and Maurice Bucaille. Tripoli: Islamic Call Society, 1978.

Burton, John. *The Collection of the Qurʾān.* Cambridge: Cambridge University Press, 1977/1979.

Cabello, Felipe. "El gran europeo Georg Friedrich Nicolai: médico y pacifista. Berlín, Alemania, 1874–Santiago, Chile, 1964." *Revista médica de Chile* 141.4 (2013): 535–539.

Casewit, Yousef. "A Muslim Scholar of the Bible: Prooftexts from Genesis and Matthew in the Qurʾān Commentary of Ibn Barrajān of Seville (d. 536/1141)." *Journal of Qurʾānic Studies* 18.1 (2016): 1–48.

Chaudhary, Muhammad A. "Orientalism on Variant Readings of the Qur'an: The Case of Arthur Jeffery." *The American Journal of Islamic Social Sciences* 12.2 (1995): 170–184.

Chaudhary, Muhammad A. "Oryantalizmin Kıraat Farklılıklarına Bakışının Tenkidi-Arthur Jeffery Örneği." çeviren Mahmut Ay. *İstanbul Üniversitesi İlahiyat Fakültesi Dergisi* 25 (2011): 189–204.

Christopher, Marcinkowski. "The Safavid Presence in the Indian Ocean: A Reappraisal of the Ship of Solayman, A Seventeenth-Century Travel Account to Siam." In *Iran and the World in the Safavid Age*, edited by Willem Floor and Edmund Herzig, 379–406. London: I. B. Tauris, 2012.

Clifford, James. "*Orientalism* by Edward W. Said." *History and Theory* 19.2 (1980): 204–223.

Clode, Danielle. "Review: Encyclopedia of Exploration: Invented and Apocryphal Narratives of Travel." *Transnational Literature* 6.1 (2013): 1.

Crawford. Robert. *The God/Man/World Triangle: A Dialogue between Science and Religion*. New York: St. Martin's Press, 1997.

Crisafulli, Alessandro S. "A Neglected English Imitation of Montesquieu's Lettres Persanes." *Modern Language Quarterly* 14.2 (1953): 209–216.

Crone, Patricia, and Michael J. Cook. *Hagarism: The Making of the Islamic World*. Cambridge: Cambridge University Press, 1977.

Daneshgar, Majid. "159 Einstein's Theory of Relativity: [Naẓariyya Nisbiyya Anshtayn]." In *Ṭanṭāwī Jawharī and the Qurʾān: Tafsīr and Social Concerns in the Twentieth Century*, 159–161. London: Routledge, 2017.

Daneshgar, Majid. "Behind the Scenes: A Review of Western Figures' Supportive Comments Regarding the Qurʾān." *al-Bayan Journal of Qurʾān and Hadith Studies* 11.2 (2013): 131–153.

Daneshgar, Majid. "David S. Powers, *Zayd*." *Der Islam* 94.1 (2017): 299–304.

Daneshgar, Majid. "Dhū l-Qarnayn in Modern Malay Commentaries and Other Literature on Qurʾanic Themes." In *The Qurʾān in the Malay-Indonesian World: Context and Interpretation*, edited by Majid Daneshgar, Peter G. Riddell, and Andrew Rippin, 212–228. London: Routledge, 2016.

Daneshgar, Majid. "'Father of Ignorance': How and Why Marginal Figures within Islam Remain Marginal." FRIAS Lunch Lecture 2018, Ignorance-What We Don't Know. Freiburg: Freiburg Institute for Advanced Studies, University of Freiburg, June 2018.

Daneshgar, M. "The Qurʾān, Orientalists and Western Scholars." *al-Bayan Journal of Qurʾān and Hadith Studies* 10.2 (2012): 4–9.

Daneshgar, Majid. "The Study of Persian Shiʿism in the Malay–Indonesian World: A Review of Literature from the Nineteenth Century Onwards." *Journal of Shiʿa Islamic Studies* 7.2 (2014): 191–229.

Daneshgar, Majid. "The Study of Qurʾān Interpretation in the Malay-Indonesian World: A Select Bibliography." In *The Qurʾān in the Malay-Indonesian World: Context and Interpretation*, edited by Majid Daneshgar, Peter G. Riddell, and Andrew Rippin, 7–22. London: Routledge, 2016.

Daneshgar, Majid. *Ṭanṭāwī Jawharī and the Qurʾān: Tafsīr and Social Concerns in the Twentieth Century*. London: Routledge, 2017.

Daneshgar, Majid. "Tarjuma, Naqd va Barrisi-yi Kitab-e Qurʾān va ʿilm, Sazigari ya Nasazigari, Dr. Zakir Naik." MA thesis, University of Qum, 1389/2010.

Daneshgar, Majid, and Donald Kerr, *Middle Eastern and Islamic Materials in Special Collections, University of Otago*. Dunedin: University of Otago Special Collections, 2017.

Daryaee, Touraj. "The Study of Ancient Iran in the Twentieth Century." *Iranian Studies* 42.4 (2009): 579–589.

Donner, Fred M. *Narratives of Islamic Origins: The Beginnings of Islamic Historical Writing.* Princeton, NJ: The Darwin Press Inc., 1998.

Edalatnejad, Saeid. "Books of Scholars of the Time of Nāṣir al-Dīn Shāh." In *Encyclopaedias about Muslim Civilizations,* edited by Aptin Khanbaghi, 138. Edinburgh: Edinburgh University Press in association with the Aga Khan University, 2009.

Elshakry, Marwa. "Global Darwin: Eastern Enchantment." *Nature* 461: 7268 (2009): 1200–1201.

Elshakry, Marwa. *Reading Darwin in Arabic, 1860–1950.* Chicago: University of Chicago Press, 2014.

Erdoğdu, A. Teyfur. "Osmanli Devrinde Son Sadrazamlar." In *Encyclopaedias about Muslim Civilizations,* edited by Aptin Khanbaghi, 141–142. Edinburgh: Edinburgh University Press in association with the Aga Khan University, 2009.

Fanon, Frantz. *A Dying Colonialism.* Translated by Haakon Chevalier. New York: Grove Press, 1994.

Filfil, Ahsan bu l. *Nash'at al-Kawn wa Hayrat al-'Ulama'.* Beirut: Dar al-Kutub al-'ilmiyya, 2010.

Foucault, Michel. "The Subject and Power." *Critical Inquiry* 8.4 (1982): 777–795.

Fudge, Bruce. "Philology and the Meaning of Sūrat al-Burūj." In *Islamic Studies Today: Essays in Honor of Andrew Rippin,* edited by Majid Daneshgar and Walid A. Saleh, 239–259. Leiden and Boston: Brill, 2016.

Furlow, Christopher A. "Intersections of the Qur'ān and Sience in Contemporary Malaysia." In *The Qur'ān in the Malay–Indonesian World: Context and Interpretation,* edited by Majid Daneshgar, Peter G. Riddell, and Andrew Rippin, 229–250. London: Routledge, 2016.

Fārūqī, Ismā'īl Rājī al. "Islamization of Knowledge: Problems, Principles and Prospective." In *Conference Proceeding on Islam: Source and Purpose of Knowledge,* 15–63. Herndon, VA: International Institute of Islamic Thought, 1988.

Gabrieli, Giuseppe. "Fakhr-al-din al-Razi." *Isis* 7.1 (1925): 9–13.

Goldberg, Ori. *Shi'i Theology in Iran: The Challenge of Religious Experience.* London and New York: Routledge, 2012.

Goldziher, Ignaz. *Schools of Koranic Commentators, with Introduction on Goldziher and Hadith from "Geschichte des Arabischen Schrifttums" by Fuat Sezgin.* Edited and translated by Wolfgang H. Behn. Weisbaden: Harrassowitz, 2006.

Graham, William A. "Those Who Study and Teach the Qur'ān." In *Proceedings of the International Congress for the Study of the Qur'ān, Australian National University,* Canberra, May 8–13, 1980, 9–28. Canberra: Australian National University, 1981.

Griffith, Sidney. *The Bible in Arabic: The Scriptures of the People of the Book.* Princeton, NJ: Princeton University Press, 2015.

Habib, 'Abd al-Maqsud. "Fakhr al-Shabab al-Muslim: Zayd b. Haritha." *Minbar al–Islam* 42.2 (1404/1983): 70–72.

Haddad, Gibril Fouad. "A Response to Andrew Rippin's Review of The Integrated Encyclopedia of Qur'ān, Volume I." *Islamic Sciences* 14.1 (2016): 91–94.

Hallaq, Wael. *An Introduction to Islamic Law.* Cambridge: Cambridge University Press, 2009.

Haqqani, Sakina. "Barrasi–yi ara–yi duktur Bucaille va Professor Arberry piramun–e masuniyyat–e Qur'ān az tahrif." *Bayinnat* 69 (1390/2011): 89–96.

Hassan al–Himyari, Bashir B. "Mushaf of Tübingen University No (MaVI165): Descriptive and Analytical Study." *Journal of al-Imam al-Shatibi Institute for Qur'anic Studies* 20 (1436/2015): 13–84.

Haywood, Eliza. *Adventures of Eovaai Princess of Ijaveo: A Pre–Adamitical History.* Edited by Earla Wilputte. Ontario: Broadview Press Ltd., 1999.

Hefner, Robert W., and Muhammad Qasim Zaman, eds. *Schooling Islam: The Culture and Politics of Modern Muslim Education.* Princeton, NJ: Princeton University Press, 2007.

Helfrich, O. L., W. R. Winter, and D. M. J. Schiff. "Het Hasan–Hosein of Taboet-feest te Bengkoelen." *Internationales Archiv für Ethnographie* 1 (1888): 191–196.

Heller, B. and Andrew Rippin, "Yāfit̲h̲." In *Encyclopaedia of Islam*, 2nd ed. Edited by P. Bearman, Th. Bianquis, C. E. Bosworth, E. van Donzel, and W. P. Heinrichs, vol. 11, 236–237. Leiden: Brill, 1994–2001.

Hilmi, Muhammad. *'Ulama' al-Gharb Yadkhulun al-Islām.* Cairo: Dar al-Nahda al-'Arabiyya, 1994.

Himmich, Bensalem. *Al-'Arab wa l-Islam fi Maraya al-Istishraq.* Cairo: Dar al-Shuruq, 2011.

Houellebecq, Michel. *Soumission.* Paris: Flammarion, 2015.

Howgego, Raymond J. *Encyclopedia of Exploration: Invented and Apocryphal Narratives of Travel.* New South Wales: Hordern House, 2013.

Hughes, Aaron W. *Situating Islam: The Past and Future of an Academic Discipline.* Sheffield: Equinox Publishing Ltd, 2007.

Hughes, Aaron W. *Theorizing Islam: Disciplinary Deconstruction and Reconstruction.* London: Routledge, 2014.

Huntington, Samuel P. "The Clash of Civilizations?" *Foreign Affairs* 72.3 (1993): 22–49.

Husayini, S. Mehdi. "Faraz va furud-e qadi 'Abd al-Jabbar-e Mu'tazili by Gabriel S. Reynolds." *Ittila'at–e Hikmat va Ma'rifat* 28 (1387/2008): 17–25.

Hussein, Haziya. "Qur'ānic Exegesis in Malaysia." In *The Qur'ān in the Malay-Indonesian World,* edited by Majid Daneshgar, Peter G. Riddell, and Andrew Rippin, 137–164. London: Routledge, 2016.

Ibn Muhammad Ibrahim. *The Ship of Sulaiman.* Edited by J. O'Kane. London: Routledge & Kegan Paul, 1972.

Iqbal, Muhammad. "First World Conference on Muslim Education and Its Possible Implications for British Muslims." *Learning for Living* 17.3 (1978): 123–125.

Iqbal, Muzaffar. *The Qur'an, Orientalism and the Encyclopaedia of the Qur'an.* Selangor: Islamic Book Trust, 2009.

Irwin, Robert. *The Arabian Nights: A Companion.* New York: Tauris Paperbacks, 2010.

Islamic World Science Citation Center (ISC). *Policy Plan.* Tehran: The Supreme Council for Cultural Revolution, 2008.

Izutsu, Toshihiko. *God and Man in the Koran: Semantics of the Koranic Weltanschauung.* Tokyo: Keio Institute of Cultural and Linguistics Studies, 1964.

Jammer, Max. *Einstein and Religion: Physics and Theology.* Princeton, NJ: Princeton University Press, 2011.

Jan Nezhad, Mohsen, and Jalal-e-Din Jalali. *English for the Students of Qur'anic Sciences and Tradition.* Tehran: SAMT, 2014.

Jeshurun, Chandran. *Malaysia: Fifty Years of Diplomacy, 1957–2007.* Kuala Lumpur: The Other Press, 2007.

Jones, William. *A Grammar of the Persian Language.* London: Printed for J Murray and J Sewell, 1797.

Karimi-nia, Morteza. "The Qur'an supposedly handwritten by Imam Reza, kept at the Astan-e Quds Library (Mashhad) and its supplements: a comparison between MS 1586 and MS 4354a, and a few Qur'anic folios at London's auctions." *Ayini-yi Miras* 60 (1396/2017): 31–70.

Keddie, Nikki R., and Hamid Algar, eds. *An Islamic Response to Imperialism: Political and Religious Writings of Sayyid Jamal al-Din al-Afghani.* Berkeley and Los Angeles: University of California Press, 1968.

Kennedy, Hugh. *The Prophet and the Age of the Caliphates: The Islamic Near East from the Sixth to the Eleventh Century.* 3rd ed. London: Routledge, 2016.

Kermani, Navid. "From Revelation to Interpretation: Nasr Hamid Abu Zayd and the Literary Study of the Qur'ān." In *Modern Muslim Intellectuals and the Qur'ān*, edited by Suha Taji-Farouki, 169–192. Oxford and London: Oxford University Press in association with the Institute of Ismaili Studies, 2004.

Kerr, Malcolm. H. "Said Edward W., Orientalism (New York: Pantheon Books, 1978). Pp. xiii+ 368." *International Journal of Middle East Studies* 12.4 (1980): 544–547.

Khalifa, Mohammad. *Al-Quran dan Orientalisme.* Translated by Zakaria Stapa and Mohamad Asin Dollah. Kuala Lumpur: Dewan Bahasa dan Pustaka, 1993.

Khalifa, Mohammad. *The Sublime Quran and Orientalism.* 2nd ed. Karachi: International Islamic Publisher, 1989.

Khalil Hamad, Nadia 'Ali. "Abu-Dib's Translation of Orientalism: A Critical Study." MA thesis, an–Najah National University, 2006.

Khattab, Mahmud Sh. "Zayd b. Haritha al-Kalbi: al-Qa'id al-Shahid." *al-Buhuth al-Islamiyya* 15 (1406/1985): 205–236.

Khomeini, Ruhullah. *Islamic Government.* Najaf: n.p., 1971.

Khurramshad, Muhammad Baqir. *Danishgah-e tamaddun-saz: tamaddun-e nuvin-e Islami-Irani.* Edited by Mustafa 'Abbasi Muqaddam. Tehran: Ministry of Research, Science and Technology, 1386/2007.

Khurramshahi, Baha'iddin. "Muqaddama bar Tarjuma-yi Qur'ān-e Richard Bell, edited/revised by Montgomery Watt." *Tarjuman-e Wahy* 1 (1376/1997): 83–103.

Khvansari, Muhammad Baqir. *Rawdat al-Jannat fi Ahwal al-'Ulama' wa l-Sadat.* 8 vols. Tehran: Maktabah–i Isma'iliyan, 1970.

"Kitab-e Da'ira al-Ma'arif-e Qur'an bar rushd-e Qur'ān-pazhuhi dar Iran athar guzasht." *Mehr News*, Khurdad 1396/June 2017.

Kotz, David. "The State of Official Marxism in China Today." *Monthly Review* 59.4 (2007): 58–64.

Koç, Mehmet Akif. "The Influence of Western Qur'ānic Scholarship in Turkey." *Journal of Qur'anic Studies* 14.1 (2012): 9–44.

Kramsch, Claire. *Language and Culture.* Oxford: Oxford University Press, 1998.

Leirvik, Oddbjørn. "History as a Literary Weapon: The Gospel of Barnabas in Muslim–Christian Polemics." *Studia Theologica* 56.1 (2002): 4–26.

Loimeier, Roman. "Translating the Qur'ān in Sub-Saharan Africa: Dynamics and Disputes." *Journal of Religion in Africa* 35.4 (2005): 403–423.

Lumbard, Joseph E. B. "Decolonizing Qur'anic Studies." Presented at the Ninth Biennial Conference on the Qur'ān. London: SOAS, 2016.

Lunatick, Sir Humphery (Francis Gentleman). *A Trip to the Moon. Containing an Account of the Island of Noibla. Its Inhabitants, Religious and Political Customs.* 2nd ed. London: S Crowder, 1765.

Ma'ayergi, Hassan. "Translations of the Meanings of the Holy Qur'an into Minority Languages: The Case of Africa." *Institute of Muslim Minority Affairs Journal* 14.1–2 (1993): 156–180.

McAuliffe, Jane Dammen. "A Concluding Appreciation." In *Islamic Studies Today: Essays in Honor of Andrew Rippin*, edited by Majid Daneshgar and Walid A. Saleh, 386–395. Leiden: Brill, 2016.

Mahdavi Rad, Muhammad 'Ali, and Nusrat Nilsaz. "Tarikhgudhari-ye Tafsir-e Mansub bi Ibn 'Abbas. Naqd-e ravish-e tahlil-e adabi-yi Wansbrough va Rippin." *Tahqiqat-e 'Ulum-e Qur'an va Hadith* 3.6 (1385/2006): 27–64.

al-Majistir al-Tanfidhi fi l-Tamwil al-Islami. Riyadh: Jami'a al-Malik 'Abd al-Aziz, n.d.

Makarim Shirazi, Nasir. *Tafsir Nemuna*. Tehran: Dar al-Kutub al-Islamiyya, 1995.

Ma'muri, 'Ali. "Danish-e Zaban Shinasi va Karburd-ha-yi an dar Mutali'at-e Qur'ani." *Qur'an va 'ilm* 1 (1386/2007): 161–176.

Manzoor, Parvez. "Method against Truth: Orientalism and Qur'anic Studies." *Muslim World Book Review* 7 (1987): 33–49.

Marchand, Suzanne L. *German Orientalism in the Age of Empire: Religion, Race, and Scholarship*. Cambridge: Cambridge University Press, 2009.

Marcinkowski, Christoph. *Shi'ite identities: Community and Culture in Changing social Contexts*. Münster: LIT Verlag, 2010.

Masataka, Takeshita. "Toshihiko Izutsu's Contribution to Islamic Studies." *Journal of International Philosophy* 7 (2016): 78–81.

Mathews, Philip, ed. *Chronicle of Malaysia: Fifty Years of Headline News, 1963–2013*. Kuala Lumpur: Editions Didier Millet, 2007.

Matulić, Tonči. "Theology: Einstein's Concept of God with the Theological Implications on the Einstein's Physical View of the World." *Filozofska Istraživanja* 26.3 (2006): 531–557.

Mesut Okumuş, "Arthur Jeffery ve Kur'an Çalışmaları Üzerine." *Ankara Üniversitesi İlahiyat Fakültesi Dergisi* 43.2 (2002): 121–150.

Mingana, Alphonse. "The Transmission of the Kur'an." *The Muslim World* 7.3 (1917): 223–232.

Mir, Raoof. "Zakir Naik and His Audiences: A Case Study of Srinagar, Kashmir." *Journal of Religion, Media and Digital Culture* 7.2 (2018): 203–222.

Moore, Keith L. "A Scientist's Interpretation of References to Embryology in the Qur'ān." *Journal of the Islamic Medical Association of North America* 18.1 (1986): 15–17.

Moore, Keith L., and 'Abdul Majid Azzindani. *The Developing Human with Islamic Additions*. 3rd ed. Jedda: Dar al-Qiblah for Islamic Literature, 1982–1983.

Morris, Paul, William Shepard, Paul Trebilco, and Toni Tidswell, eds. *The Teaching and Study of Islam in Western Universities*. London: Routledge, 2013.

Morrison, Toni. *The Origin of Others*. Cambridge and Massachusetts: Harvard University Press, 2017.

Mottahedeh, Roy. *The Mantle of the Prophet: Religion and Politics in Iran*. New York: Simon and Schuster, 1985.

Motzki, Harald. "Alternatives Accounts of the Qur'ān's Formation." In *The Cambridge Companion to the Qur'ān*, edited by Jane Dammen McAuliffe, 59–75. Cambridge: Cambridge University Press, 2006.

Mu'ini, Syed Abdul Vahid, and Muhammad 'Abdullah Qurayshi, eds. *Maqalat-i Iqbal*. Lahore: Al-Qamar Enterprises, 1963.

Mushakhkhassat-e Kulli. *Barnama va Sar–fasl–e Durus (Department of Qur'ān and Hadith)*. Isfahan: University of Isfahan, 2014.

Mutahhari, Murtaza. *Dastan-e Rastan*. Tehran: Sadra, 1980.

Muttaqi–zadeh. 'Isa and Babullah Muhammadi Nabi Kindi. "Barrisi jam' Qur'ān-e Payambar (SAW) va Imam 'Ali (AS) az Nigah-e Mustashriqan va Ahl-e Sunnat." *Qur'ān Pazhuhi-yi Khavar–shinasan* 11 (1390/2011): 31–44.

Najjar–zadegan, Fathullah. *Tafsir-e Tatbiqi: barrisi-yi tatbiqi-yi mabani-yi tafsir-e Qur'ān va ma'arifi az ayat dar didgah-e Fariqayn*. Qum: Markaz-e Jahani-yi 'Ulum-e Islami, 1388/2009.

Nasiriyan, Yadullah. "Tahqiqi darbara-yi Tabanni va Zayd b. Haritha." *Maqalat va Barrisi-ha* 57.58 (1374/1995): 51–70.

Nishihara, Daisuke. "Said, Orientalism, and Japan." *Alif: Journal of Comparative Poetics* 25 (2005): 241–253.

Nourse, Jennifer W. "The Meaning of Dukun and Allure of Sufi Healers: How Persian Cosmopolitans Transformed Malay-Indonesian History." *Journal of Southeast Asian Studies* 44.3 (2013): 400–422.

Nurul, Maghfirah. *99 Fakta Menakjubkan dalam al–Qur'ān*. Jakarta: Mizan, 2015.

Nöldeke, Theodor. *Geschichte des Qorāns*. Gottingen: Verlag der Dieterichschen Buchhandlung, 1860.

Othman, Hussain. "Conceptual Understanding of Myths and Legends in Malay History." *SARI: Jurnal Alam dan Tamadun Melayu* 26 (2008): 91–110.

Parry, Tauseef Ahmad. "West Knows How to Honor Their Academicians." *KashmirReader* (June 2018): 9.

Parry, Tauseef Ahmad. "Western Scholarship on Qur'anic Studies in 21st Century: A Brief Study of the Contribution of Jane D. McAuliffe and Andrew Rippin." *Hazara Islamicus* 1.2 (2012): 1–10.

Parsa–nia, Hamid, and Hadi Beygi Malik Abad. "Sharq-shinasi-yi Postmodern: Zamina-ha va Payamad-ha." *Contemporary Islamic Thought Studies* 2.1 (2016): 33–55.

Pollock, Sheldon. "Future Philology? The Fate of a Soft Science in a Hard World." *Critical Inquiry* 35.4 (2009): 931–961.

Powers, David S. *Muḥammad Is Not the Father of Any of Your Men: The Making of the Last Prophet*. Philadelphia: University of Pennsylvania Press, 2009.

Pregill, Michael E. "I Hear Islam Singing: Shahab Ahmed's What Is Islam? The Importance of Being Islamic." *Harvard Theological Review* 110.1 (2017): 149–165.

Pregill, Michael E. "Some Reflections on Borrowing, Influence, and the Entwining of Jewish and Islamic Traditions; or, What the Image of a Calf Might Do." In *Islamic Studies Today: Essays in Honor of Andrew Rippin*, edited by Majid Daneshgar and Walid A. Saleh, 164–197. Leiden–Boston: Brill, 2016.

Quandt, William B. "The Middle East Crises." *Foreign Affairs* 58.3 (1979): 540–562.

Rabi'i Navidehi, Ruqayya, and Mahdi Bakuyi. "Naqd va Barrisi-yi Barjam va Pasa-barjam az Didgah-e Qur'an-e Karim." *Conference-e Melli-yi ruykard-ha-yi nuvin-e 'Ulum Insani dar Qarn-e 21*. Rasht: Imam Sadiqh University Campus, 1396/2017.

Raghib, Subhi. *Haqaiq Majhoulah 'an al–Kawn*. Homs, Syria: n.p., 1927.

Rahman, Rizwanur. "Urdu Da'irah-yi Ma'arif-e Islamiyya." In *Encyclopaedias about Muslim Civilizations*, edited by Aptin Khanbaghi, 174. Edinburgh: Edinburgh University Press in association with the Aga Khan University, 2009.

Ramsay, Chevalier. *The Travels of Cyrus to Which Is Annexed, A Discourse upon the Theology and Mythology of the Ancients*. Dublin: S. Powell, 1728.

Readings, Bill. *The University in Ruins.* Cambridge, MA: Harvard University Press, 1996.

Rezaei Haftadur, Hassan. "Barrisi-e Kitab-e Jamʿ Avari-yi Qurʾān-e John Burton." *Qurʾān Pazhuhi Khavar–shinasan* 7 (1388/2009): 103–132.

Riddell, Peter G. *Islam and the Malay–Indonesian World: Transmission and Responses.* Honolulu: University of Hawaii Press, 2001.

Riddell, Peter G. "Reading the Qurʾān Chronologically." In *Islamic Studies Today: Essays in Honor of Andrew Rippin*, edited by Majid Daneshgar and Walid A. Saleh, 297–316. Leiden-Boston: Brill, 2016.

Riddell, Peter G. "The Sources of Abd al-Raʾūf's Tarjumān al–Mustafīd." *Journal of the Malaysian Branch of the Royal Asiatic Society* 57.2 (247) (1984): 113–118.

Ringer, Monica M., and A. Holly Shissler. "The al–Afghani–Renan Debate, Reconsidered." *Iran Nameh* 30.3 (2015): 28–45.

Rippin, Andrew. "Analisis Sastra Terhadap al-Qurʾān, Tafsir, dan Sirah. Metodologi John Wansbrough." In *Pendekatan Kajian Islam Dalam Studi Agama.* Translated by Zakiyuddin Bhaidhawy. Surakarta: Muhammadiyah University Press, 2001.

Rippin, Andrew. "Kurân 7/40: Deve İğnenin Deliğinden Geçinceye Kadar." çeviren Mehmet Dağ. *Dinbilimleri Akademik Araştırma Dergisi* 2.4 Samsun (2002): 1–7.

Rippin, Andrew. *Muslims: Their Religious Beliefs and Practices.* 4th ed. London–New York: Routledge, 2012.

Rippin, Andrew. "The Qurʾān on the Internet: Implications and Future Possibilities." In *Muslims and the New Information and Communication Technologies*, edited by Thomas Hoffman and Göran Larsson, 113–126. Dordrecht: Springer, 2013.

Rippin, Andrew. "Review: The Integrated Encyclopedia of the Qurʾān, vol. 1: Allah, Ahmad, A--Beautiful Names of Allah by Muzaffar Iqbal." *Journal of the American Oriental Society* 136.1 (2016): 222–225.

Rippin, Andrew. "Tefsir Çalışmalarının Bugünkü Durumu." çeviren İsmail Albayrak. *Sakarya Üniversitesi İlahiyat Fakültesi Dergisi* 8 (2003): 139–156.

Rippin, Andrew. "Tefsir Çalışmalarının Mevcut Durumu." çeviren Erdoğan Baş. *İslâmi Araştırmalar Dergisi* 16.3 (2003): 454–461.

Rippin, Andrew, et al. "Arabic Software for the IBM." *Courseware Reviews (Journal of Compute and the Humanities)* 25.6 (1991): 445–465.

Rouhani, Kamal. *Din-suzi-yi Muʿasir.* Sanandaj: Aras, 1390/2011.

Ryad, Umar. "Islamic Reformism and Christianity: A Critical Reading of the Works of Muhammad Rashid Rida and His Associates (1898–1935)." PhD diss., Leiden University, 2008.

Sahab, Abu l-Qasim. *Farhang-i Khavar-shinasan dar Sharh-e Hal va Khadamat-e Danishmandan-e Iran-shinas va Mustashriqin.* Tehran: Shirkat-e Tabʿ-e Kitab, 1317/ 1938.

Said, Edward W. *Culture and Imperialism.* New York: Vintage, 1994.

Said, Edward W. "The Idea of Palestine in the West." *MERIP Reports* 70 (1978): 3–11.

Said, Edward W. "Iran and the Press: Whose Holy War?" *Columbia Journalism Review* 18.6 (March-April 1980): 23–33.

Said, Edward W. *The Myth of the "Clash of Civilizations": Professor Edward Said in Lecture.* Northampton, MA: Media Education Foundation, 1998.

Said, Edward W. "On the University." *Alif: Journal of Comparative Poetics* 25 (2005): 26–36.

Said, Edward W. *Orientalism.* New York: Vintage, 1978.

Said, Edward W. *The Question of Palestine.* New York: Vintage, 1979.

Said, Edward W. *Reflections on Exile.* Cambridge, MA: Harvard University Press, 2000.

Said, Edward W. *Şarkiyatçılık: Batının Şark Anlayışları.* 3rd ed. Translated by Berna Yıldırım. Istanbul: Metis, 2017.

Said, Edward W. *Sharq-shinasi.* 7th ed. Translated by ʿAbdul-Rahim Gavahi. Tehran: Dafter-e Nashr-e Farhang-e Islami, 1395/2016.

Said, Edward W. *Sharq-shinasi.* 3rd ed. Translated by Lotf ʿAli Khunji. Tehran: Amir Kabir, 1394/2015.

Said, Edward W. "Zionism from the Standpoint of Its Victims." *Social Text* 1 (1979): 7–58.

Saleh, Walid A. *In Defense of the Bible: A Critical Edition and an Introduction to al-Biqāʿīʾs Bible Treatise.* Leiden: Brill, 2008.

Saleh, Walid A. "A Fifteenth-Century Muslim Hebraist: Al–Biqāʿī and His Defense of Using the Bible to Interpret the Qurʾān." *Speculum* 83.3 (2008): 629–654.

Saleh, Walid A. "Review of Muḥammad Is Not the Father of Any of Your Men: The Making of the Last Prophet, by David S. Powers." Translated by ʿAli Aghaʾi. *Kitab-e Din* 10.193 (1392/2013): 10–18.

Saleh, Walid A. "Review of Muḥammad Is Not the Father of Any of Your Men: The Making of the Last Prophet, by David S. Powers." *Comparative Islamic Studies* 6.1–2 (2010): 251–264.

Saleh, Walid A. "Sublime in Its Style, Exquisite in Its Tenderness: The Hebrew Bible Quotations in al–Biqāʿīʾs Qurʾān Commentary." In *Adaptions and Innovations: Studies on the Interaction between Jewish and Islamic Thought and Literature from the Early Middle Ages to the Late Twentieth Century,* edited by Y. Tzvi Langermann and Joseph Stern, 331–347. Leuven: Peeters, 2007.

Salem, Feryal. "Introduction to the Muslim World: The Challenges and Opportunities of Teaching Islam in Theological Seminaries." Special issue, *The Muslim World* 108.2 (2018): 211–213.

Salim Khan, Muhammad. *Islamic Medicine.* London: Routledge, 2013.

Saʿdi al–Shirazi, Muslih al-Din. *Gulistan: Taman Mawar.* Kuala Lumpur: Islamic Book Trust, 2017.

Schedel, Hartmann. *First English Edition of the Nuremberg Chronicle: Being the Liber Chronicarum of Dr. Hartmann Schedel.* Madison: University of Wisconsin Digital Collections Center, 2010.

Schirrmacher, Christine. *Mit den Waffen des Gegners.* Berlin: Klaus Schwarz, 1992.

Schöller, Marco. "Post–Enlightenment Academic Study of the Qurʾān." In *Encyclopaedia of the Qurʾān,* edited by Jane Dammen McAuliffe, 187–208. Leiden and Boston: Brill, 2004.

Shah, Ahmad. *Miftah-ul-Quran.* Lahore: The Book House, 1906.

Shoemaker, Stephen J. *The Death of a Prophet: The End of Muhammad's Life and the Beginnings of Islam.* Philadelphia: University of Pennsylvania Press, 2011.

Siraisi, Nancy G. *Avicenna in Renaissance Italy: The Canon and Medical Teaching in Italian Universities after 1500.* Princton, NJ: Princeton University Press, 2014.

Sobhe, Khosrow. "Education in Revolution: Is Iran Duplicating the Chinese Cultural Revolution?" *Comparative Education* 18.3 (1982): 271–280.

Steenbrink, Karel A. "Jesus and the Holy Spirit in the Writings of Nūr al-Dīn al-Ranīrī." *Islam and Christian-Muslim Relations* 1.2 (1990): 192–207.

Stenberg, Leif. *The Islamization of Science: Four Muslim Positions Developing an Islamic Modernity.* Stockholm: Almqvist & Wiksell International, 1996.

Stewart, Devin, and Gabriel Said Reynolds. "Afterword: The Academic Study of The Qurʾān—Achievements, Challenges, and Prospects." *Journal of the International Qurʾanic Studies Association* 1 (2016): 173–183.

Stone, John R. "Reflections on the Craft of Religious Studies." In *The Next Step in Studying Religion: A Graduate Guide*, edited by Mathieu E. Courville. London and New York: Continuum, 2007.

Stubbe, Henry. *An Account of the Rise and Progress of Mohametanism*, edited by Hafiz Mahmud Khan Shairani. London: Luzac & Co., 1911.

"Sukhani az Shiʿayan–i Thailand." Translated by Muhammad Ali Muhammadi. *Darshaʾi az Maktab-e Islam* 11 (1357/1979): 59–60.

Sulaymani, Nasrullah. "Nishast-e ʿilmi–yi Qurʾan va Mustashriqan: Jamʿi az Asatid ba Hudur-e Hazrat-e Ayatollah al-ʿUzma Makarim Shirazi." *Qurʾān va Mustashriqan* 2 (1386/2007): 13–60.

Sönmezsoy, Selahattin. *Kurʾan ve Oryantalistler*. Ankara: Fecr Yayınevi, 1998.

al–Tabrisi, Fadl b. Hassan. *Jawamiʿ al-Jamiʿ*. Tehran: Intisharat Danishgah Tehran va Mudiriyyat–e Hawza ʿIlmiyya Qum, 1377/1998.

Tantawi Jawhari, *al-Jawahir fi Tafsir al-Qurʾān al-Karim*. 26 vols. Cairo: Matbaʿa Mustafa al-Babi al-Halabi, 1923–1935.

Taraqqi Jah, Masʿud. "Istita Mihwar: al-Islam fi Tayland wa-duwar al-Shaykh Ahmad al-Qummi." *al-Tawhid* 83 (1375/1996): 130–142.

Tehrani, Muhammad Muhsin Agha Buzurg. *Tabaqat aʿlam al-Shiʿa*. Qum. Ismaʿilian, n.d.

The Persian Letters, Continued; or, the Second Volume of Letters from Selim at London, to Mirza at Ispahan. London: E. Davis, 1735.

Thurston, Alexander. "Interactions between Northern Nigeria and the Arab World in the Twentieth Century." MA thesis, Georgetown University, 2009.

Thurston, Alexander. "Nigerian Universities: Islamic Studies in Secular Universities." *The Revealer: A Review of Religion and Media* (2012).

Tolan, John Victor. *Sons of Ishmael: Muslims through European Eyes in the Middle Ages*. Gainesville: University Press of Florida, 2013.

Tottoli, Roberto. "Origin and Use of the Term Isrāʾīliyyāt in Muslim Literature." *Arabica* 46.2 (1999): 193–210.

Traboulsi, Fawwaz. "Edward Said's *Orientalism* Revisited." *The Translator* 15.1 (2009): 179–183.

al–Tustari. *Tafsir al-Tustari*. Beirut: Dar al-kutub al-ʿilmiyyah, 1423/2002.

Ummu Muhammad. *Protokol-Protok Mesyuarat Para Pemimpin Ilmuwan Zions: Dengan Prakata dan Nota-Nota Penjelasan*. Batu Cave: Crescent News (K.L) Sdn. Bhd., 2014.

Varisco, Daniel Martin. *Reading Orientalism: Said and the Unsaid*. Seattle and London: University of Washington Press, 2007.

Venuti, Lawrence. *The Scandals of Translation: Towards an Ethics of Difference*. London and New York: Routledge, 1998.

Vika Gardner, and Salman Hameed. "Creating Meaning through Science: 'The Meaning of Life' Video and Muslim Youth Culture in Australia." *Journal of Media and Religion* 17.2 (2018): 61–73.

Vika Gardner, E. Carolina Mayes, and Salman Hameed. "Preaching Science and Islam: Dr. Zakir Naik and Discourses of Science and Islam in Internet Videos." *Die Welt des Islams* 58.3 (2018): 357–391.

Vrolijk, Arnoud, and Richard van Leeuwen. *Arabic Studies in the Netherlands: A Short History in Portraits, 1580–1950*. Leiden: Brill, 2013.

Wan Zahidi, *Mengenal Hakikat Syiah*. Putra Jaya: Jabatan Perdana Menteri, 2013.

Wansbrough, John. *Qur'ānic Studies: Sources and Methods of Scriptural Interpretation.* Edited with a foreword, translations and expanded notes by Andrew Rippin. Amherst, New York: Prometheus, 2004.

Warnk, Holger. "The Role of Translations in the Development of Modern Malay Literature, 1850–1950." *Journal of the Malaysian Branch of the Royal Asiatic Society* 80.1 (292) (June 2007): 91–113.

Wasti, S. Razi. "Dr Muhammad Iqbal from Nationalism to Universalism." *Iqbal Review* 1.19 (1978): 35–45.

Watt, William Montgomery. *Muhammad Salli Allah alayh wa alih wa salam fi Mecca.* Translated by 'Abdulrahman 'Abdallah al-Shaykh. Cairo: al-Hay'a al-Masriyya al-'Amma li l-Kitab, 1415/1994.

Watt, William Montgomery. *Muslim-Christian Encounters: Perceptions and Misperception.* London: Routledge, 1991.

White, Elwyn Brooks. *Here Is New York.* New York: The Little Bookroom, 1999.

Wilson, M. Brett. *Translating the Qur'an in an Age of Nationalism: Print Culture and Modern Islam in Turkey.* Oxford: Oxford University Press in association with the Institute of Ismaili Studies, 2014.

Wokoeck, Ursula. *German Orientalism: The Study of the Middle East and Islam from 1800 to 1945.* New York: Routledge, 2009.

Yamanaka, Yuriko, and Tetsuo Nishio, eds. *The Arabian Nights and Orientalism: Perspectives from East and West.* New York: I. B. Tauris, 2006.

Yasir Qadhi, Abu Ammar. *An Introduction to the Sciences of the Qur'ān.* Birmingham, AL: al-Hidayah, 1999.

Yusuf Abdullah Puar. *Perjuangan Ayatullah Khomeini.* Jakarta: Pustaka Antara Jakarta, 1979.

al-Zamakhshari. *al-Kashshaf.* Beirut: Dar al–Kutub al–'Arabi, 1986.

Zarnett, David. "Edward Said and the Iranian Revolution." *Democratiya* 3.9 (2007): 43–53.

Zorvani, Mojtaba, et al. "A Study of Gabriel Reynolds' Ideas regarding the Guardianship over Mary in the Quran." *Pajuhash-ha-ye Quran va Hadith* 49.2 (2016–2017): 269–284.

II Online Sources

Agha Tehran, Morteza. Access date December 28, 2018. http://aghatehrani.ir/.

"Albert Einstein in a Letter to Ayatollah Brujirdi: 'I Prefer Islam.'" (*Albert Einstein dar namei bi Ayatollah Brujirdi*: "Islam ra bar tamami-ye Adyan-e Jahan tarjih midaham"). http://www.taghribnews.com/vdcgwt9x.ak93x4prra.html.

"Andiru Ribin, Biritaniy." Last modified November 2016. http://www.iicss.iq/?id=2252.

Ansari, Hasan. "Edward Said va miras-e u." Access date December 28, 2018. http://ansari.kateban.com/post/1368.

"Ayin-e Ru-namai az Danishnama-yi 'Ulum-e Qur'ān dar Qum Surat Girift." News No. 5318, Esfand 21, 1395/Februrary 2017. http://www.iict.ac.ir/index.aspx?fkeyid=&siteid=1&fkeyid=&siteid=1&pageid=1212&newsview=5318.

"Einstein Was a Shiite Muslim." Access date December 28, 2018. http://www.azarmehr.info/2012/12/einstein–was–shiite–muslim.html.

"Einstein's 'God Letter' to Eric B. Gutkind: On the Existence of God." Access date December 28, 2018. http://my.umbc.edu/discussions/5472.

"Bunnag." Access date December 28, 2018. http://www.bunnag.in.th/english/.

Casciani, Dominic. "Who Was Khalid Masoud? (Khalid Masʿud ki bud?)." *Persian BBC*. Access date December 28, 2018. http://www.bbc.com/persian/world–39392530.

Coghlan, Andy. "Iran Is Top of the World in Science Growth." New Scientist/Daily News, March 28, 2011. Access date December 28, 2018. https://www.newscientist.com/article/dn20291-iran-is-top-of-the-world-in-science-growth/.

Daneshgar, Majid. "al-Mizan Pazhuhi bi Zaban-ha-yi Uruppa-yi va Asiya-yi." *Center and Library for Islamic Studies in European Languages* (2015). Access date December 28, 2018. http://clisel.com/al–mizan-fi-tafsir-al-quran/.

Daneshgar, Majid. "New Zealand and Islam Deserve Deeper Joint Study." *Otago Daily Times* (March 2015). Access date April 15, 2019. https://www.odt.co.nz/opinion/new-zealand-and-islam-deserve-deeper-joint-study.

Daneshgar, Majid. "Philosophical Perspectives on Modern Qur'anic Exegesis: Key Paradigms and Concepts, by Massimo Campanini." *Reading Religion*, 2018. Access date December 28, 2018. http://readingreligion.org/books/philosophical-perspectives-modern-quranic-exegesis.

"Dar Sayeh-yi Aftab: Guft-u-gu-yi Qur'ān Pazhuhana ba Ustad Bahaʾiddin Khurramshahi." *Maʿarif* 56,1387/2008. Access date December 28, 2018. https://library.tebyan.net/fa/Viewer/pdf/2841069/1.

"DFAJ." Access date December 28, 2018. http://www.dfaj.net.

"Did Einstein Write a Letter to the Late Ayatollah Boroujerdi?." Access date December 28, 2018. http://www.shiachat.com/forum/index.php?/topic/234937890-did-einstein-write-a-letter-to-the-late-ayatullah-boroujerdi/page–2.

"Dr. S Parvez Manzoor: Method Against Truth: Orientalism and Qur'anic Studies." Access date December 28, 2018. https://www.imamreza.net/old/eng/imamreza.php?id=1350.

"Dr. William W. Hay's Comments about the Holy Koran." Access date December 28, 2018. https://www.youtube.com/watch?gl=SN&hl=fr&v=te4CQ0fIzXk.

"Einstein and Islam." Access date October 3, 2013. http://einstein2007.persianblog.ir.

Formichi, Chiara. "Lovers of the Ahl al-Bayt: Indonesia's Shiʿism from the Keratin to Qum." *Inside Indonesia*, July-September 2011. Access date December 27, 2018. www.insideindonesia.org/weekly-articles/lovers-of-the-ahl-al-bayt.

Gardet, L. "ʿIlm al-Kalām." In *Encyclopaedia of Islam*, 2nd ed. Edited by P. Bearman, Th. Bianquis, C. E. Bosworth, E. van Donzel, and W. P. Heinrichs. Access date December 27, 2018. http://dx.doi.org/10.1163/1573–3912_islam_COM_0366.

"Genesis 19." Gill's Exposition. Access date December 28, 2018. http://biblehub.com/commentaries/gill/genesis/19.htm.

"Genesis 20." Gill's Exposition. Access date December 28, 2018. http://biblehub.com/commentaries/gill/genesis/20.htm.

"Gharb talash mikunad marjaʿiyyat-e ʿilmi dar Qur'ān ra az ma bigirad." Access date November 2016. http://www.iqna.ir/fa/print/1428402/.

"Harvard Business School Professor Emeritus Louis 'By' Barnes Dies at 81." Access date December 28, 2018. www.hbs.edu/news/releases/Pages/louisbarnes.aspx.

"Imam Sadiq University." Access date December 28, 2018. https://www.isu.ac.ir/page.aspx?ID=Mission–fa.

"Interdisciplinary Qur'anic Studies Journal." Access date December 28, 2018. http://jiqs.ir/.

"Iranian Shii Diaspora Malaysia." Access date December 28, 2018. www.mei.edu/content/iranian-shii-diaspora-malaysia.

"Islamic World Science Citation Center (ISC)." Access date December 28, 2018. http://isc.gov.ir/en/page/15/about–us.

Iqbal, Muzzafar. "Barrisi va naqd-i Qurʾān-pazhuhi dar sunnat-i daʾirat al-maʿrif-yi gharb (1913–2013)." Access date December 28, 2018. http://www.fathimiah.com/index.aspx?fkeyid=&siteid=125&pageid=35395.

Kapadia, Zakir. "Einstein's Theory in the Holy Quran." Access date December 28, 2018. https://khutbahbank.org.uk/v2/2007/07/13/einsteins-theory-in-the-holy-quran/.

Keller, Raoul. Virale Verbreitung einer Ideologie: Islamistische Fundamentalisten nutzen die Wissenschaft [unavailable online source].

"Kutub wa Dirasat ʿan al-Istishraq." Access date December 28, 2018. http://www.fisalpro.net/?p=99.

"Malaysia Citation Centre." Access date December 28, 2018. http://www.myjurnal.my.

"Masa Sih Albert Einstein Seorang Syiah." Access date December 28, 2018. http://ejajufri.wordpress.com/2010/09/25/masa–sih–albert–einstein–seorang–syiah/.

"Mengenal Hakikat Syiah." Access date May 2014. http://www.islam.gov.my/en/pelancaran–buku–%E2%80%9Cmengenal–hakikat–syiah%E2%80%9D.

"Noor Specialized Magazines Website." Access date December 28, 2018. www.noormags.ir.

"Ordering the Orient: A History of the Publication of Eastern Texts in Europe and America and the Production of a Cultural Economy of Orientalism, 1850–1939." Access date December 28, 2018. https://www.hist.cam.ac.uk/research/research-projects/world-history/ordering-the-orient-a-history-of-the-publication-of-eastern-texts-in-europe-and-america-and-the-production-of-a-cultural-economy-of-orientalism-1850-1939.

"Quran from the Point of View of Non–Muslims." Roshd. http://www.roshd.org/eng/beliefs/?bel_code=112.

"Rakaman bagi Tafsir al-Qurʾan in the 17th Century Malay World oleh Professor Dr. Peter G Riddle di Balai Ilmu, Akademi Pengajian Islam pada 23 September 2014." Access date December 25, 2018. https://www.youtube.com/watch?v=coMr3_FHWb0.

Randerson, James. "Childish Superstition: Einstein's Letter Makes View of Religion Relatively Clear." The Guardian, May 13, 2008. Access date December 28, 2018. Acchttps://www.theguardian.com/science/2008/may/12/peopleinscience.religion.

"Relativity and Quantum Physics, International Catholic University." Access date November 2013. https://icucourses.com/pages/023-a06-relativity-and-quantum-physics.

"Some Notes of Einstein's Final Treatise (Guzid–ei az akharin risali–yi Einstein)." Translated by ʿIsa Mahdavi. Accessed August 10, 2013. http://broujerdi.org/images/book–anishtain.pdf.

"Syiah di Malaysia." Portal Rasmi Fatwa Malaysia. 1996..

"Tafsir Ibn ʿAbbas." Translated by Mokrane Guezzou. Access date: December 28, 2018. www.altafsir.com.

"The Arabian Nights in European Literature – An Anthology," in Encounter with the Orient. Access date December 28, 2018. https://www.kent.ac.uk/ewto/projects/anthology/index.html.

"The Comprehensive Muslim e–Library." Access date December 28, 2018. http://www.muslim-library.com.

"The Letter of Einstein to Ayatullah Brujirdi" (matn-e name-yi Einstein bi Ayatollah Brujirdi). Access date August 10, 2013. http://www.rasadnws.com/?p=1428.

"Warnings about Potential Muslim Radicalization Went Ignored, Ex–U of C Prof Says." CBC News, June 25, 2014. Access date December 28, 2018. http://www.cbc.ca/news/

canada/calgary/warnings-about-potential-muslim-radicalization-went-ignored-ex-u-of-c-prof-says-1.2687016.

"Why Are Some Books Banned in Malay but Allowed in English?" Access date December 28, 2018. http://www.malaysia-today.net/why-are-some-books-banned-in-malay-but-allowed-in-english/.

Yaakub, Nazmi. "Gulistan karya Sa'di bukan hanya warisan Parsi, Iran." *Bharian*, September 2017. https://www.bharian.com.my/rencana/sastera/2017/09/322721/gulistan-karya-sadi-bukan-hanya-warisan-parsi-iran.

Index

Printed in the USA/Agawam, MA
September 5, 2024

871766.003